THE STRATEGY OF RHETORIC

THE
STRATEGY
OF
RHETORIC

Campaigning for the American Constitution

WILLIAM H. RIKER

Edited by
Randall L. Calvert
John Mueller
Rick K. Wilson

Yale University Press   New Haven & London

Published with assistance from the Mary Cady Tew Memorial Fund.

Designed by James J. Johnson and set in Baskerville type by Keystone Typesetting, Inc., Orwigsburg, Pennsylvania. Printed in the United States of America by BookCrafters, Inc., Chelsea, Michigan.

Library of Congress Cataloging-in-Publication Data

Riker, William H.
    The strategy of rhetoric : campaigning for the American constitution / William H. Riker ; edited by Randall L. Calvert, John Mueller, Rick K. Wilson.
        p. cm.
    Includes index.
    ISBN 0-300-06169-2 (alk. paper)
    1. United States — Politics and government — 1783-1789. 2. United States — Constitutional history. 3. Rhetoric — Political aspects — United States — History — 18th century. I. Calvert, Randall L., 1953-   . II. Mueller, John, 1937-   . III. Wilson, Rick K. IV. Title.
    JK116.R55 1996
    324.7′2′0973 — dc20   96-12669

A catalogue record for this book is available from the British Library.

The paper in this book meets the guidelines for permanence and durability of the Committee on Production Guidelines for Book Longevity of the Council on Library Resources.

10 9 8 7 6 5 4 3 2 1

Contents

IV THE HERESTHETIC OF THE RATIFICATION CAMPAIGNS

V   CONCLUSIONS

Figures

Tables

Editors' Preface

When William Riker died in June 1993, he left this remarkable manuscript substantially completed. He had been writing the book on and off for years, and it was the culmination of a project dealing with issues and a historical era that were of great interest to him throughout his career. As in all his writings, it gives evidence of—and is a tribute to—his unflagging zest for explaining in both a detailed and an abstracted way how real politicians, at once flawed and dedicated, argue and maneuver their way through difficult and important undertakings.

In editing the manuscript, we have not changed the exposition in any notable way. In particular, we have made no attempt to alter any of the formal theory presentation. We have appended a chronology, rearranged and retitled a couple of chapters, divided the book into titled parts, reformatted some of the tables and figures, inserted a few section titles within chapters, cleaned up some inconsistent notation, labeled or relabeled a few tables and figures, cleared up a mystery or two by going back to the handwritten original, checked many of the references and statistical computations, and added within double brackets some explanatory, summary, and connecting paragraphs and footnotes to help the reader—particularly the nontechnical reader—follow the argument and exposition. The manuscript has also undergone light copy-editing.

Regrettably, Bill never wrote an acknowledgments section, but in various publications and convention papers that used material from this book he had the following to say: "National Science Foundation Grant #SES-8410092 supported the work on this paper. I am deeply indebted to several students for help in summarizing and interpreting rhetorical themes: Patrick Fett, John Huber, William Kubik, Thomas O'Donnell, Margaret Raymond, and especially Evelyn Fink. Also, several colleagues have given me important insights, especially Peter Aronson and Norman Schofield. I am also greatly indebted to seminar participants at the universities of Iowa, North Carolina, and Rochester, especially David Austen-Smith, John Conybeare, Calvin Jillson, George Rabinowitz, David Weimer, Thomas Schwartz, and Kenneth Shepsle."

In addition, we would like to thank Bertha Santirocco for her labors in typing the manuscript, deciphering some of Bill's handwritten material, and arranging the various drafts; Roger James for his comments on a late version of the manuscript and for rechecking many of the quotes; William Kubik for helping to clarify a few data issues; David Austen-Smith for valuable advice at several points; and Bill's wife, M.E., for moral support.

During his highly productive career, Bill Riker exhibited great skill as an institution-builder, teacher, and social scientist. However, in the eyes of his colleagues at the University of Rochester and elsewhere, these could never overshadow his qualities as a colleague and mentor. His energy and enthusiasm were infectious; his commitment to political science exemplary; and his store of knowledge awe-inspiring. He had time for every colleague and every student and a knack for the encouraging word that continually spurred others on. Bill's influence on those who knew him, like his influence on his department and on the discipline, will prove long-lasting, and perhaps the publication of this, his last book, can stand at once as a capstone to his career and as a tribute from his colleagues to the qualities that so deeply affected them and so many others.

RANDALL L. CALVERT
JOHN MUELLER
RICK K. WILSON

Abbreviations

CC: John Kaminski and Gaspare Saladino, *The Documentary History of the Ratification of the Constitution: Commentaries on the Constitution: Public and Private* (Madison: State Historical Society of Wisconsin, 1981– 86), 4 volumes. CC is followed by the number of the document, except for material in the appendices, in which case CC is followed by the volume and page numbers.

RCS: John P. Kaminski and Gaspare Saladino, *The Documentary History of the Ratification of the Constitution: Ratification of the Constitution by the States* (Madison: State Historical Society of Wisconsin, 1990). RCS is followed by the volume and page number.

Chronology

1788 Apr 28   Maryland ratifies, 63–11

1788 May 23   South Carolina ratifies, 149–73

1788 Jun 21   New Hampshire ratifies, 57–47

1788 Jun 25   Virginia ratifies, 89–79

1788 Jul 26   New York ratifies, 30–27

1789 Jan 7   First presidential election is held

1789 Mar 4   First Congress convenes

1789 Apr 30   Washington inaugurated as president

1789 Nov 21   North Carolina ratifies, 197–77

1790 May 29   Rhode Island ratifies, 34–32

1791 Dec 15   Bill of Rights becomes part of Constitution

I

Introduction

1

The Core of Campaigning: Rhetoric and Heresthetic

LECTORAL CAMPAIGNS are a distinguishing feature of modern representative democracies worldwide. For most citizens in most polities, campaigns provide a compelling incentive to think about government. Campaigns thus are a main point—perhaps *the* main point—of contact between officials and the populace over matters of public policy. If, as democratic theorists postulate, rulers are responsible to the ruled, responsibility is imposed during campaigns and the elections in which they culminate.

Yet as crucial as campaigns are to the operation of large-scale representative government, we have only begun to accumulate knowledge about how they are involved in the transmission and approval of political ideas. We have learned quite a bit about voters' preconceptions, habits, and decisions.[1] We have learned something too about coalition formation and the dynamics of coalition development in campaigns.[2] We also know something about the way issues evolve.[3] We know quite a bit about how the

1. Paul F. Lazarsfeld, Bernard K. Berelson, and Hazel Gaudet, *The People's Choice* (New York: Duell, Sloan and Pearce, 1944); Angus Campbell, Philip E. Converse, Warren E. Miller, and Donald E. Stokes, *The American Voter* (New York: John Wiley and Sons, 1960); William H. Flanigan and Nancy H. Zingale, *Political Behavior of the American Electorate*, 5th ed. (Boston: Allyn and Bacon, 1983); and James Enelow and Melvin J. Hinich, *The Spatial Theory of Voting* (Cambridge: Cambridge University Press, 1984).

2. William H. Riker, *The Theory of Political Coalitions* (New Haven: Yale University Press, 1962); Benjamin I. Page, *Choices and Echoes in Presidential Elections: Rational Man and Electoral Democracy* (Chicago: University of Chicago Press, 1978); John H. Aldrich, *Before the Convention: A Theory of Campaigning for the 1976 Presidential Nomination* (Chicago: University of Chicago Press, 1980); William H. Riker, *Liberalism against Populism* (1983; repr. Prospect Heights, Ill.: Waveland Press, 1989); Larry M. Bartels, *Presidential Primaries and the Dynamics of Public Choice* (Princeton: Princeton University Press, 1988); and John Kessel, *Presidential Campaign Politics*, 3d ed. (Chicago: Dorsey Press, 1988).

3. Riker, *Liberalism against Populism*, chap. 8; William H. Riker, *The Art of Political Manipulation* (New Haven: Yale University Press, 1986); Robert Axelrod, "Presidential Election

3

media influences the way voters think.[4] And we have some fine efforts to calculate particular campaign strategies.[5]

But we have very little knowledge about the rhetorical content of campaigns, which is, however, their principal feature. Consequently, we do not know much substantively about how policies are presented, discussed, and decided upon. Consequently also, we cannot explain campaigns, and we cannot even give good advice to campaigners.

It is true that we have some good descriptions of particular campaigns,[6] but particular descriptions uninformed by general theory fail to provide cumulative knowledge. We can use isolated data to ferret out, by analogical reasoning, some helpful hints for campaigners, although these hints may be devastatingly counterproductive if we happen to choose the wrong analogy. So the fact remains that we know very little about what to say in campaigns — but this is what both political scientists and candidates want to know.

THE FAILURE TO UNDERSTAND CAMPAIGNS IS A FAILURE TO UNDERSTAND RHETORIC

That we fail to understand campaigns is not surprising. Campaigns are rhetorical exercises: attempts to persuade voters to view issues in the way the candidate wishes them to. And our knowledge of rhetoric and persuasion is itself minuscule. Despite the fact that the formal study of rhetoric is twenty-five hundred years old, despite the fact that during all this time it has been an important element of the school curriculum, despite the fact that the best students of politics from Gorgias and Aristotle to Machiavelli

Coalitions in 1984," *American Political Science Review* 80 (March 1986): 281–84; John Kingdon, *Agendas, Alternatives and Public Policies* (Boston: Little Brown, 1984); and Edward G. Carmines and James A. Stimson, *Issue Evolution: Race and the Transformation of American Politics* (Princeton: Princeton University Press, 1989).

4. Donald Kinder and Shanto Iyengar, *News that Matters: Television and American Opinion* (Chicago: University of Chicago Press, 1987).

5. Ithiel de Sola Pool, Robert P. Abelson, and Samuel Popkin, *Candidates, Issues, and Strategies: A Computer Simulation of the 1960 and 1964 Presidential Elections* (Cambridge: Massachusetts Institute of Technology Press, 1964); Gerald H. Kramer, "A Decision Theoretic Analysis of a Problem in Political Campaigning," in *Mathematical Applications in Political Science*, vol. 2, ed. Joseph L. Bernd (Dallas: Arnold Foundation of Southern Methodist University, 1966), 137–60; Steven J. Brams, *The Presidential Election Game* (New Haven: Yale University Press, 1978); and Gary A. Mauser, *Political Marketing: An Approach to Campaign Strategy* (New York: Praeger, 1983).

6. Theodore H. White, *The Making of the President, 1960* (New York: Atheneum, 1961); and John Kessel, *The Goldwater Coalition: Republican Strategies in 1964* (Indianapolis: Bobbs Merrill, 1968).

and Madison have themselves been skilled rhetoricians as well as thoughtful commentators on rhetoric — despite all this, we have no general systematic knowledge, only a vast accumulation of examples, classified and reclassified in myriad ways without explanatory theory and even without tested hypotheses.

The remedy for ignorance is investigation. So I start with the evidence that we know little about persuasion. Perhaps the best evidence is the controversy over whether persuasion takes place: if we do not know whether it exists, we probably also do not know what makes it work. On the one hand, the commonsense conviction, expressed in the very word *persuade* (that is, through advice), is that rhetoric changes opinion: in faith (as by conversion), in trade (as by advertising), and in politics (as by eloquence).

On the other hand, many specialists doubt that opinion changes. Economists typically assume — without doing much damage to their results — that tastes are constant in the short run of several months or years.[7] In practical matters they say, for example, that it is far cheaper for a merchant to provide what consumers want than to persuade them to buy what they do not want. By this account — and contrary to popular opinion — advertising informs but does not persuade. Similarly, political theorists assume that tastes are constant over a campaign so that the best strategy for candidates is to position themselves at the median of voters' opinions and not try, as did the failures Barry Goldwater and George McGovern, to change opinions.[8] By this account — again contrary to popular opinion — propaganda informs but does not persuade. I am not, however, inclined to reject out of hand popular opinion about matters of daily experience, especially since recent experiments on the effects of television news programs suggest that much persuasion, or at least agenda setting, takes place.[9]

Altogether, the controversy between common sense and professional judgment convinces me that we know very little about persuasion. The reason for our ignorance is, I believe, that we have not systematically investigated how people change their values and opinions. It is surprising but true that in the twenty-five hundred years of the study of rhetoric, scholars have not discovered, and have only recently tried to discover, how rhetoric persuades auditors.

For the kind of full understanding of rhetoric and the process of persuasion in campaigns, we need a set of tested generalizations about the

7. George J. Stigler, *The Theory of Price*, 4th ed. (New York: Macmillan, 1987), 32–33.
8. Anthony Downs, *An Economic Theory of Democracy* (New York: Harper and Brothers, 1967); Mauser, *Political Marketing*; and Enelow and Hinich, *Spatial Theory*.
9. Kinder and Iyengar, *News that Matters*.

process itself and about the content of rhetorical appeals. Given such generalizations we could develop a science of rhetoric by which, perhaps, we might predict the course of campaigns and explain what kind of rhetoric works and why. At present, however, we have little in the way of such generalizations and hence little systematic knowledge about campaigns.

To illustrate what I mean by generalizations about rhetoric, I offer one of the main generalizations put forward in this book. Of course, I do not claim this generalization is well verified. After all, the evidence for it comes from only a single campaign from which, furthermore, I induced it. I set it forth here simply to give an example of the kind of knowledge that is necessary in order to understand rhetoric and campaigns:

> When one side dominates in the volume of rhetorical appeals on a particular theme, the other side abandons appeals on that theme (the Dominance Principle), and when neither side dominates in volume, both sides abandon it (the Dispersion Principle).

Assuming this generalization is valid, we can infer from it, first, that when rhetors abandon appeals on a theme they have discovered that their appeals have failed; and, second, that when they continue to make appeals they have discovered that these appeals are persuasive. A generalization like this and the inferences drawn from it do not tell us how persuasion works in the individual, but together they do tell us that professional rhetors, presumably relying on feedback from something like what we now call focus groups, have concluded that a particular appeal is or is not persuasive. This inference about rhetors' decisions is especially impressive because it is based on observation of their choices in situations in which their interests are deeply involved. In particular cases, then, we have a solid basis for concluding that a particular appeal is or is not widely persuasive. Ideally, students of rhetoric, like the students of any practical subject, would use such laws, if they existed, to practice their art, just as, say, physicians use the laws of biology and chemistry to practice theirs. Unfortunately, such laws are not as easy to come by in rhetoric as in biology, though in the infancy of rhetoric Aristotle sought to utter some: "We must also take into account the nature of our particular audience." "It adds much to an orator's influence that his own character should look right." "Clearly the orator will have to speak so as to bring his hearers to anger."[10] These are at best prudential rules, however, and they are patently false if interpreted as implicit generalizations about behavior.

Owing to the difficulty, therefore, of uttering generalizations, rhetori-

10. W. Rhys Roberts, trans., *Rhetoric*, bk. 1, ch. 9, 1367 b 7; bk. 2, ch. 1, 1377 b 25; bk. 2, ch. 2, 1380 a 1.

cians aimed at more attainable goals: rules of thumb based on experience and a vast storehouse of carefully described exemplars that learned rhetors could examine for analogies to their own immediate tasks of communication. The rhetorical tradition became one of collecting and classifying techniques — not on the basis of some theoretical scheme that might be used to generate hypotheses, but instead on the untheoretical basis of rhetorical usage (figures of speech, kinds of appeals, and so on). Furthermore, most rhetoricians justified the selection of exemplars with highly subjective evidence of the efficacy of appeals, namely, the fact that they and their friends judged the item persuasive. In the extreme case, the only evidence is the rhetor's own "shiver down the spine."[11] So whether or not the collected and classified exemplars were in fact widely persuasive remains unknown.

In the past forty years or so, however, social psychologists have indeed tried to study persuasion scientifically. Initially motivated, perhaps, by the fear of the presumed success of totalitarian propaganda,[12] psychologists narrowed the subject down to persuasion. They succeeded in supporting some of the traditional themes of rhetorical analysis:

- that the credibility of the source improves the acceptability of the message,[13]
- that the order of presentation makes little difference,[14] and
- that prior rebuttal induces resistance to appeals.[15]

And they added one new theme of considerable importance: that much persuasion fails because the intended audience is listening selectively.[16]

---

11. A. E. Housman, *The Name and Nature of Poetry* (New York: Macmillan, 1933), 46.

12. Leonard Doob, *Propaganda: Its Psychology and Technique* (New York: Holt, 1935); and Ernst Kris and Hans Speier, *German Radio Propaganda: Report on Broadcasts during the War* (London: Oxford University Press, 1944).

13. William J. McGuire, "The Nature of Attitudes and Attitude Change," in Gardner Lindzey and E. Aronson, *The Handbook of Social Psychology* (New York: Addison Wesley, 1969), 136–314; and David O. Sears and Richard E. Whitney, *Political Persuasion* (Morristown, N.J.: General Learning Press, 1973).

14. Carl I. Hovland et al., *The Order of Presentation in Debate* (New Haven: Yale University Press, 1957).

15. William J. McGuire and D. Papageorgis, "Effectiveness of Forewarning in Developing Resistance to Persuasion," *Public Opinion Quarterly* 26 (1963): 24–33; William J. McGuire, "Inducing Resistance to Persuasion: Some Contemporary Approaches," in *Advances in Experimental Social Psychology*, ed. Leonard Berkowitz (New York: Academic Press, 1964), 191–221; and Richard E. Petty and John T. Cacioo, "Forewarning, Cognitive Responding, and Resistance to Persuasion," *Journal of Personality and Social Psychology* 35 (1977): 645–55.

16. Leon Festinger, *A Theory of Cognitive Dissonance* (Evanston, Ill.: Row, Peterson, 1957); and Thomas Patterson and Robert McClure, *The Unseeing Eye: The Myth of Television Power in National Politics* (New York: Putnam, 1976).

Some social psychologists, while seeking to study decision making rather than rhetoric, have nevertheless revealed some psychic features of persuasion. Investigating the effects of the presentation of alternatives on the actual choice that subjects make, particularly when the alternatives presented involve risk and ambiguity, these experimenters have shown that the framing of a choice (that is, the language used to set forth the alternatives) significantly affects the subjects' response in systematic and apparently replicable ways.[17] Unfortunately, the direct relevance of this extensive literature to persuasion has not been explored, especially not in the setting of controversy.

As this discussion suggests, however, the social psychologists have not supplied much beyond adding some experimental or observational support to traditional rhetorical wisdom. The contemporary students of communication, a field that combines rhetoric and psychology, have been somewhat more successful. These scholars have contributed some genuinely new insights into persuasion, such as the observation that, for relatively passive auditors, rhetors' intense language tends to reduce credibility,[18] although this feature may vary among cultures.

I believe that the reason psychologists have improved only slightly over the traditional wisdom of rhetoricians is that psychologists have concerned themselves with ancillary circumstances of persuasion rather than with its substantive content. They have examined attributes and attitudes of rhetors and auditors, which are, of course, the traditional subject matter of the science dealing with the psyches of individual persons. Doubtless these properties are significant features of the circumstances under which persuasion takes place, but they only indirectly concern the social interaction of persuasion.[19] Rhetoricians and students of political campaigns want to discover generalizations about messages themselves. Scholars in the field

17. Amos Tversky and Daniel Kahneman, "The Framing of Decisions and the Rationality of Choice," *Science* 211 (1981): 453–58; Kahneman and Tversky, "Prospect Theory: An Analysis of Decision under Risk," *Econometrica* 47 (1979): 263–91; Paul Slovic, Bernard Fischoff, and Sarah Lichtenstein, "Behavioral Decision Theory," *Annual Review of Psychology* 28 (1977): 11–39; and Daniel Kahneman, Paul Slovic, and Amos Tversky, *Judgement under Uncertainty: Heuristics and Biases* (Cambridge: Cambridge University Press, 1982).

18. Michael Burgoon, "Empirical Investigation of Language Intensity," *Human Communication Research* 1 (1975): 251–54; and Michael Burgoon and Erwin P. Bettinghaus, "Persuasive Message Strategies," in *Persuasion: New Directions in Theory and Research*, ed. Michael E. Roloff and Gerald R. Miller (Beverly Hills: Sage, 1980), 141–70.

19. My view of the shortcomings of the psychological approach is shared by some specialists in communication, e.g., Gerald R. Miller, "On Being Persuaded," in *Persuasion: New Directions in Theory and Research*, ed. Michael E. Roloff and Gerald R. Miller (Beverly Hills: Sage, 1980), 25–26.

of communications do occasionally study messages, which is why, I believe, they have had more success than psychologists.

The challenges to political science are that the literature of rhetoric is particularistic, that it consists mostly of anecdotal accounts of presumed successes and failures, and, worst of all, that its evidence for interpretive criticism is suspiciously tendential and subjective. This book is a response to that challenge. Although it deals with only one campaign, its goal is to derive generalizations that may be tested on others.

RHETORIC AND HERESTHETIC

Because the subject matter is a whole campaign, the book also deals with other arts of language. In the medieval trivium there were three of these: logic, grammar, and rhetoric. There should also have been a fourth, heresthetic. [[Logic is concerned with the truth value of sentences, grammar with the communication value of sentences, rhetoric with the persuasion value of sentences, and heresthetic with the strategy value of sentences.]][20]

Heresthetic is a word I coined from a Greek root for choosing and deciding, and I use it to describe the art of setting up situations — composing the alternatives among which political actors must choose — in such a way that even those who do not wish to do so are compelled by the structure of the situation to support the heresthetician's purpose. [[Heresthetic differs from rhetoric because there is much more than eloquence and elegance involved in heresthetic. People win politically by more than rhetorical attraction. Typically they win because they have set up the situation in such a way that other people will want to join them — or will feel forced by circumstances to join them — even without any persuasion at all. And this is what heresthetic is about: structuring the world so you can win. For a person who expects to lose on some decision, the fundamental heresthetical device is to divide the majority with a new alternative, one the person prefers to the alternative previously expected to win.]]

The line between heresthetic (manipulation) and rhetoric (persuasion) is wavy and uncertain, just as, in another comparison, is the line between rhetoric and grammar. Indeed, some ancient writers (for example, the false Dionysus of Halicarnassus) discussed clearly heresthetical maneuvers as if they were rhetorical ones. But the limitation of rhetoric to single orations (as in the works of Cicero and Quintillian) or to figures of

---

20. [[The material added in double brackets has been adapted from Riker, *Art of Political Manipulation*, ix–x, 1.]]

speech and single sentences (as in the works of medieval rhetoricians) effectively cuts rhetoric off from heresthetic, which is usually observed in committee, legislative, and electoral interactions. In the real events of campaigns, however, heresthetic and rhetoric are inseparably linked and must be analyzed together. As I will show in this study, heresthetical considerations twist and transform rhetorical appeals in campaigns, even as rhetorical appeals constrain heresthetical arrangements.

THE PLAN OF THE BOOK

In this book, as I examine the rhetoric and heresthetic of the campaign of 1787 and 1788 to ratify the American Constitution, I seek to arrive at some descriptive generalizations about both kinds of efforts and about the interplay between them.

[[The analysis begins, in part II, with an extensive qualitative and quantitative examination of the content of the campaign's rhetoric. This analysis reveals distinct rhetorical patterns in the campaign, including especially an emphasis on negative themes. There is also a notable failure by both the Federalists and the Antifederalists to address all the issues of the campaign, or indeed even to address the same issues.

To try to explain this failure, part III begins with a theoretical analysis of the strategy of rhetorical interaction, and this leads to the derivation of the Dominance Principle (when one side dominates in the volume of rhetorical appeals on a particular theme, the other side abandons appeals on that theme) and the Dispersion Principle (when neither side dominates in volume, both sides abandon it).[21] The value of these principles is then buttressed by an analysis of the rhetorical dynamic of the ratification campaign.

Part IV turns from the rhetoric to the heresthetic of the campaign, employing both historical analysis and rational actor theories of political choice. Although the rhetorical contest was important in developing the issues of the campaign, the Federalists' heresthetical maneuvers were also crucial to their narrow victory. The first and most important maneuver was the Constitutional Convention itself, in which, rather than proposing re-

21. These can also be put another way. When one side successfully wins the argument on an issue, that is, is more persuasive, the other side ceases to discuss it, while the winner continues to exploit it (the Dominance Principle). When both sides fail to persuade — to win the argument on an issue — both cease to discuss it and search for some other, more profitable issue (the Dispersion Principle). This formulation is from William H. Riker, "Rhetorical Interaction in the Ratification Campaigns," in *Agenda Formation*, ed. William H. Riker (Ann Arbor: University of Michigan Press, 1993), 81–82.

forms to the Articles of Confederation, the delegates proposed a completely new constitution that, in the degree of centralization it imposed,
went significantly beyond what the majority of citizens probably would
have preferred. In addition, they designed the ratification process as a
take-it-or-leave-it proposition, thereby preventing any ratifying state from
altering the proposal. Also, they used procedural maneuvers to gain quick
approval by the first several states, before the Antifederalists could coordinate their own strategies. When progress toward ratification appeared to
stall in Massachusetts despite these maneuvers, they made a credible promise to later alter the document without opening the way to amendment
during the ratification process itself. And finally, in New York the Federalists insisted on ratification before amendment for a state to participate in
the new government, and this forced the votes of Antifederalists who did
not want to be left out.

Part V concludes the book by examining the relation between rhetoric
and heresthetic. Both were necessary for the Federalist victory: rhetoric, to
build support for Federalist positions; and heresthetic, to structure the
choice process in such a way that that level of support would be sufficient.
These concepts yield a new understanding of the ratification campaign.
Moreover, the tools and approaches developed here lead us toward the
further development of the science of political campaigns.]]

II

The Rhetoric of the
Ratification Campaigns

2

Shaping the Alternatives:
The Proposed Constitution of 1787

I N ORDER TO STUDY the rhetoric and heresthetic of a campaign, we
must interpret concrete events and utterances of campaigns themselves. Unfortunately, scholars have not collected and arranged data
about campaigns in a convenient form. Hence I have undertaken to
do so for one campaign, the campaign in 1787–88 for the ratification of
the United States Constitution.

THE PATH TO THE RATIFICATION CAMPAIGN

The ratification campaign occurred at the midpoint of a centralizing,
nationalizing political movement that began in the late 1770s and ended
with the inauguration of Thomas Jefferson as president in 1801. The movement for centralization began as a reaction to inflation and to the military
inefficiencies of the revolutionary effort. But the roots were deeper. They
went back to the structure of the Revolution itself. The Revolution began in
1774 and 1775 as rebellious subjects and state legislatures drove out the
representatives of the London government. As a result the colonies ceased
to be colonies and became independent states, de facto ones at first, then,
in 1776, legitimate ones, as they adopted constitutions under the self-
created authority of the Second Continental Congress.

Although the new states on their own could easily manage the domestic
functions of the old colonies, after the expulsion of British officials, they
still lost contact with the intercolonial functions of the London government that had coordinated the actions of the colonial governors. The
Congress was then the only national organization left. It had begun in
1774 as the First Continental Congress, which the irregular state legislatures had called for the purpose of coordinating political views toward
England. In 1775 the Second Continental Congress, called for the same
reason, became willy-nilly the continuing national level body, regularly
renewed by delegates dispatched from state legislatures. This Congress,

more an alliance-negotiator and ideology-rationalizer than a government, necessarily undertook legislative and executive functions, appointing generals and officials, negotiating treaties, borrowing money and issuing paper, buying supplies and paying soldiers, legislating military structure, and so on, as well as simpler tasks like running a post office and establishing and maintaining admiralty courts.

The two levels of government, states and Congress, developed together during the period from 1775 to 1781, when the Articles of Confederation (written in 1777) gave what was intended to be a permanent shape to the relation of states and Congress. Although the two levels had different functions, they were competitors in the sense that officials at each level wanted to control decisions at the other. For example, state officials wanted to direct military affairs, and Congress wanted a hand in local taxation. The state legislatures had the advantage in this competition because they selected and instructed the members of Congress, and they did not acknowledge any authority over themselves, except by their own unanimous agreement.

As a consequence, Congress was a weak body, weaker perhaps than the estates of the Dutch Republic, which, while similar in structure, had the advantage of being dominated by a single province and city, Holland and Amsterdam. During the 1770s Congress operated without a coordinated, hierarchical executive except in the army. Congress's committees were ad hoc and unspecialized, and all decisions, both legislative and executive, even tiny details, were made on the floor. Consequently, diplomatic, military, and financial affairs were managed slowly, awkwardly, and usually inefficiently. Only the exigencies of war, which fostered cooperation, enabled this weak government to work at all.[1]

Such was the setting for the nationalist movement's attempt to strengthen the federal government. In the nationalists' opinion, the Articles of Confederation did nothing to improve the operation of Congress. Instead they froze the Congress into becoming a committee of an alliance rather than a government, and in some respects this paralyzed Congress even more — for example, the Articles required that a state's vote count only if two (instead of the previous one) of its delegates were present to cast it, with the result that Congress often lacked a quorum.

Nevertheless, nationalists reasonably hoped for reform because their faction gained control of Congress in 1781.[2] This faction consolidated civil

1. Calvin Jillson and Rick K. Wilson, *Congressional Dynamics: Structure, Coordination, and Choice in the First American Congress, 1774–1789* (Stanford: Stanford University Press, 1994).

2. See detail on nationalist sentiment in chapter 9.

functions under three departments — Finance, Foreign Affairs, and War — and elected Robert Morris superintendent of finance, a kind of prime minister. Under Morris, Congress ceased issuing paper and, to cope with the immediate problem of inflation, proposed a 5 percent impost (tariff). The nationalists' long-term plan included the transfer of western lands to Congress (as a source of funds and a function for Congress), the consolidation of the state war debt under Congress (as a function for Congress), and the regulation of interstate and foreign trade by Congress.

Though nationalists continued to control Congress (except possibly for 1784), they failed to enact most of their proposals. The impost, which was interpreted as an amendment to the Articles, twice failed to surmount the Articles' barrier of unanimity among the thirteen states — Rhode Island refused it in 1781 and New York did so in 1784–85. While Morris initiated the consolidation of debt, states began to reclaim their portions when Congress lacked funds to repay. Although the nationalists were able to call a convention in Annapolis in 1786 for consideration of trade, so few states sent delegates that it was unable to act. Thus, by 1786–87, nationalists ended up with only one small part of their program: the transfer of some western lands to the United States and the organization of the Northwest Territory.

This was the setting for the Constitutional Convention. In the state legislative elections of 1786–87, nationalists regained full control of most state legislatures and sent ten or eleven nationalist-controlled delegations to Congress and eleven nationalist-controlled delegations to the Philadelphia convention. Both eighteenth-century and contemporary writers have attributed the nationalist sweep to, at least, the following sentiments:

1. The disappointment over the continuation of the wartime economic crisis (for example, inflation, depressed trade) into the postwar period, a development that violated expectations raised by the political and military success of the Revolution.

2. The revelation of the international insignificance of the United States by, for example, the failure to negotiate a trade treaty with Britain and by the British retention of the forts on the Great Lakes, even though the peace treaty assigned these forts to the United States.

3. The shock of Shays' Rebellion in Massachusetts in 1786, which seemed entirely unexpected in republican theory: how and why would citizens rebel against the government they had elected?

4. The regional resentments over the Jay-Gardoqui negotiations in 1786 for a Spanish trade treaty, the proposed terms of which pleased the north (by opening Spanish ports to United States shipping) but

offended the south (by closing the Mississippi to United States trade for twenty years).[3]

The relative strength of these sentiments in the nationalist sweep in 1786–87 may not be assessable. We can say that the first two sentiments underlay the development of the nationalist movement from 1781 and 1783 onward. The latter two, which were responses to events that occurred in 1786, especially affected people in the large, relatively self-sufficient states of Massachusetts and Virginia, where the nationalist faction had been relatively weaker than elsewhere prior to 1786–87. Indeed the change in these two states, piled on top of the nationalist strength in smaller states, produced the nationalist sweep in 1787.

The results of this sweep were that some states, and then Congress, called for the Philadelphia convention and that the convention contained an overwhelming majority of nationalists. In many state legislatures that nationalist majority was narrow, but the legislatures acted as filters, sending only members of the nationalist majority on to Congress in New York and, in May 1787, to the convention in Philadelphia. About half of the delegates were extreme nationalists — men like Washington, Madison, Hamilton, Gouverneur Morris, and James Wilson. By the end of the convention on 17 September 1787, they had converted most of the moderate nationalists, like Roger Sherman, to their extreme position. Out of fifty-five delegates, forty-eight signed or supported the final document.

As a consequence, the Constitution as written embodies the goals of one faction. Considering how weak the government of the Articles of Confederation was, I think it is amazing that the framers dared to produce a Constitution that provided for a far greater degree of centralization than had existed under the colonial regime. Still, the nationalists had an overwhelming voice in the convention, and they produced what they wanted. Exercising their election-endowed control of the agenda, they chose a method of ratification that forced moderate voters over to their extreme position, and this is also what gave the nationalists a popular majority.

SHAPING THE RATIFICATION CAMPAIGN: A SPATIAL REPRESENTATION

To understand the framers' achievement, [[it is helpful to think of the alternative possible constitutions in the form of a "spatial voting model," a simplifying analytic device used by social scientists. Such a model repre-

3. Richard Bernstein, with Kym S. Rice, *Are We to Be a Nation?: The Making of the Constitution* (Cambridge: Harvard University Press, 1987).

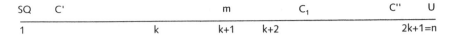

SQ	C'		m	C$_1$	C''	U
1	k		k+1	k+2	2k+1=n	

Figure 2.1   Schematic Diagram of the Distribution of Opinions on and
Alternatives for the Constitution

sents alternatives as more or less proximate to one another depending on
their substantive content, and it presents each voter's preferences over
those alternatives as a function of the resulting distance from each alternative to some ideal.[4] If one examines the problem in this way, it becomes
clear how successful the nationalists were in manipulating the process to
achieve an outcome much more to their liking than would have resulted
under a more neutral voting procedure.]]

We can think of possible constitutions as placed on a continuum on
which constitutions become progressively more centralized as one moves
from left to right (see fig. 2.1). At the left extreme is provincial autonomy
under the Articles (that is, the status quo, SQ); at the right extreme is full
unification (that is, a unitary government, U). There are n voters and they
too are arrayed along this continuum, at their ideal points — that is, at the
constitution each would like best. For convenience we can assume that,
when choosing between any two possible constitutions, all voters prefer
the constitution that is closer to their ideal — that is, preferences depend
solely on distance.

If the procedure for choosing a constitution had been unconstrained,
the voters would have been able to amend any proposed constitution. By a
sequence of such amendments, the voters would then have arrived at an
equilibrium outcome, a constitution from which they as a group would not
have chosen to deviate. By the well known median voter theorem, this
equilibrium would have been the ideal point, m, of the median voter.[5] With
$n = 2k + 1$, the point m has k voters' ideal points to its left and k such points
to its right, as indicated in figure 2.1. [[That is, as many voters would prefer
constitutions lying to the left as to the right, and thus any attempt to move
away from this point would fail to get a majority.]]

In historical fact, however, the framers had full control of the agenda in
the convention and in Congress, and they used their control to constrain
the procedure of ratification. In effect, they prohibited amendments to

4. For an introductory discussion of the spatial voting model, see, for example, William
H. Riker, *Liberalism against Populism* (Prospect Heights, Ill.: Waveland Press, 1989), chap. 3.

5. Duncan Black, "On the Rationale of Group Decision Making," *Journal of Political
Economy* 56 (1948): 23–34; Duncan Black, *The Theory of Committees and Elections* (Cambridge:
Cambridge University Press, 1958).

their proposed constitution, C_1, until they agreed to accept amendments of which they approved. By forcing the voters to choose between SQ and C_1, they were able to carry a Constitution that was probably far to the right of m.[6]

Note that in figure 2.1 it takes at least a majority, $k + 1$, to win. But as can be seen from the figure, there is no particular constraint on what part of the continuum these $k + 1$ voters come from. Assume there is one voter's ideal point at SQ and another at U, and that the remaining $n - 2$ voters are scattered evenly between. If the framers had written a constitution, C', at the ideal point of the second voter on the left, that constitution would have passed with $2k$ votes for C' and one vote for SQ. If, at the other extreme, they had written a constitution, C'', at the ideal point of the $(n-1)$th voter on the right, the nth voter and k voters to the left of the nth would have preferred C'' to SQ by a vote of $k + 1$ to k. [[(This is necessarily true because the voter ideals are evenly spaced and because we assumed that preference depends solely on distance from the ideal point.)]] Assuming a fairly uniform distribution of voters, the framers were, therefore, in a position to choose a constitution at the ideal point of any one of the $n-2$ voters not at the extremes on the dimension. In accordance with the size principle,[7] they chose a constitution that they believed would pass with a small majority, not greatly in excess of $k + 1$. Because they did not have good information about the actual distribution of the voters or the location of the nth voter on the dimension, they of course allowed for some excess over a minimal winning coalition. Still, their proposed constitution, C_1, was far from the Articles (SQ), and in fact called for a more centralized government than the median voter would have preferred.

As it turned out, they probably did err on the construction of their coalition. As early as October 1787, shortly after the Constitution had been created, it was apparent that the outcome was going to be close. Jackson Turner Main estimates the division of opinion to have been about 48 percent for the Constitution and 52 percent against, but he does not explain how he arrives at the split.[8] Evelyn Fink and I have argued that the

6. The theory behind their maneuver is developed in Thomas Romer and Howard Rosenthal, "Bureaucrats versus Voters: On the Political Economy of Resource Allocation by Direct Democracy," *Quarterly Journal of Economics* 93 (1979): 563–87; and Romer and Rosenthal, "Political Resource Allocation, Controlled Agendas, and the Status Quo," *Public Choice* 33 (1978): 27–44.

7. William H. Riker, *The Theory of Political Coalitions* (New Haven: Yale University Press, 1963).

8. *The Antifederalists: Critics of the Constitution* (1961; rept., New York: W. W. Norton, 1974), 249.

division was about 50 percent to 46.[9] Regardless of who is correct, both are close splits, suggesting that C_1 was pretty close to U.

Further evidence of the closeness of the split is the fact that the Federalists were obliged to compromise their no-amendment rule. As discussed in chapter 13, in the Massachusetts ratifying convention they carried out a remarkable heresthetical maneuver, promising to support a set of recommended amendments to C_1 provided some antifederalists join them in an immediate ratification. This promise was repeated in four subsequent state conventions and may well have been the marginally necessary compromise to ratify the Constitution. This possibility suggests that the original Federalist coalition may have been too small, less than enough to win in the nine required states.

The consequence of the Federalists' proposal of a Constitution that was extreme within its political space was of course an intense political campaign. It lasted for nine months and engaged at least as large a proportion of the electorate as do our contemporary presidential campaigns. But the Federalists' gamble on an extreme Constitution paid off. Their manipulation of the agenda effectively did force a choice between their Constitution and the status quo. And in 1787–88 eleven states ratified the Constitution as submitted — subject, however, to potential revisions proposed by five ratifying states. In 1789 and 1790 the two remaining states ratified, and in 1788 the people and the state legislatures elected a Federalist president and Congress. The Federalists retained control for most of the next twelve

9. "The Strategy of Ratification," in Bernard Grofman and Donald Wittman, *The Federalist Papers and the New Institutionalism* (New York: Agathon Press, 1988), 220–55. Our difference with Main is that Main apparently assumed that voters' opinions were accurately represented by the electoral platforms or announced positions of the delegates to state ratifying conventions, while Fink and I assumed that voters' opinions were more accurately represented by delegates' final votes on ratification. We justify our assumption with the following argument: The election was between C_1 and not-C_1. Certainly all candidate/delegates located from SQ to C_1 in figure 2.1 belong to not-C_1. Yet it seems unlikely that voters supporting these not-C_1 candidates were all against the Constitution. For example, given a binary choice, voters whose ideal point was near the median might very well vote for a not-C_1 candidate also at their ideal point, even though on balance the voter would prefer C_1 to SQ. A better estimate of voters' opinions is derived from the delegates' votes. In a representative system, the representative who wishes to continue in office must decide what his constituents really want. In some cases delegates apparently changed their minds when they thought they had many constituents who preferred C_1 to SQ. Consider, for example, Samuel Jones of Queens, New York. He was elected on a Clintonian Antifederalist platform, but he ultimately voted for the Constitution when it became apparent that rejection by New York would at least exclude New York from the Union and might even lead to the partition of the state. Presumably the Queens voters approved of Jones's reversal because they continued to elect him to public office.

years, during which they completed the constitutional amendments to their satisfaction and established the basis for a strong national bureaucracy. The Jeffersonians, who were the heirs of the provincials of the 1780s and who dominated the national government for most of the time from 1801 to 1861, modified the nationalism of the central government, but they certainly did not dismantle it. Consequently, the nationalist themes of 1787–88 continue to dominate our life today.

3

Data and Methods for the Study of Campaigns

NEITHER TRADITIONAL RHETORIC nor contemporary scientific psychology has been able to construct generalizations about campaign messages. I will attempt to do so in this study, and I begin by assembling the messages of one specific campaign to provide a base for analysis and interpretation.

The huge number of messages in this campaign presents a formidable obstacle, of course, even with modern techniques of data management. At least the primary data — messages in the campaign for the ratification of the United States Constitution — have already been assembled and arranged so as to facilitate systematic investigation. Under the initial direction of Robert E. Cushman, then of Merrill Jensen, and finally of John P. Kaminski and Gaspare K. Saladino, the Project for the *Documentary History of the Ratification of the Constitution* has collected all surviving national and local publications and private letters relating to the ratification campaign.[1] These consist of newspaper stories and editorials, pamphlets, and broadsides that circulated in more than one state as well as private letters of nationally significant politicians.

[[This research required a fairly complete record of campaign materials from some specific arena of conflict, one in which the contending rhetors reacted to one another's strategies and to the responses of a com-

---

1. John Kaminski and Gaspare Saladino, *The Documentary History of the Ratification of the Constitution: Commentaries on the Constitution: Public and Private* (Madison: State Historical Society of Wisconsin, 1981–88), 4 vols. This source is cited as CC followed by the number of the document, except in the case of material from the appendices, which is cited as CC followed by the volume and page numbers. [[Bernard Bailyn has more recently published an abridged version of the Kaminski and Saladino documents, *The Debate on the Constitution: Federalist and Antifederalist Speeches, Articles and Letters during the Struggle over Ratification* (New York: Library of America, 1993), 2 vols. A few new documents are contained in these volumes. Bailyn's volumes are a slightly more accessible but limited collection of many of the documents used in this book.]]

mon public. The national campaign was one such arena; particular local campaigns, in which there may have been different public reactions and different local rhetorical use of the same issues, represent other arenas. Therefore even though the local materials have not all been published yet, the national materials will suffice as one case in which to examine the rhetorical strategies of a campaign.]]²

RELEVANCE OF AN EIGHTEENTH-CENTURY CAMPAIGN

An eighteenth-century campaign may seem irrelevant to twentieth-century concerns, but there are important advantages in studying the ratification campaign that make it as relevant as a contemporary one. It was the first national campaign in a popularly based, territorially extended, representative government. Indeed, prior to 1787, the necessary conditions for a national campaign — a large territory and a large electorate — did not exist. In the earliest usage, the essence of a campaign is that political leaders coordinate in many constituencies the election of candidates of one faction or party or ideological grouping who, if elected, are expected to cooperate in running the government or, as in 1787, in making a decision. Later usage extended the word *campaign* to refer also to the coordination of voters in many districts to elect a single candidate for office or to elect adherents of one party to all offices. In either case the essence of a campaign is the coordination of voters and candidates of one faction.

Only in the late eighteenth century did there come to exist appropriate conditions to call forth a campaign. Ancient democracies and medieval cities with a popular element were not representative, except sometimes for executive officers. Neither were they territorially extended. Furthermore, no other modern representative governments were popularly based until at least a half-century after the United States. True, Britain had during the previous century a partially representative government over a large territory, and it was, until 1781, unique in the world. But only a few parliamentary constituencies were popular in the sense of having an electorate that included men of modest means.³ In the United States, on the other hand,

2. Private letters, if they remain private, are also irrelevant for the study of the public rhetoric of a campaign. Public speeches, the eighteenth-century equivalent of television and radio advertisements and reports, do in principle belong in the study. None of these survived, however, unless reported in newspapers. If they were not reported or if they were reported only locally, they necessarily pertain to local campaigns, not to the national one. Consequently, it is reasonable to say that the published work of Kaminski and Saladino presents us with the entire national campaign.

3. Sir Lewis Namier, *The Structure of Politics at the Accession of George the Third* (London: Macmillan, 1929); Sir Lewis Namier and John Brooke, *The House of Commons 1754–1790*, 3

suffrage, although narrower than today, was extremely wide by eighteenth-century standards. Of a total population of just under 4 million in 1790, approximately 500,000 were white men. Some urban "mechanics" (but seldom farmers) were excluded by property qualifications.[4] So the electorate was likely composed of some 450,000 eligible voters, of whom possibly half voted. This is clearly a mass electorate in the contemporary sense, large enough that a media campaign was politically advantageous.

Of course, there had been local campaigns before. In colonial times the elite dominated elections, which consequently were usually staid, often uncontested, and typically manipulated by small cabals. During the Revolution, however, popular groups keenly contested elections. Although the contests were local, campaignlike coordination began to appear. In cities, self-appointed groups began nominating and endorsing sets of candidates for city and state offices. In many states, when men of similar political beliefs acted together in the legislature, the rhetors and voters recognized this cooperation and used it as a cue at election time. In Pennsylvania the rhetors gave names to the ideological groupings, Constitutionalist and Republican, recognizing, respectively, support for and opposition to the Pennsylvania Constitution of 1777. This semantic device legitimated factions as nascent political parties. And in 1787–88 editors and politicians introduced the words *Federalist* and *Antifederalist* to designate groups that did in fact act together in such matters as presenting arguments, distributing literature among states, copying editorials from one paper to another rather like syndicated columnists today, and even participating quietly in the decisions of conventions of states other than their own.

So the campaigns of 1787–88 were indeed national—the very first in history. The significance of the fact is that our study of it may reveal universal features of the campaign situation. These first campaigners were naive in the sense that no one had as yet analyzed and rationalized campaign techniques. Of course, they already knew how to contest elections intensely, how to harangue voters, how to discredit opponents, how to manipulate candidates, how to bribe voters (with whiskey and rum), and so on. But these first campaigners had not yet had occasion to think about the organization of a campaign. Consequently, if we can identify a property of

vols. (London: Secker and Warburg, 1986); and Edward Porritt and Annie B. Porritt, *The Unreformed House of Commons*, 2 vols. (Cambridge: Cambridge University Press, 1909).

4. Robert E. Brown, *Middle-Class Democracy and the Revolution in Massachusetts, 1691–1780* (Ithaca: Cornell University Press, 1953); Robert E. Brown, *Reinterpretation of the Formation of the American Constitution* (Boston: Boston University Press, 1963); and Robert E. Brown and B. Katherine Brown, *Virginia 1705–1786: Democracy or Aristocracy?* (East Lansing: Michigan State University Press, 1964).

messages in this campaign that recurs in many later campaigns, then we can be sure that the property is obviously related to campaigners' interest. If naive campaigners utilize a technique widely used in later campaigns, then it is more than a recent invention and probably is, therefore, a general feature of campaign rhetoric.

Some have argued that an initial campaign, by reason of its constitutional nature, may have unique rhetorical features and thus be incomparable with subsequent campaigns. It is certainly true that writers on both sides emphasized the primacy and magnitude of the decision — as indeed often happens in more ordinary campaigns. But they tied their comments in with their rhetorical strategy, Federalists saying that the crisis necessitated constitutional revision and Antifederalists saying that the revision ought not to be so hasty,[5] which, as I will show, are main themes on either side. So perhaps the constitutional nature of the contest makes little difference. Whether it does is, of course, an empirical question, not to be settled by a prior argument: If subsequent campaigns display similar features, then the constitutional nature of this one will make little difference for generalizations about rhetoric. And since I will in fact offer generalizations about what, even casually, appear to be regular features, I will thus have established the value of the study of this initial campaign.

THE DATA

The media material of this campaign is modest in size in comparison with twentieth-century campaigns. Consequently it is physically possible to analyze a large sample of the rhetorical material. The sample used here consists of all the editorials, news stories, and pamphlets published in volumes 1–4 of *Commentaries on the Constitution,* which covers the period from September 1787 through March 1788.

There are 617 items, of which, as indicated in table 3.1, 371 were substantial essays and 246 were briefer squibs. Although 617 items is a large number, a scholar can study this campaign in detail.

The method of selection of the sample guarantees that it contains only the materials that the editors and publishers, who were also campaigners, thought were important and convincing. Lacking syndicated columnists and cooperative reporting services like the Associated Press, the editors of 1787–88 subscribed to one another's papers and unabashedly copied editorials, news stories, and squibs. Naturally they chose items that appealed to their partisan tastes because many of them were intense partisans.

---

5. See, for example, the first *Federalist* paper (CC 201) and the first paper by Federal Farmer (CC 242).

Table 3.1   Number of Items of the Public Campaign, September 1787
through March 1788

	Federalist	Antifederalist	Total
Substantial essays	256	115	371
Squibs	192	54	246
Total	448	169	617

Sometimes, in an effort to satisfy subscribers' demand for a wider range of
political opinion, they accepted new essays from their political opponents.
When they copied old essays they usually chose items by their political
friends. Kaminski and Saladino used this editorial filter in their selection
of items published in more than one state; they avoided their personal
judgments of quality and importance and relied entirely on the editors'
judgments of 1787–88. This means that the sample not only contains the
material of the national campaign, but also, and more significantly, that it
comprises what the campaigners of 1787–88 thought was both important
and rhetorically effective.

The significance of this selection rule for the study of rhetoric is that it
allows analysts to ignore their own and other scholars' subjective impression of rhetorical quality. Because scholars disagree among themselves and
often with popular opinion, it is difficult to interpret rhetorical behavior.
Consider, for example, the *Federalist*, a set of essays written under the pen
name Publius. To my taste and to the taste of many other teachers, it
contains penetrating political philosophy and cogent political argument.
The most intellectual of Publius's contemporaries thought so too. But this
was not the judgment of editors, who reprinted James Wilson's speeches
far more frequently and even ranked such relatively pedestrian writers as
Landholder (Oliver Ellsworth) over Publius.[6] When analyzing the impor-

6. Among Publius's contemporaries, Washington, for example, wrote to John Arm-
strong, Sr., that the defenders of the Constitution "have thrown new lights upon the science of
Government, they have given the rights of man a full and fair discussion, and have explained
them in so clear and forcible a manner as cannot fail to make a lasting impression upon those
who read the best publications on the subject, and particularly the pieces under the signature
of Publius": John P. Kaminski and Gaspare Saladino, *Ratification of the Constitution by the States*
(Madison: State Historical Society of Wisconsin, 1990), 9:760. (This publication will hereafter
be cited as RCS followed by the volume and page number.) On the other hand, Rufus King,
perhaps more immediately concerned than Washington about winning delegates in New
England and New York, observed to Jeremiah Wadsworth (December 23), " 'The Landholder'
will do more service our way, than the elaborate works of Publius" (CC 368). This was probably
written after he had seen Landholder's personal attacks on Elbridge Gerry and George Mason
(CC 295, 316, 335, on 26 November, 3 December, and 10 December, respectively).

tance and effect of messages, whose judgment matters? Clearly, the editors'. Certainly not mine, and only incidentally those of the Federalist elite. The combined judgment of the editors tells us what was believed to be rhetorically convincing in 1787, and that is what the analyst wants to know.

The use of editors' judgments not only enables us to transcend our subjectivity in selection, but it also solves a major problem in our study of rhetorical messages, namely, how to discover whether a message effectively persuades. Because they were close to the scene, their judgments are probably reliable, perhaps even as reliable as the results of tests by survey research of the effectiveness of political persuasion today. In studying the editors' choices, we can be fairly sure that we are analyzing the messages that editors believed actually persuaded.

In spite of these significant advantages, there are obvious questions about the data. As can be seen in table 3.2, about 80 percent of the essays and squibs originated in Boston, in New York City, and especially in Philadelphia, which was the largest city and the main publishing center. What I call the national campaign is, therefore, based on the campaign as it was developed in these urban centers, though the provincial editors who selected from the urban campaigns of course chose by their own provincial standards, typically ignoring or downplaying local issues of the originating place. Unavoidably, therefore, the campaign is more Federalist than Antifederalist, simply because the editors lived and sold papers in cities, all of which were enthusiastically Federalist. (Indeed, Federalists carried every city: Portsmouth, Newburyport, Salem, Gloucester, Marblehead, Boston, Providence, Newport, New London, Norwich, Hartford, New Haven, Albany, New York, Philadelphia, Lancaster, Baltimore, Norfolk, Richmond, Charleston, and Savannah.) Not surprisingly, newspapers were considerably more Federalist than not, as can be seen in table 3.1. This fact does not distort the analysis, however, so long as we interpret the Federalist and Antifederalist campaigns separately.

A TECHNIQUE FOR STUDYING CAMPAIGNS

To analyze campaign messages, we need to know, first, the arguments and sentiments uttered and, second, the weight that the campaigners placed on them. To obtain both kinds of information, research associates and I summarized each of the essays, stories, and squibs in the sample into one or several sentences, each of which is devoted to a single argument or sentiment. Of course, what constitutes a single unit of meaning is itself a matter of dispute. But we do know that sense units exist — sentences, for example, and even paragraphs — that are typically recognized as such by

Table 3.2   Distribution of News Items, September 1787 to April 1788

Contribute to	NH	MA	RI	CT	NY	NJ	PA	DE	MD	VA	NC	SC	GA	Items published in state Total	%
NH	14	101	24	47	37	8	161	5	5	6	—	3	—	411	7
MA	19	316	41	90	114	13	530	7	18	23	—	8	2	1,181	19
RI	6	7	18	30	29	4	156	3	4	8	—	2	—	331	5
CT	9	157	13	150	63	11	273	6	4	13	—	8	—	712	12
NY	8	159	11	48	454	7	363	7	22	19	—	7	—	1,105	18
NJ	5	46	5	11	23	4	82	2	6	4	—	2	—	190	3
PA	18	254	29	71	169	10	606	10	59	40	1	6	—	1,273	21
DE	—	—	—	—	1	—	7	1	—	—	—	—	—	9	
MD	7	72	6	18	35	3	150	—	28	6	—	4	—	329	5
VA	1	58	6	6	35	4	139	1	7	27	—	4	—	288	5
NC	—	4	—	—	1	—	4	—	—	3	3	—	—	15	
SC	—	33	3	10	19	1	77	1	13	8	—	7	—	172	3
GA	1	10	4	2	7	3	27	1	1	3	—	—	1	60	1
Items originating in state Total	88	1,281	165	483	987	68	2,575	44	167	160	4	51	3	6,076	
%	1	21	3	8	16	1	42		3	3		1	3		100

literate readers within a culture. We have used a team approach to reach agreement on the boundaries of sense units, attempting thereby to eliminate idiosyncratic judgments. Typically, paragraphs were our sense units, but we did not hesitate to break them up or combine parts of different paragraphs if we agreed that the sense unit dictated such divisions.

Typically our summaries reduced the bulk of the writing to about one-tenth of the number of words in the original. The 617 items in the sample yielded 3,268 summary sentences, an average of slightly more than five sentences per item.

We then assigned each of the summary sentences to a category, hereafter designated as c, based on subject matter, partisan origin, and argument or sentiment. In the event of doubt about the best assignment, we assigned the same sentence to two or even three categories. Initially there were about 1,200 categories, but by frequently redefining, broadening, and combining categories, we reduced the number to 178: 101 for Federalist ideas and 77 for Antifederalist ones (see Appendix). By the time the categories were reduced, there was little doubt about the appropriate assignments, and secondary assignments were subsequently ignored.

The process of reducing the number of categories is, of course, very little different from the effort of literary critics to discern the fundamental themes of a body of writings. All such enterprises are subjective by reason of their dependence on the scholar's sense of meaning and on the purposes in categorization. Meaning is, however, necessarily communal and in that sense objective, even for the most romantic or mystical interpreter. I have tried to enhance the objectivity, partly by involving two readers in each step of the reduction — and I have myself been involved in every judgment — but mainly by including all of the writings in the national campaign so that we could neither ignore what we thought trivial nor overemphasize what we thought important.

Of course the main purpose of summarizing and categorizing is to arrive at some judgment of the significance of various arguments and sentiments in the campaign. What ideas are most important? How are ideas related? To arrive at answers, we have weighted each summary sentence by the number of words that it summarizes and the number of times that these words were printed, as reported in the *Commentaries*. For each summary sentence, s_i, $i = 1, \ldots 3{,}268$, there is a weight l_i, which is the number of words, v_i, in the original material that s_i summarizes, times the number of printings, p_i. So $l_i = v_i \, p_i$. For each category, c_j, $j = 1, \ldots, 178$, there is a weight

$$w(c_j) = \Sigma \; l_i.$$
$$i \, \varepsilon \, c_j$$

To illustrate, the tenth *Federalist,* probably now the most frequently read of the items in the sample, is summarized into about twenty sentences, the first two of which summarize the first paragraph:

1. Popular government needs a cure for its propensity to faction, which often causes its failure and the specious condemnation of it.

$$v_i = 129, \, p_i = 8, \, l_i = 1,032$$

2. American constitutions have improved popular government, but they fail to obviate the dangers of faction, as witness instability, overbearing majorities, unreliable public engagements and dangers to private rights.

$$v_i = 258, \, p_i = 8, \, l_i = 2,064$$

Ultimately, these sentences were classified in category no. 18253 (see Appendix): "Union and republicanism cure the disease of faction." This rubric contains altogether nineteen summary sentences from various essays and $w(c_{18253}) = 23,421$.

Of course, what the analyst wants to know is not this raw weight, but rather the ratio of the weight of this category to the weight of all categories in a campaign. So I assign a superscript, k, to each category, where $k = 1,2$ and $k = 1$ stands for Federalist and $k = 2$ stands for Antifederalist. Each category $c_j^k \in C^k$ where C^k is the set of all categories, respectively 101 or 77 in number in each campaign. Then the normalized weight of c^k is derived:

$$\hat{w}(c_j^k) = \frac{w(c_j^k)}{\displaystyle\sum_{c \in C^k} w(c)}$$

Thus, for category c_{18253}, this value is .0073 or, as it is usually expressed below, 0.73 percent. These normalized weights make it possible to analyze themes, T^k, that are (proper) subsets of C^k, with c^k chosen for T^k according to the analyst's judgment of meaning.

4

Campaign Themes

HE CONSTRUCTION OF THEMES is the first step in the analysis of
the campaigns.

THE ANTIFEDERALIST THEMES

It is easy to characterize the Antifederalist themes: they were extremely
negative. Some themes are direct denunciations of Federalists, their campaign, and the Constitution. Others warn that if the Constitution should
be adopted individuals would lose their liberty in an unrepresentative,
aristocratic, or despotic government, and states would lose their identity in
a consolidated nation. Direct denunciation of the other side is, of course,
to be expected in an emotionally intense campaign. But name-calling is
probably not intellectually sufficient to sustain the kind of convincing argument that is necessary to attract and satisfy supporters. And for this
purpose one might expect the presentation of a positive program for the
future of America. But no, the Antifederalists developed an almost entirely
negative two-pronged attack: the threat to liberty and the danger of consolidation.

Consolidation was, no doubt, the main substantive issue for both sides.
The Constitution was intended to consolidate and did so, and this was its
main departure from the Articles. Appropriately, Antifederalists attacked
it in a variety of ways, and their main attack was directed against the threat
to liberty that they perceived in the Constitution.

Occasionally Antifederalists connected their two main themes with the
proposition that liberty is a function of the small size of states, which to
them implied that consolidation would destroy liberty. This connection
was seldom emphasized, however, so I consider their two themes as independent attacks on the Constitution.

To demonstrate the profound and pervasive negativity of the Anti-

Table 4.1   Distribution of Antifederalist Campaign Themes

Themes	$w(T)$	%$W(T)$	$w(T)$	%$W(T)$
Direct criticism of Federalists			383,161	22
Theme: The Constitution threatens liberty				
In general	244,720	14		
With respect to civil liberties	251,195	14		
With respect to govern- mental structure	246,507	14		
With respect to federal powers	126,796	7		
Total for theme			869,218	50
Theme: Consolidation threatens states			363,067	21
Positive Antifederal arguments and utterances			126,988	7
Total			1,742,434	100

federalists, I summarize in table 4.1 the themes of their campaign, starting with their direct attacks on Federalists. These attacks, of course, include ad hominem remarks (in the Appendix, code numbers 8007, 8513, 8514, 10108, and 10116 with $w(T)$ = 98,064 words), which did include, however, some claims that Federalists sought to deprive Americans of liberty. Another direct attack consisted simply of news reports that the ratification was in electoral trouble — code #88705, with $w(c_{88705})$ = 93,019 words. (Hereafter all references to weight will be simply the number $w(c_j)$ following the number of c_j.) In addition, Antifederalists devoted much attention to discussion of alternative methods of defeating ratification:

Strategy of amendments as a condition of ratification (#97105) 45,207
Strategy of a second convention (#97301)   28,602
Advice to ignore famous supporters, who might err (#10305)   19,191
Complaint that 9/13 ratification violated the Articles (#88013)   15,394
Admonitions for caution and delay in consideration (#97501)   49,980
    Total   158,374

There were also a few direct attacks on provisions of the Constitution not clearly related to the broad Antifederalist themes of liberty and consolidation. These were attacks on the provision permitting the slave trade to continue (#19001, 18,805 words), claims that the Constitution unfairly advantaged the south by the three-fifths rule for counting slaves in the census (#21105, 4,118), and, conversely, claims that it unfairly advantaged the northeast with navigation laws (#90001, 10,781), and so on. Altogether these direct negatives (ad hominem, strategic, and miscellaneous) accounted for 383,161 words, or about 22 percent of the campaign.

On the substantive issues, the Antifederalists' primary argument was that the Constitution threatened liberty. They presented this argument both abstractly, as a philosophical principle, and concretely, with evidence drawn from the Constitution and the campaign. They often coupled the abstract argument itself (#1001, 30,105; #84001, 7,907) with admonitions to citizens to oppose the Constitution because of its implicit threat (#97601, 11,332; #1005, 11,403). Sometimes they interpreted consolidation as an attack on liberty because it eliminated the small states, where they thought liberty flourished (#18302, 33,222). Repeatedly they asserted that the Constitution would establish an aristocracy or monarchy or despotism (#4002, 48,988); and they supported their contention by calling the framers (for example, Washington) incipient despots or dupes of despots (#8501, 15,624; #8503, 2,551; #8505, 8,796) and by calling Federalists aristocrats (#10304, 8,427) and conspirators against liberty (#10136, 10,321; #14005, 9,567). (The attacks in these categories differ from those mentioned in the previous paragraph—for example, #8007—because these materials usually do not involve named persons.) Antifederalists confirmed their suspicions about Federalists' intentions by pointing to the Federalists' efforts to obtain a speedy ("hasty") ratification (#97511, 26,371); and, predicting that the Constitution would be ratified only by force, they insisted that this act would destroy freedom (#51001, 15,910; #88301, 4,196). Altogether this condemnation for nonspecific threats to liberty accounted for 244,720 words, or 14 percent of the campaign.

These abstract assertions probably had more force when coupled with concrete evidence of validity. Their most frequently repeated (and probably most potent) evidence of the putative threats was the omission from the Constitution of the then-standard protection of civil rights. There was, they pointed out, no bill of rights (#1501, 35,407), which, they inferred, permitted rulers to invade liberty (#1502, 21,095).

Early in the campaign, the Federalist ideologue James Wilson had "explained" that a bill of rights was not necessary in a government of delegated powers, only in the directly responsible state governments. The Antifederalists poured forth many words in refutation (#1503, 13,656). Mostly, however, they raised an alarm about the absence of protection for particular rights. There was, they said, no guarantee of a free press (#2001, 21,705), and they dramatized the inherent danger of the omission by their accusation that the Federalist postmaster general delayed Antifederalist newspapers (#88006, 58,464) and by their complaint that Federalist editors refused to print unsigned Antifederalist letters (#88001, 22,584).

Furthermore, the Antifederalists said that the Constitution did not guarantee trial by jury, not always making clear that they referred either to the absence of guarantees of juries in civil trials and juries of the vicinage or to their theory that appeals on facts invalidated jury decisions (#2301, 50,429). Finally, they also noted the absence of protection for other civil rights, such as liberty of conscience (mostly, an appeal to Quakers, #2502, 10,203) and freedom from search and seizure and other traditional liberties as well as the "right to hunt" on public lands and other oddities (#2801, 13,025). Perversely, they complained about the constitutional provision against ex post facto laws, which they regarded as unenforceable and as a protection for "public defaulters" (#2401, 4,627). Altogether, this concrete evidence of the supposed threat to civil liberty accounted for 251,195 words, or about 14 percent of the campaign.

Alongside evidence about civil liberties, Antifederalists discovered threats to liberty in the proposed institutions of government. They argued that the framers had mixed, not separated, the branches of government, thus violating, in their opinion, Montesquieu's admonitions about the separation of powers as a protection of liberty (#20802, 35,877). Their argument seems to me to mean that they wanted to perpetuate the populist, unlimited legislatures of the states; and, indeed, some Pennsylvania Constitutionalists (that is, members of the radical party favoring the unicameral constitution of Pennsylvania) directly condemned bicameralism (#21501, 17,818). The Antifederalists' more specific criticisms of institutions as threats to liberty were

- that Congress was to control features of its election (#21,011, 22,551);
- that the House was relatively small — too small to represent all interests in all states (#21,101, 47,247) and to provide for the proper sort of representation (#21,107, 3,366);
- that the House lacked annual elections, rotation in office, and other putative protection against tyranny (#21104, 4,095);
- that the Senate was, in their opinion, too powerful and aristocratic (#22201, 16,313; #4102, 3,361);
- that the single-person executive, without a council, was strong and potentially a monarch (#24001, 41,609; #24210, 6,473); and
- that the national judiciary was likely to be oppressive (#26001, 27,275; #26204, 20,522).

Altogether, criticism of constitutional structures that tended toward tyranny accounted for 246,507 words, or about 14 percent of the Antifederalist campaign.

Finally, the Antifederalists frequently found threats to liberty in the powers granted to the federal government. The presumably open-ended powers in the general welfare clause and the necessary and proper clause made them quite apprehensive (#21301, 17,576). But two grants of authority disturbed them most: the powers of purse and sword. They saw a real threat to liberty in a supposedly unlimited power to tax (#43001, 37,851) — a theme reminiscent of the agitation that took place before the Revolution. Their propaganda laid the greatest stress, however, on the prospect of a standing army (#48101, 64,394; #48103, 6,975) — and properly so because the radical party had throughout the previous decade declared a preference for militia as against a regular army, whereas Washington and other Federalists distrusted militia as a military force. Altogether, Antifederalists' criticism of federal powers accounted for 126,796 words, or about 7 percent of their campaign.

The theme of a threat to liberty in the Constitution thus accounted for 869,218 words, or about half of the content of the campaign.

As for consolidation, the Antifederalists pursued this theme both in abstract philosophical terms and with concrete evidence of constitutional defects. The abstract theme was the assertion that the Constitution transformed the confederation into a consolidated national government. The campaign was just a bit ambiguous on this point, however, because some Antifederalists admitted that military and foreign affairs and interstate trade required more centralization than the Articles provided — a theme that parallels the campaign's ambiguity on the existence of crisis, #13001. Nevertheless, all Antifederalist editors agreed that the constitutional consolidation went too far, as evidenced by the necessary and proper clause, the general welfare clause, and the supremacy clause; by the limits on state powers and the absence of limits on federal power (that is, no reservations to states of undelegated powers, as was later provided in the Tenth Amendment); and by the "absurdity" of two sovereigns. Specifically, their attacks on consolidation consisted of

- interpretations of consolidation as a major defect (#5006, 49,812), along with a denial that a crisis sufficient to justify consolidation existed (#13002, 27,821) and rebuttals of Wilson's argument that the method of electing senators preserved confederation (#5004, 15,397);
- attacks associating consolidation with threats to liberty (#5039, 40,373);
- arguments that consolidation was impractical for the United States (#5010, 10,271) and that representation should be equal among states (#20501, 58,625);
- assertions that the framers exceeded their authority in consolidating (#5020, #11896), that the convention was called to amend the Articles,

not to produce a new constitution (#14004, 27,363), and that there were very few if any Antifederalist delegates (#14101, 10,748); and
• arguments that particular institutions provided for in the Constitution consolidated and destroyed the confederation, specifically:

a. that the federal judiciary would absorb the state judiciary (#26201, 31,028),

b. that the difficulty of amendment preempted revision (#30001, 4,658),

c. that the federal government would preempt most tax resources, thus starving state governments (#43002, 64,072); and

d. that the federal government would have all treaty-making power (#45001, 6,643) and all interstate commerce power (#46002, 4,360).

Altogether, these attacks on constitutional consolidation accounted for 363,067 words, or about 21 percent of the total Antifederal campaign.

Finally, the Antifederalists were not always negative but rather tried occasionally to be positive or at least neutral. Sometimes, they were quite positive, as, for example, in offering and justifying their own version of the future with proposed amendments to the Constitution (#97201, 52,382). Either as rhetorical devices or as true reflections of their tastes, they sometimes also presented themselves and their opinions as reasonable, middle-of-the-road positions (#98101, 31,212). Thus, they occasionally agreed with Federalists that a crisis existed and necessitated reform (#13001, 15,225). And they offered themes otherwise out of character for Antifederalists: that the Senate should be proportional to population (#20503, 2,016) and that the national Judiciary should interpret treaties (#26004, 479). Furthermore, they offered positive justifications for their own positions when they defended paper money (#81001, 4,682) and when they defended Antifederalist leaders against the Federalists' ad hominem attacks (#8012, 18,033; #96201, 2,959). Altogether, these positive portions accounted for 126,988 weighted words, or about 7 percent of the campaign.

It has long been recognized that the Antifederalist campaign was extremely negative. Cecelia Kenyon characterized the Antifederalists as "men of little faith," and the appellation has stuck[1] — and quite properly, as the foregoing analysis shows. Only 7 percent of their national campaign can be described as positive in the sense of proclaiming and justifying their programs. The other 93 percent consisted of negative elements, attacks on Federalists or on the Federalist program of centralization.

---

1. "Men of Little Faith: The Antifederalists on the Nature of Representative Government," *William and Mary Quarterly,* 3d series, 12 (1955): 3–43.

On reflection, it is hard to see how it could have been otherwise. Consider the Antifederalists' position. Those who were to become Antifederalists — the proto-Antifederalists of the early and middle 1780s — would have been content to make mild reforms to the Articles of Confederation. Suddenly they were faced with a proposal to change the system radically, a proposal moreover that had been framed entirely without their participation. One would not expect them to be able, on the spur of the moment, to work out a counterproposal. Indeed, one of the reasons that R. H. Lee and other Antifederalists wanted a second convention was to give themselves time to work out an effective alternative. In the actual circumstances, the best they could do was to defeat the proposal at hand. So their campaign was necessarily given a negative twist. It is not, as Kenyon argued, that Antifederalists were essentially pessimistic, but rather that the framers and the Federalists put the Antifederalists on the defensive. Once there, they put first things first and attempted to defeat the Federalists' proposal before concocting any of their own.

The surprising feature of modern interpretations of the Antifederalist campaign is that anyone should ever have believed that it was not almost entirely negative. In the nineteenth century, most scholars regarded the main Antifederalist writers like Federal Farmer and Centinel as carping and petty. Only in the twentieth century, under the influence of populist historians like J. Allen Smith and Charles Beard, has the Antifederalist position been romanticized and treated as if it were intellectually coherent philosophy with both positive and negative elements. Once the Antifederalist position became regarded as coherent, scholars have, with great effort, teased positive beliefs out of the Antifederalists' negative writings.[2] Apparently, it is hard for scholars to accept that politicians, caught by surprise, might lash out with negative denunciations and have nothing coherent to say in positive justification of their position. Fortunately, Kenyon's clearheaded reading of the texts reintroduced the understanding that they were overwhelmingly negative. I hope that her perception is reinforced by my more comprehensive demonstration.

THE FEDERALIST THEMES

The Antifederalists' negativity has long been and is now again generally recognized. But it has not usually been thought that the Federalists were, after allowing for their somewhat different circumstances, almost equally negative. Yet that is the case.

2. Herbert Storing, *What the Anti-Federalists Were For*, vol. 1 of *The Complete Anti-Federalist* (Chicago: University of Chicago Press, 1981).

Negative Themes

The proto-Federalists had indeed been conducting a campaign for reform even before the Articles of Confederation were ratified in 1781. Almost immediately after ratification, they took control of the federal government by electing Robert Morris to be the superintendent of finance. Morris, as the acknowledged leader of the faction, then sought to reform the Articles by adopting an impost (that is, a tariff to be collected by nationally appointed collectors). The proto-Antifederalists succeeded in treating this proposal as an amendment to the Articles, the adoption of which required a unanimous vote of the states. This proposal was twice defeated by the vote of one state. Frustrated by the failure of the impost, the proto-Federalists, as noted in chapter 2, promoted first the Annapolis convention in 1786, which failed to produce a proposal for reform, and then the Philadelphia convention in 1787, which succeeded.

Thus for seven years prior to the ratification campaign the proto-Federalists had been running a highly negative campaign that was the mirror image of the later Antifederalist campaign. Whereas the Antifederalists of 1787–88 said that the proposed reform would destroy American liberty, the proto-Federalists had been saying for seven years that the failure to reform would destroy America. Naturally, they continued this theme into the campaign for ratification.

Like the Antifederalists, the Federalists devoted a portion of their campaign to direct personal attacks on the opposition (#8056, 34,404; #8062, 43,617), whom they accused of being job seekers (#10152, 28,988) and demagogues, Shaysites, and Tories (#10155, 11,859) and of offering generally weak, sinister, hypocritical, and sophistical arguments (#10158, 55,227; #10172, 98,314). They denounced Rhode Island, of course (#96251, 32,164), and sought to show that New York mulcted Connecticut and adjacent states mulcted North Carolina (#96253, 17,769). Federalists also dissected specific Antifederalist arguments to demonstrate, presumably, that they were mere propaganda, consciously and sophistically intended to mislead inexperienced voters. So interpreted, the Antifederalists' alarms about liberty (#1158, 16,939), free speech (#2051, 9,745), consolidation (#5051, 10,501), and executive authority (#24153, 9,730) were said to be spurious rhetorical manipulation, as were the Antifederalists' calls for a second convention and warnings against hasty ratification (#97555, #8469). Altogether, these direct denunciations are 317,726 weighted words, or about 10 percent of the 3,204,819 in the Federalist campaign.

The primary Federalist assertion, however, was that the country was in crisis (see table 4.2). The Articles, they said, were a wartime expedient,

Table 4.2   Distribution of Federalist Campaign Themes

Themes	w(T)	%W(T)	w(T)	%W(T)
Direct criticism of Antifederalists			317,726	10
Theme: The national crisis				
In general	265,747	8		
Responses to crisis	335,752	10		
In military and foreign affairs	278,258	9		
In economic affairs	158,985	5		
The constitutional crisis	139,588	4		
Total for theme			1,178,330	37
Theme: Populist legislatures			183,228	6
Defense against Antifederal criticism				
With respect to liberty	577,533	18		
With respect to consolidation	199,932	6		
With respect to miscellaneous charges	63,675	2		
Total for theme			841,140	26
Defense against Federalist criticism			34,720	1
Cheers for the campaign			649,675	20
Total			3,204,819	100

now inadequate, both generally (#11052, 8,057) and in specific ways that I will soon discuss, causing a pervasive crisis (#13056, 67,484). So profound was this crisis, according to the Federalist presentations, that the Union was in danger of dissolving into separate confederacies or states (#12053, 84,146). Turning the Antifederalists' alarm about liberty back on them, the Federalists argued that the real threat to liberty was the present anarchy (#1151, 78,400; #4051, 27,660).

Against this, they offered the ideals of Union, Federation, and Constitution, which were not entirely consistent except in the sense that each theme depended on the Federalist emphasis on crisis. In categories to be described shortly, Federalists presented these ideals positively, but in a number of categories the Federalists' presentation of these ideals is negative and inseparable from their criticism of the Articles. Union, they said, would save the nation from pervasive localism (#12151, 81,861). They contrasted Federation (that is, compound government or what we today would call centralized federalism) with the government of the Articles (which I have elsewhere called peripheralized federalism). The latter, they said, depended on legislation for states, not for individuals, and was therefore extremely weak (#53152, 55,903). They pointed out that similar governments had typically failed (#53160, 53,725), but that a compound republic could make the federal government work and avoid incipient civil war (#53257, 57,689), even though states would continue to dominate (#53251, 25,262). Thus the main merit of the Constitution was that it would save the United States from the present crisis (#13052, 39,547; #97054, 21,765).

In their definition of crisis, the Federalists laid greatest stress on the danger of war, both foreign and civil. The Articles could not provide the military framework for national survival (#11060, 9,046), as concretely illustrated by the dangers Canada posed to New Hampshire (#96257, 15,217). Only a Union under the Constitution could provide the military strength necessary for gaining international respect and military preparedness (#12350, 59,162; #51052, 78,988). This implied, of course, national powers to tax (#43051, 19,334), a standing army (which, as Federalists emphasized, states then had, but which would be competent only under the Constitution) (#48151, 68,876), and national institutions to make and interpret treaties (#45051, 27,635). Somewhat less important in the Federalists' presentation of crisis were economic matters, although these were associated mainly (but not entirely) with foreign trade and hence are not clearly distinguishable from the military crisis. The Articles were, the Federalists said, commercially inadequate (#11053, 3,496), as illustrated by paper money (#81051, 15,686, together with the previously mentioned attacks on Rhode Island); but under the Constitution, with a government able to regulate trade (#46152, 8,522), peace and prosperity would be achievable (#85054, 96,087; #85051, 28,589), so much so that West Indians would migrate here (#85951, 6,605).

As their presentation of the military and economic crisis illustrates, the Federalists thought there was indeed a constitutional crisis under the Articles: simply, the federal government could not support itself (#11058, 69,171). So this was what consolidation meant. It was the Federalists' solution to crisis (#5082, 13,694). Naturally, therefore, they explained the political structures set out in the Constitution as the concrete solution. Congress was, they pointed out, arranged to provide for energetic government (for example, the necessary and proper and general welfare clauses, #21350, 25,231), as were the single-person executive (#24151, 22,187) and the federal courts (#26152, 9,305). Altogether, the theme of crisis accounted for 1,178,330 weighted words, or about 37 percent of the Federalist campaign.

A subordinate negative theme, one that the framers felt deeply and that occupies a large place in Madison's *Notes*,[3] is the populist structure of the governments, especially as expressed in unicameral legislatures and omnipotent legislative bodies. The Federalists generally, as distinct from the framers and from Madison when writing as Publius, did not emphasize their antipathy to populism, which indicates that they did not believe it would win as many votes as would the theme of crisis. But Madison's Publius and James Wilson both emphasized the dangers of populism, and, because their writings were frequently reprinted, this distinct negative theme does have a minor, but significant, weight. They emphasized that a strong Union (#18253, 23,421) and the extended republic (#18257, 55,928) would cure the disease of faction. The institutional embodiment of the control over populist legislatures was the separation of powers (#20851, 73,338; #20860, 11008) and bicameralism (#21551, 19,533). Altogether, the theme of populist legislatures accounted for 183,228 weighted words, or about 6 percent of the Federalist campaign.

Positive Themes

Just as the "plaintiff" position of the Antifederalists forced them to be negative, so the "defendant" position of the Federalists forced them to be positive in the sense that they had to refute the Antifederalists' criticisms. Thus, Federalists sought to refute the main Antifederalist charge that the Constitution threatened liberty by developing republicanism as a theme, emphasizing that federal power derived from the people and was popularly controlled (#18151, 138,412). To the Antifederal alarm about liberty, the Federalists directly responded that liberty depends on social conditions, not on specific constitutional provision (#1152, 26,493). Furthermore, they refuted Antifederalists' supposed evidence of censorship by editors and postmasters by pointing to the intense debate on ratification and the public denials of censorship (#88052, 9,086; #88060, 8,454). Somewhat inconsistently they also argued that a bill of rights was unnecessary (#1551, 24,417; #1556, 6,708), that the Constitution already contained guarantees of specific rights (#1552, 1,629; #2351, 21,804; #2551, 13,854; #2851, 9,375), and that certain "rights" (for example, unappealable jury decisions on facts and religious tests) ought not to be protected (#2354, 4,125; #2452, 5,723). As for the institutional threats to liberty, the Federalists asserted that the methods of electing Congress (#21057, 23,674; #21158, 11,511) and the president (#24052, 5,150; #24057, 33,926) were no

---

3. Max Farrand, ed., *Records of the Federal Convention of 1787*, 4 vols. (New Haven: Yale University Press, 1964).

threats to liberty. Neither were there any such threats in the size of Congress (#21154, 39,757) or in the powers of the president (#24261, 8,307; #24351, 22,754; #26251, 13,980). Similarly, the Federalists asserted that the upper house, unlike that in Rome or Britain, was neither aristocratic (#4152, 14,491) nor excessively powerful (#22252, 24,389) and that federal taxes and a standing army would not be oppressive because both would be popularly controlled (#43054, 72,244; #48252, 36,820).

Responding to the allegations about consolidation, the Federalists sought to prove that the states would retain essential functions (#5053, 87,580) and concurrent jurisdictions and functions (#5552, 27,641) and that the Antifederalists misunderstood and misquoted Montesquieu on large republics (#53157, 84,711).

On several more or less unrelated points, the Federalists defended themselves by saying that Pennsylvania delegates were fairly chosen (#14151, 627), that the Constitution provided for elimination of the slave trade (#19251, 14,843), that the amendment process and the provision for new states prevented rigidity (#30152, 4,824), and that ratification by ⁹/₁₃ was fully justified (#88951, 3,148). I include here the instances in which Federalists attempted to appear moderate (#98151, 34,745) as well as some neutral formalities (#99998, 5,488). Altogether, Federalists' positive response to Antifederal criticism accounted for 841,140 weighted words, or about 26 percent of the Federal campaign.

In a few cases, Federalists felt obliged to defend themselves from criticism that probably came from other Federalists. For example, while admitting that the three-fifths rule for counting slaves was dubious (#21152, 6,861) and that equality in the Senate was equally so (#20552, 26,634), they argued that these arrangements were compromises, politically necessary for ratification. Several also admitted that there were possible improvements that could be made in the structure of the executive (#24054, 1,225).

Other Themes

To conclude this analysis of the Federalist campaign, I note that the Federalists, who were, of course, winning most of the time, boasted positively about the progress of the campaign (#88751, 265,340; #88051, 11,818; #96902, 2,590) and encouraged their supporters with enthusiastic cheers (#98053, 53,218), including the blasphemous claim that God favored the Constitution (#99060, 32,854). They also urged immediate ratification (#97051, 36,074; #97152, 8,587; #97551, 11,179) and mightily praised Federalist politicians (#8576, 56,815), especially Washington and Franklin (#8551, 37,194; #8553, 16,256; #8554, 10,107) and other framers (#10360, 13,140; #14052, 61,765; #14054, 1,032), who, they said, wrote an excellent Constitution, even if they might have exceeded their authority (#14051, 11,195). They even had some good words for the Antifederalists who publicly acquiesced in state ratification once it occurred (#96199, 20,511). Altogether, this positive encouragement accounted for 649,675 weighted words, or about 20 percent of the Federalist campaign.

Conclusions

As is apparent from table 4.2, more than half of the Federalist campaign (53 percent, to be exact) was criticism of the status quo and its Antifederal defenders. Furthermore, most of its positive features derived from the Federalist position that, as reformers, they were obliged to justify their proposed reform against Antifederal attacks. Consequently, the main part of the positive Federalist argument is not a balanced rationale for their reforms, but rather simply an answer to the particular Antifederal criticisms.

Thus, although the Federalist campaign was not as negative as the Antifederalist, the greater part of the Federal campaign was also negative. To characterize the whole campaign, therefore, we can say that Federalists were campaigning against the crisis of the status quo, while Antifederalists were campaigning against the reforms that the Federalists offered.

THE RELIABILITY OF THESE CAMPAIGN SUMMARIES

How useful and reliable is my summary of the campaign messages? So far as I know, no other research has aimed at exactly the same kind of summarizing. There are, however, at least two efforts to state Antifederalist beliefs in systematic detail: one by Jackson Turner Main, the other by Herbert Storing.[4] Fortunately, their summaries of Antifederalist beliefs can be compared with my summary of public campaign messages to estimate the reliability of all three studies.

---

4. Federalist beliefs have not been similarly studied, possibly because *The Federalist*, which many people regard as the heart of the Federalist campaign, has itself been analyzed repeatedly. Actually, *The Federalist* was far too intellectually superior to be typical, although it was indeed a significant portion of the Federalist campaign. The *Federalist* papers in my sample are 817,059 weighted words, or about 25 percent of the Federalist campaign. Incidentally, more than half of the weight of *The Federalist* lies in five subjects: standing army, 77,246; national defense, 76,069; advantages of federation, 121,764; advantages of union, 130,121; and separation of powers, 39,181. This constitutes 494,381 weighted words, about 55 percent of *The Federalist* in my sample.

Main distills the principles on which Antifederalists were "in basic agreement" from (1) debates in the ratifying conventions, mostly in Massachusetts, Virginia, and North Carolina, (2) private letters of Antifederal leaders, and (3) Antifederal writings, mostly those collected by Ford and by MacMaster and Stone,[5] which perhaps overweighs Main's sample with the more intellectually respectable Antifederalist writings. Main seems to rely most heavily on private letters, which, he points out, were more likely to reveal true beliefs.[6] This contrasts with my procedure because, with my exclusive concern for the public campaign, I ignore private letters unless they were published during the campaign (as were several by Washington) and speeches in the ratifying conventions unless they were published in time for the campaign in other states.

In spite of these differences in sources, Main's listing of Antifederalist ideas is remarkably similar to mine. Naturally, since he is concerned with principles, he does not mention campaign-specific material:

1. Antifederalists' presentation of themselves as moderates (#98101, 31,212);
2. Antifederalists' crowing about Federalist failures (#88705, 93,019);
3. Antifederalists' planning of a strategy to defeat the Constitution by prior amendments (#97105, 45,207), by a second convention (#97301, 28,602), by delay (#97501, 49,980), by advice to ignore "great names" (#10305, 19,191), and by emphasizing that the ⅔ rule violated the Articles (#88013, 15,394);
4. Antifederalists' defense of their publicists and politicians against Federalist attack (#8007, 49,898; #8513, 11,053; #8012, 18,033; #96201, 2,959);
5. Antifederalists' complaints that Federalist editors refused to print anonymous Antifederal contributions (#88001, 22,584) and that the postmaster general delayed distribution of Antifederal newspapers (#88006, 58,464); and
6. Antifederalists' citation of Federalists' haste to call ratifying conventions as evidence that the Federalists conspired to overthrow the Articles (#97511, 26,371).

Although these omissions are substantial (471,967 weighted words, or

5. Paul Leicester Ford, *Pamphlets on the Constitution of the United States* (1888; rept. New York: Da Capo Press, 1968); Paul Leicester Ford, *Essays on the Constitution of the United States* (1892; rept. New York: Burt Franklin, 1970); and John Bach MacMaster and Frederick D. Stone, *Pennsylvania and the Federal Constitution, 1787–88* (Philadelphia: Historical Society of Pennsylvania, 1888).
6. Jackson Turner Main, *The Antifederalists: Critics of the Constitution* (1961; rept. New York: W. W. Norton, 1974), 127.

about 27 percent of the campaign), they are outside of Main's concern for Antifederalist principles, and hence it is consistent for him to omit them. Turning to the remaining items on my listing, one finds that Main discusses almost all of them. His omissions are trivial: Antifederal allegations that the constitution supported slavery (#19001, 18,805), Antifederal opposition to the three-fifths rule (#21105, 4,118), Antifederal claims that states should be represented equally (#20501, 58,625) and conversely, proportionally (#20503, 2,016), and Antifederal approval (#26004, 479) or disapproval (#45001, 6,642) of federal interpretation of treaties. Although these omissions total 90,685 weighted words, or about 5 percent of the campaign, most of them derive from Luther Martin's obsession with equal representation. Consequently, it is fair to say that Main's listing of principles includes all of the important ones that I identified.

Furthermore, Main does not include any principles that are not on my list. He does discuss at considerable length the attitude of Antifederalists toward democracy, but this is based on an interpretation of themes that he previously lists and, though somewhat anachronistic, is merely an effort to reconcile their antidemocratic utterances with his presentation of them as populists.

Thus, with the noted omissions, which are for the most part consistent with his goal and which, if not consistent, are trivial, Main records all and only the themes I list. I did not look at Main's work during the period in which I made my list, and so our fundamental agreement convinces me that we both captured the essence of the Antifederal campaign.

Main and I do differ, however, on our assessment of the relative importance of these themes. Main identifies the Antifederalists' concern about consolidation as their primary theme. He then derives their concern about liberty from their belief that a national, consolidated government would deprive citizens of the freedom they enjoyed in the small republics of the states. In my analysis, on the other hand, the Antifederalists' theme of liberty is most important — emphasized, indeed, two and a half times as much as the theme of consolidation. Furthermore, I treat liberty as mostly an independent theme, although I acknowledge that Antifederalists sometimes inferred threats to liberty from consolidation. Thus, although we agree on what the Antifederalists talked and wrote about, we disagree sharply on the relative significance of their ideas.

There are two ways to reconcile this disagreement. One or the other of us may simply have erred, but I believe that we were both careful and that it is more likely that we disagreed because we had different goals in our work. Main seeks to identify Antifederalist principles and thus to interpret the meaning behind their public utterances, whereas I seek simply to say what their public utterances were. On that charitable reconciliation, there is no necessary inconsistency between our accounts. Quite possibly they believed what he asserts they believed while they uttered what I say they uttered.

Such a difference between private thoughts and public words can be variously interpreted. Assuming Antifederalists' principles were in fact as Main interprets them, the difference between thought and utterance might result simply from editors' choices of the most newsworthy themes. Certainly, threats to liberty are intellectually uncomplicated and easy for the common reader to understand and to fear. The consequences of consolidation, on the other hand, are not as obvious and surely not as immediate. Consequently, editors in search of essays to arouse the common reader would presumably prefer ones about threats to liberty to ones about consolidation. Of course, there is a more cynical interpretation: Antifederalist writers themselves, not just editors, might have emphasized the theme of liberty for rhetorically manipulative reasons and concealed what Main thought was their primary concern lest an intense antipathy to consolidation reveal them to be, as many Federalists alleged, mainly interested in preserving their jobs. However, whether editors or authors reversed in utterance the hierarchy of opinion, the best explanation of the divergence between Main's interpretation and mine is that some self-interested persons sought some sort of rhetorical advantage.

Turning now to Storing's summary, I begin by noting that he makes no effort to be inclusive. Although he bases his analysis on his six-volume collection of Antifederalists' essays, he says in his introduction, "In searching for the underlying unity in the Anti-Federal position we are not tabulating the frequency of different arguments. We are looking not for what is common so much as for what is *fundamental*. We might well find the foundations laid in a very few writings, even a single one. Thus, on the Federalist side, a James Madison is more important in this kind of quest than a Tench Coxe, not because he (Madison) is more typical or more influential in a direct sense, but because he sees farther and better. He can *explain* more."[7] As might be expected, therefore, Storing omits much of what Main and I summarize, so much so that it does not seem worthwhile to examine his omissions. (His analysis adds nothing to my summary, except the assertion that Antifederalists sought to revitalize religion;[8] but none of the writers cited for this opinion are in the Kaminski-Saladino collection, and they are thus, by definition, irrelevant to the national campaign.)

But while Storing's themes are a proper subset both of Main's themes

7. Herbert Storing, *What the Anti-Federalists Were For,* vol. 1 of *The Complete Anti-Federalist* (Chicago: University of Chicago Press, 1981), 6.

8. Ibid., 22.

and mine, he supports Main against me on our primary difference. Like Main, Storing believes that consolidation is the primary issue and that, to the Antifederalists, the threat to liberty was not an independent feature of the Constitution but derived from its consolidation of the states.

Because neither they nor I can read the minds of eighteenth-century men, I do not—indeed cannot—dispute their assertion that in the minds of Antifederal pamphleteers consolidation was the primary evil of the Constitution. Similarly, they cannot prove their assertion. But I do dispute the contention that consolidation is primarily what Antifederalists wrote about. As far as Antifederal publications indicate, the Constitution threatened liberty not so much because of consolidation itself, but because of the tax and military powers granted to Congress, because of the congressional power over its own selection (something not mentioned at all by Storing, though included in every state proposal for prior amendments), because of the absence of a bill of rights, and because of what Antifederalists believed were improper structures in the federal government. As even Storing himself inferentially suggests when he asserts that the Antifederalists agreed to the Union, the Antifederalists objected less to the closer union than to the institutions provided in the Constitution. So I conclude from Storing's analysis that the disjunction between Antifederalists' opinions and Antifederalists' utterances is real. Perhaps they believed one thing, but they certainly said, or their editors made them say, something quite different. They believed, perhaps, that consolidation was the primary defect of the Constitution, but they certainly said that the primary defect was the implicit threat to liberty.

I have undertaken this comparison with Main and Storing to investigate the reliability of my assessment. I conclude that we all properly identify Antifederal themes, but our estimates of the importance of themes vary according to our goals and our procedures, that is, whether we examine the supposed logic of the argument or measure the weight of the words. Our different emphases reveal an unexpected feature of the campaign: the Antifederalists' presentation is different from their probable beliefs. I conclude, therefore, that some persons, either editors or publicists or both, rhetorically emphasized not what they believed, but what they imagined to be persuasive.

We know pretty surely, then, that the negative content of the Antifederal campaign was a rhetorical stance, and it is appropriate to ask why reasonable men would adopt a stance of this sort. The same question is appropriate as to the Federalist campaign. Even though I cannot use the same method to assess the reliability of my interpretation of it, I assume, since my method of interpretation of Federalists is the same as that for Antifederalists, that Federalist negativity was also a rhetorical stance.

5

The Utility of Negative Themes

[[Much of the ratification campaign, on both sides, was negative. How does one explain the prevalence of negative campaigning? This chapter develops a model of strategic choice of campaign rhetoric. In doing so it demonstrates the advantage campaigners often find in adopting persistently negative stances.]]

COMMONPLACE EXPLANATIONS OF NEGATIVE CAMPAIGNING

ONE POSSIBLE EXPLANATION, which I immediately reject, for the widespread use of negative campaign themes is that negativity is simply an aberration of this particular campaign or, at most, of the revolutionary era. It is true that the ideology of the Revolution stressed some of the later Antifederalist themes holding powerful government to be a threat to liberty.[1] Conceivably, then, the Antifederalists' negativity was no more than the application of a rhetorical stance that was previously locally successful. Certainly, some of their themes, for example, the dangers to liberty from a standing army, owed much to revolutionary events, to revolutionary propagandists, and, as Bailyn shows, to early eighteenth-century Whig radicals like John Trenchard, one of the authors of the immensely popular *Cato's Letters*.[2] But there is an obvious defect in this simple attribution of Antifederalists' negativity to a local tradition: The Federalists also were negative, but in a way that owed nothing to revolutionary rhetoric. Their criticism was aimed at the status quo of weak government and thus emphasized the threat to liberty from anarchy or resubjection to a European power. The Federalists were Whigs, of course, but they were not radical Whigs, and, as developers

---

1. Bernard Bailyn, *The Ideological Origins of the American Revolution* (Cambridge: Belknap Press of Harvard University Press, 1967).
2. Ibid., 62, 112–19.

rather than revolutionaries, they neither needed nor desired to elaborate on revolutionary arguments.

So it is difficult to attribute the negativity of *both* campaigns to a unique eighteenth-century rhetorical style. The Antifederalists doubtless picked up themes from the revolutionaries and earlier Whig radicals, but, because both sides were negative, there must be a deeper reason for the negativity, especially since it has reappeared in many, perhaps all, subsequent political campaigns.

Another possible explanation of negativity is that the campaigners, deeply involved as they were, became intensely irritated and then assuaged their anger by denouncing the other side. Under this account, the negativity of this (and other) campaigns is no more than self-prescribed, self-administered therapy for the campaigners. I find this explanation just as inadequate as the previous one. True, this explanation is not idiosyncratic — therapy might be a feature of all campaigns. And it is possible that some ideologists of 1787 did indeed obtain relief by means of verbal aggression, especially the Pennsylvanians like Philadelphiensis and Centinel, who had already lost in their state when they wrote their most vituperative pieces. But the proposition that two-thirds of the writers and editors of 1787 were mainly seeking to repair their own psychic damage and had indeed no particular political goal renders the whole Constitution decision genuinely absurd.

So I reject the explanation of private satisfaction and look instead for some public purpose in the campaigners' stance. What might have led calculating, goal-oriented, self-interested campaigners to emphasize negative criticism rather than positive justifications? Presumably the campaigners wanted to win. Given this goal and given that they were rational calculators who would try, within the limits of their knowledge and abilities, to find and use the best strategy to win, the fact that they used negative appeals implies that they believed such appeals improved their chances of winning. Our question is, What intuitions might reasonably lead them to this belief?

To appeal negatively is to point out the danger implicit in the opponents' program, while not emphasizing the advantages of the campaigners' own program.[3] Why emphasize dangers rather than advantages? It must be that the rhetor believes some voters to be extremely risk averse or, perhaps, mainly concerned to minimize their worst possible regrets in

3. For an excellent discussion of the difference between positive and negative campaigning, see Gideon Doron, "A Rational Choice Model of Campaign Strategy," in *The Elections in Israel, 1981*, ed. Asher Arian (Tel Aviv: Ramot, Tel Aviv University, 1983), 213–31.

their choices among alternatives. [[Throughout this discussion, *regret* refers to the utility difference, as seen *after* true outcomes are revealed, between the utility of the actual outcome and the highest utility one could have obtained had one known what would happen.]] If so, then their response to the risk implied by potential danger may lead them to agree with the campaigner's assessment of the opponents' program. That potential agreement may well be what motivates campaigners' negativity.

THEORIES OF DECISION MAKING UNDER RISK

Social science theory has a great deal to tell us about an individual's attitudes toward risk. [[We can define a decision made under risk as one that yields the decision maker not an immediate payoff or a determinate outcome, but rather a *risky* outcome whose final result is the product of some further, random process beyond the decision maker's control. The economic theory of decision making under risk begins with the assumption that decision makers have consistent preferences over such risky outcomes, just as over determinate outcomes. This theory has long been called into question by experimental research in which subjects have made choices inconsistent with the theory. Economists and psychologists have suggested new theoretical principles to better describe the observed patterns of choice.]]

This section briefly reviews this literature and derives from it three principles that are highly relevant to campaigning: (1) people often prefer certainty to risk in ways that confuse the analysis of preference, (2) many people dislike losses more than they like gains, and (3) for ambiguous events with low probabilities, subjective probabilities are larger than objective ones. [[Later sections of this chapter then apply these principles to campaigning.]]

Milton Friedman and Leonard Savage worked out the idea of risk aversion in an effort to explain how a single person might simultaneously be willing to buy a lottery ticket (to gamble) and to buy insurance (to avoid a gamble). Their answer is that the person's utility for money (or any other good) might be curvilinear.[4] To illustrate, let I' be the expected monetary value of a gamble between a pair of incomes, I_1 and I_2.[5] That is, $I' = pI_1 + (1-p)I_2$, where p is the probability with which the gambler receives I_1.

---

4. "The Utility Analysis of Choices Involving Risk," *Journal of Political Economy* 56 (1948): 279–304.
5. [[The expected monetary value of any gamble is the sum of the various amounts that could be won, weighted by the probabilities of winning them.]]

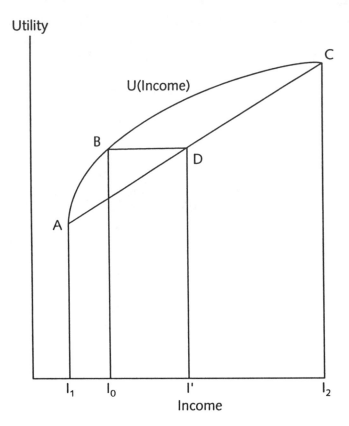

Figure 5.1   A Utility Function Exhibiting Risk Aversion

Choose another income level, I_0, such that the utility of I_0, $U(I_0)$, is just equal to the expected utility of the gamble, $pU(I_1) + (1-p) U(I_2)$. In figure 5.1, drawn with $I' > I_0$ to illustrate risk aversion, the utility curve between I_1 and I_2 is the curve ABC, with line ADC as its chord and, by assumption, line $I_0B = U(I_0)$ = line I'D.[6] In this case, the person desires to avoid risk (that is, the danger that the gamble might give only I_1 when the certain gain is I_0) and is willing to buy insurance up to the cost $(I'-I_0)$ to guarantee I_0 instead of the "actuarial value" of the lottery, I'.[7] Conversely, in figure 5.2, drawn with $I_0 > I'$ to illustrate risk acceptance, the actor

6. [[The second equality holds because ADC is a straight line; hence, since $I' = pI_1 + (1-p)I_2$, it can easily be shown (by using the algebraic formula for a straight line) that [I'D] = $p[I_1A] + (1-p)[I_2C]$, where the bracketed terms indicate line segment lengths. But the latter expression is just $pU(I_1) + (1-p)U(I_2)$, which by definition is equal to [I'D], as required.]]

7. Ibid., 291.

Utility

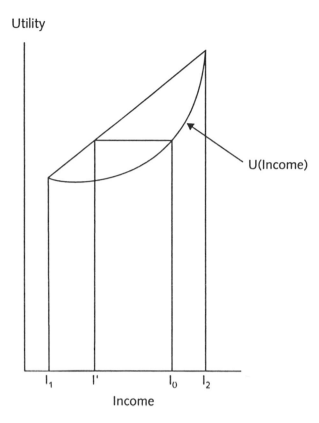

U(Income)

I_1 I' I_0 I_2

Income

Figure 5.2   A Utility Function Exhibiting Risk Acceptance

would pay up to the amount $(I_0 - I_1)$ for a lottery ticket. Combining figures 5.1 and 5.2 in figure 5.3, we get the utility curve of a person who is simultaneously willing, on different ranges of income, to buy insurance and to gamble.

The recognition that a person might be willing to forego significant expected income in order to guarantee certain income was then explored by other writers. For example, Harry Markowitz shows that risk aversion and acceptance are affected as much by whether the risks undertaken are gains or losses as by the relative size of the gamble.[8] He argues that the utility curve for losses is likely to be the negative of that for gains. Peter Fishburn and Gary Kochenberger somewhat confirm this proposition through their examination of utility curves for persons making investments. Almost half are convex (risk acceptant) for losses and simultaneously concave (risk

8. "The Utility of Wealth," *Journal of Political Economy* 60 (1952): 151–58.

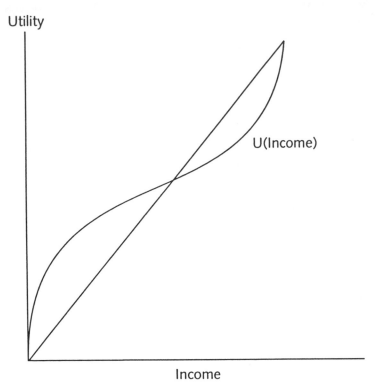

Figure 5.3   A Utility Function Exhibiting both Risk Aversion and Acceptance over Different Ranges of Income

averse) for gains, as shown in figure 5.4, while another fourth are exactly the opposite.[9] This fits pretty well with the observation by Amos Tversky and Daniel Kahneman that many people are risk acceptant for losses and that consequently utility curves in the third (negative) quadrant are images multiplied by a constant, c, $c < 0$, of curves in the first (positive) quadrant.[10]

The significance of this observation for rhetorical strategy is clear: that utility is convex for losses means that the voter is willing to accept risk in order, if possible, to minimize the expectation of loss. An appropriate rhetorical strategy is for the rhetor to seek to place the voter in the third quadrant, where he must, rationally, accept the risk of voting as the rhetor wishes. In the campaign of 1787, therefore, Antifederalists emphasized

9. Peter C. Fishburn and Gary A. Kochenberger, "Two Piece von Neumann-Morgenstern Utility Functions," *Decision Sciences* 10 (1979): 503–18.

10. "The Framing of Decisions and the Rationality of Choice," *Science* 211 (1981): 453–58.

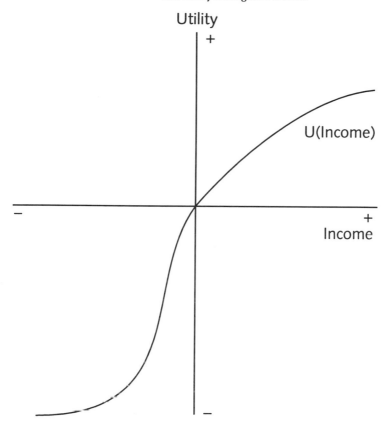

Figure 5.4   A Utility Function Exhibiting Risk Aversion and Acceptance in Gains and Risk Acceptance in Losses (Fishburn and Kochenberger, 1979)

the large potential loss in ratifying the Constitution and urged voters to accept the risk implicit in the Articles. Federalists minimized the risks inherent in the Constitution while magnifying the losses in staying with the Articles.

This feature of risk is, however, merely the first of several important discoveries. Allais's paradox and the huge array of work that it has spawned are probably even more significant because they show that decisions made under risk are subject to manipulation in a large variety of ways.[11] Maurice

11. Maurice Allais, "Le Comportment de l'Homme Rational devant le Risque: Critique des Postulats et Axioms de l'Ecole Américaine," *Econometrica* 21 (1953): 503–46; and Maurice Allais, "The So-Called Allais Paradox and Rational Decision under Uncertainty," in *Expected Utility Hypothesis and the Allais Paradox*, ed. Maurice Allais and O. Hagen (Boston: Reidel, 1979).

Allais gave subjects (mostly economists) thought experiments on pairs of choices on alternatives. The first choice was between (A) getting $1 million for certain and (B) a lottery in which there was an 0.89 chance of getting $1 million, a 0.10 chance of getting $5 million, and a 0.01 chance of getting zero. The tiny chance of getting zero frightened some people away from the lottery, which has, of course, the larger expected monetary value. The second choice, offered at a later time, was between two lotteries: (C) one in which there was an 0.11 chance of getting $1 million and an 0.89 chance of getting zero, and (D) one in which there was a 0.10 chance of getting $5 million and a 0.90 chance of getting zero. Some of those initially frightened by the 0.01 chance of getting zero now greedily chose the larger expected value with the additional 0.01 chance of reward. Though such choosers clearly preferred A over B and D over C, simple algebra shows that if the expected utility of A exceeds that of B, then the expected utility of C *must* exceed that of D.[12] Such choice is, on its face, inconsistent. The inconsistency arises because, as between A and B, the chooser uses the standard of minimizing the regret that would be felt at receiving zero but then, as between C and D, uses the standard of maximizing the expected utility. Allais's sleight of hand in presentation, of course, encouraged choosers to change standards. Still, in repetitions of Allais's experiment in which there was no time lapse between choices, some persons continue to choose inconsistently, and, in my opinion, it is hard to say that such choosers behave unreasonably.

In recent years, psychologists and economists have greatly expanded on the insights of Allais and Markowitz. Sarah Lichtenstein and Paul Slovic demonstrate the existence of so-called preference reversals, in which, as between bets P and D, the chooser prefers to play a bet P, which has a high probability of winning a small amount, but assigns a higher monetary value to D, which has a low probability of winning a large dollar amount.[13]

---

12. [[Let EU(B) denote the expected utility of lottery B, and similarly for lotteries C and D. Naturally, EU(A) = U(A). Then,

$$EU(A) > EU(B)$$
$$\Rightarrow U(\$1M) > .89\, U(\$1M) + .1\, U(\$5M) + .01\, U(o)$$
$$\Rightarrow \text{all } U(\$1M) > .1\, U(\$5M) + .01\, U(o);$$

adding .89 U(o) to both sides gives

$$.11\, U(\$1M) + .89\, U(o) > .1\, U(\$5M) + .9\, U(o)$$

which is identical to

$$EU(C) > EU(D)]]$$

13. "Reversals of Preference between Bids and Choices in Gambling Decision," *Journal of Experimental Psychology* 89 (1971): 46–55; Lichtenstein and Slovic, "Response Induced

It is difficult to explain such behavior by any theory of utility, yet it is quite robust. David Grether and Charles Plott tested it in an experiment designed to show its nonexistence and find instead that one-third to three-eights of the choices are inconsistent (that is, displayed such preference reversal).[14] Robert Reilly even instructed subjects in the notion of expected value and still found some reversal, although less than that found by Grether and Plott.[15] While it is difficult to offer a good explanation of this phenomenon, it does suggest that judgments about risk are very much affected by the circumstances of judgment. Apparently risk aversion and regret minimization are more salient when people are actually betting because then they choose the bet with the higher probability of winning; but risk aversion is less salient when people set a selling price because then they place the higher price on the bet with the higher dollar win. The circumstances affect the choice.

Tversky and Kahneman have elaborated even more extensively on the fluctuation of choice in different circumstances.[16] Their work is probably the most useful for rhetorical analysis, mainly because they have shown how, by offering alternatives in different ways, the experimenter can systematically affect the choices made. Such effect is, of course, the rhetor's main concern, and Tversky and Kahneman offer assurance that manipulation is possible. Thus, in one kind of experiment, they presented different versions of the same risky alternatives and produced substantially different choices. For example, with two pairs of alternatives about the adoption of proposed public health responses to an anticipated epidemic that in the absence of a response is expected to kill six hundred people, they offered: (1) if A is adopted, two hundred will be saved, and (2) if B is adopted, the probability is one-third that all six hundred will be saved and two-thirds that no one will be saved. Well over half of the subjects chose A, the certain alternative, over B, the risky one, despite the fact that the expectations are identical. The experimenters also presented the same choice (in numbers of deaths) with grammatically negative statements of alternatives: (3) if C

Reversals of Preference in Gambling: An Extended Replication in Las Vegas," *Journal of Experimental Psychology* 101 (1973): 16–20; Slovic and Lichtenstein, "Preference Reversals: A Broader Perspective," *American Economic Review* 73 (1983): 596–605.

14. "Economic Theory of Choice and the Preference Reversal Phenomenon," *American Economic Review* 69 (1979): 623–38.

15. "Preference Reversal: Further Evidence and Some Suggested Modifications in Experimental Design," *American Economic Review* 72 (1982): 576–84.

16. "The Framing of Decisions"; Kahneman and Tversky, "Prospect Theory: An Analysis of Decision under Risk," *Econometrica* 47 (1979): 263–91; and a collection of essays by many writers, Kahneman, Paul Slovic, and Tversky, *Judgement under Uncertainty: Heuristics and Biases* (Cambridge: Cambridge University Press, 1982).

is adopted, four hundred will die, and (4) if D is adopted, the probability is one-third that no one will die and two-thirds that six hundred will die. In this presentation, well over half chose D, the risky alternative, over C, the certain one, thus reversing the choice between A and B. This result confirms the Markowitz and Fishburn and Kochenberger observations about risk aversion in the positive quadrant and risk acceptance in the negative quadrant. More significant, it shows that the experimenter's manipulative presentation influences the majority of choices in the sense that it apparently encourages the subjects to carry out different calculations in the two circumstances, even though the algebra of probability is the same.

For rhetoricians the lesson is obvious: if it can be done in the laboratory, it can be done in the campaign. Of course, in the laboratory no one exposes the experimenter's manipulation, whereas in campaigns rhetors do sometimes expose each other. Still, refutation is incomplete, and manipulation is always possible. So rhetoricians have always assumed. But even they perhaps have not suspected the extraordinary plasticity of attitudes toward risk.

One further development is important to the study of rhetoric, namely, that low-probability events are typically accorded higher subjective probability than is objectively justified. Daniel Ellsberg initiated this line of thought and discovered another paradox, this one in the probabilities rather than in the valuations of utility theory.[17] He points out that in experiments and theories based on well-defined probabilities, as in gambling, the degree of uncertainty is explicit and clearly understood; but in the real world, beliefs about uncertainty are themselves uncertain — uncertainty itself may be ambiguous. His illustrative example involves two urns, both of which contain red and black balls, and a chooser who receives $100 for drawing a red ball and zero for drawing a black one. Urn 1 (ambiguous) contains one hundred balls in unknown proportion of red and black, and urn 2 (unambiguous) contains fifty red and fifty black. Many people are indifferent between betting on drawing Red or Black from urn 1, which implies $p(R_1) = p(B_1) = 0.5$; and similarly indifferent between betting on drawing Red or Black from urn 2, which implies $p(R_2) = p(B_2) = 0.5$. Many of these same people, however, prefer to bet on drawing Red from urn 2 rather than Red from urn 1 and Black from urn 2 rather than Black from urn 1. This avoidance of ambiguity (choosing from urn 2 rather than urn 1) implies either

$$p(R_2) > p(R_1) = 0.5 \text{ and } p(B_2) > p(B_1) = 0.5;$$

17. "Risk, Ambiguity, and the Savage Axioms," *Quarterly Journal of Economics* 75 (1961): 643–69.

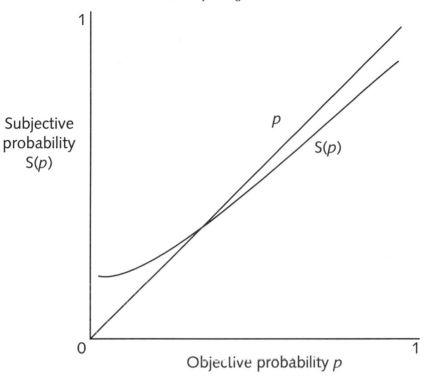

1

Subjective
probability
S(p)

p

S(p)

0   1

Objective probability p

Figure 5.5 A Subjective Probability Function Exhibiting Ambiguity Avoidance (Einhorn and Hogarth, 1987)

or

$$p(R_2) = 0.5 > p(R_1) \text{ and } p(B_2) = 0.5 > p(B_1),$$

either of which is inconsistent with the previous indifference. Yet it is hard to fault these avoiders because they seem to be seeking a security level that minimizes maximum regret. They know unambiguously the risk in urn 2, which sets a minimum on how unfavorable the bet can be. But they know nothing about urn 1, which might be much more unfavorable; so they prefer urn 2 to avoid the unlimited hazard of urn 1.

Hillel Einhorn and Robin Hogarth experimentally verified the existence of ambiguity avoidance and devised a theory to explain it in terms of adjustment on ambiguity.[18] Aversion, they argue, places greater weight on the likelihood of low (and hence undesired) probabilities, as in figure 5.5,

18. "Decision Making under Ambiguity," in *Rational Choice: The Contrast between Economics and Psychology*, ed. Robin M. Hogarth and Melvin W. Reder (Chicago: University of Chicago Press, 1986).

where the horizontal axis measures the objective probability, p, and the vertical axis measures the subjective probability, $S(p)$. This overestimation accounts for the Ellsberg paradox and is consistent with other interpretations of subjective probability.

APPLYING THE THEORIES

To summarize the inquiry launched by Markowitz, Allais, and Ellsberg, we have the following discoveries:

1. Many people so greatly prefer alternatives with certain outcomes over risky alternatives that they choose inconsistently, sometimes using the standard of minimizing maximum regret and other times using the standard of maximizing expected utility.
2. Many people [[prefer to take risks when all outcomes involve losses — that is, they appear to]] have convex utility curves for losses.
3. Many people subjectively overestimate the probability of low-probability events, especially events with undesirable outcomes.

It is difficult to determine how much these discoveries relate to real life. Although most people display some kind of risk aversion, not all people display inconsistencies and violations of the axioms of expected utility:[19] indeed, the majority usually behave as if they are maximizing expected utility. So, to some degree, the results of the experiments are superficial. For one thing, most of them are paper-and-pencil tests lacking in genuine risks for the subjects (although Grether and Plott, for example, did require subjects to risk some of the money they earned). Perhaps there would be strikingly different results if genuine risks were at stake.

Furthermore, most of the subjects have been naive. Hence the attributes discovered may be especially characteristic of people who have not previously thought about the problems of probability and utility theory. (Tversky and Kahneman attempted to avoid naivety by using, for example, physicians as subjects on public health puzzles; but physicians, however well informed about health, are often naive about probability, so of course the experimenters got their usual results.) Allais, however, did truly fool economists, who are presumably knowledgeable about probability theory, while Reilly failed to eliminate violations by instructing his subjects. We know that even extremely brilliant but arithmetically naive persons err

19. [[That is, the assumptions about individual preferences over gambles necessary to demonstrate that rational choice among risky alternatives requires that the chooser maximize expected utility. For explanation, see R. Duncan Luce and Howard Raiffa, *Games and Decisions* (New York: Wiley, 1957), chap. 2.]]

arithmetically: Thomas Hobbes thought he squared the circle and Bernoulli thought complementary probabilities added to more than one. Children learning arithmetic often have trouble with such matters as dividing by zero and, perhaps, if probability theory were as deep in the culture as the concept of zero, most adults would not violate the axioms of expected utility.

Finally, for the study of campaign rhetoric, the most superficial feature of the experimental tests of the Allais and Ellsberg paradoxes is that the experimental situation consists of a single experimenter presenting choices to subjects. No competing experimenter is present to explain to the subjects how the single experimenter is trying to fool them. By contrast, in the rhetorical situation (at least in campaigns and courtrooms and debates) there are competing rhetors presenting the auditors with at least two sides of the alternatives before them. Often, of course, several rhetors present several sides in quite sophisticated detail. Consequently, it may be that it is more difficult for rhetors to manipulate auditors than it is for the experimenter to manipulate subjects.

The drawbacks of this research notwithstanding, it seems evident that rational choosers sometimes use the standard of minimizing maximum regret instead of the usual standard of maximizing expected utility. If so, this is an important conclusion for the study of political rhetoric.

RISK AND RHETORICAL MANIPULATION

All of the odd discoveries about utility summarized in the preceding section are related in one way or another to the distaste that many people feel for making risky choices. Such distaste, or risk aversion, is what leads them to value smaller amounts of certain reward more than large amounts of risky reward. This is also what impels them to use minimax regret rather than maximum expected utility as a standard of choice. And it is just exactly this distaste that paves the way for rhetorical manipulation.

Rhetors can not only introduce risk and exploit risk aversion, but they also — perhaps especially — can exploit the standard of minimax regret because it is exceptionally sensitive to the external circumstances of choice. To illustrate this sensitivity, I offer the following example suggested in a somewhat different form by Thomas Schwartz in conversation and by John Ferejohn and Morris Fiorina.[20] Suppose that some citizens actually try to use the standard of minimizing the maximum regret that they would

20. John Ferejohn and Morris Fiorina, "The Paradox of Not Voting: A Decision Theoretic Analysis," *American Political Science Review* 68 (1974): 525–36.

feel from losses. This is a sensibly conservative standard, entirely appropriate for persons in a risk-aversion situation. It assumes that the worst outcome can well occur and then defends against it. When a citizen considers voting, he knows that he has $1/n$ chance of changing a loss to a tie or a tie to a win.[21] If the citizen does change the outcome in one of these ways, he earns a benefit, b, which is the absolute difference between losing and tying or between tying and winning. (Doubtless this b should differ according to whether voters cause a tie or a win. For the sake of brevity, however, I will treat the two cases as the same.) If he does not decide the election, he gets nothing that he would not have gotten anyway. In either case, he must bear the cost of voting, c, which may or may not be trivial. By the standard of maximizing expected utility, this citizen chooses to vote only if the expected value from voting is greater than zero.[22] If b is a small number and c and n are large, then sometimes the expected value of voting is less than zero, so the citizen chooses not to vote. Note that if $b < cn$, the citizen receives negative utility from voting, while the expected value of not voting is zero. On the other hand, by the standard of minimizing maximum regret, the citizen would, typically, choose to vote where $b > c$, as illustrated in tables 5.1 and 5.2.

The outcome matrix is simply the situation as described for the expected utility calculation. Continuing the assumption of $b > c$, the regret matrix is derived from the outcome matrix by calculating, for each cell in the outcome matrix, the difference between the outcome in the cell and the largest outcome in the column. Thus, each column in the regret matrix is a distinct potential state of the world. The entries in the cells record how much regret the chooser would feel, if the column state were to prevail and if, for each cell, the chooser were to choose the row strategy leading to that cell. Thus, in the upper left cell of the regret matrix, the entry is zero because $(b-c)-(b-c) = 0$. The chooser feels no regret because he did as well as in this circumstance. In the upper right cell, the entry is c because $0-(-c) = c$. The chooser, finding himself not decisive,

21. When the number of other voters, $n-1$, is even, there are n possible divisions of those $n-1$ voters — $(n-1$ to zero), $(n-2$ to one), . . . (zero to $n-1$) — of which exactly one is a tie that the nth voter can break in his or her favor. When the $n-1$ other voters is an odd number, there are n possible divisions of which exactly one permits the nth voter to change his or her loss into a tie. So, assuming that even and odd are equally likely and that each division of the vote is equally likely, the voter has $1/n$ chance of being decisive, either to win or to tie.

22. Note that, when voting, the voter is expected to get $b-c$ with a chance of $1/n$ and $-c$ with a chance of $(n-1)/n$. Summing these terms gives $(b-c)/n-c(n-1)/n = (b-cn)/n$. Thus, a prospective voter votes only if $b > n(c+1)$, i.e., only if his benefit exceeds everybody's costs by at least the number of voters.

Table 5.1 Outcome Matrix: Utilities from Voting and Not Voting As a Function of Whether the Voter Turns Out to be Decisive

	Eligible Citizen Is Decisive for Win (Odd) or Tie (Even) Pr = 1/n	Eligible Citizen Is Not Decisive Pr = (n − 1)/n	Expected Value of Row
Citizen votes	$b - c$	$-c$	$(b - cn)/n$
Citizen does not vote	0	0	0

Table 5.2 Regret Matrix for the Voting Problem in Table 5.1

	Decisive	Not Decisive	Maximum Regret in Row
Citizen votes	0	c	c
Citizen does not vote	$b - c$	0	$b - c$

regrets wasting the time, energy, and money for voting. Finally, the right column of the regret matrix shows the maximum regret for the row.

In this regret model of the world, the citizen would usually choose to vote because the minimum of the maximum regret column is, typically, in the "citizen votes" row. Thus, expected utility and minimax regret sometimes lead to different choices.

The choices by minimax regret can, however, be easily reversed by adding another column that, in effect, splits the left column into two parts. For an example of a strategy of inducing a reversal by adding another column, I offer Alexander Hamilton's (and John Jay's) repeated assertions in the *Federalist* papers that the failure to ratify would lead to the breakdown of the Union into several confederacies. For the citizen who assumes that there is a chance of 0.5 that Hamilton's forecast of balkanization is correct and who values the balkanization at -2b, the new outcome and regret matrices are presented in tables 5.3 and 5.4. By consulting these tables, one can easily see that, as before, utility-maximizing citizens would ordinarily not vote, unless their cost was zero. In a sharp reversal, however, the minimax-regret-using citizen would not vote either, because not voting occasions the least of the maximum regrets.

This example reveals the extreme sensitivity of the minimax regret

Table 5.3 Outcome Matrix: Utilities of Voting and Not Voting When a Decisive Vote May Have Good or Bad Consequences

	Citizen Decisive and Union Destroyed $Pr = \dfrac{1}{2/n}$	Citizen Decisive and Union Survives $Pr = \dfrac{1}{2/n}$	Citizen Not Decisive $Pr = (n-1)/n$	Expected Value of Row
Citizen votes	$-b-c$	$b-c$	$-c$	$-c$
Citizen does not vote	0	0	0	0

Table 5.4 Regret Matrix for the Voting Problem in Table 5.3

	Decisive Union Destroyed	Decisive Union Survives	Not Decisive	Maximum Regret
Citizen votes	$b+c$	0	c	$b+c$
Citizen does not vote	0	$c-b$	0	$c-b$

criterion to the style of the presentation of the alternatives. A rhetor who successfully raises doubts about the consequences of a decision can induce persons to change their choices.

Incidentally, with respect to the historical veracity of this example, it is true that Hamilton (and his associate, Jay) developed the theme of several confederacies more than any other Federalist writers. In the Appendix, this theme is code #12053, with 84,146 weighted words, about 2½ percent of the entire Federalist campaign. Publius (in the form of Hamilton and Jay) supplied about 66 percent of this theme, John Hancock about 12 percent, James Wilson about 11 percent, and Edmund Randolph about 6 percent, with the remainder scattered among six other less popular writers. Furthermore, Publius's strategy seems to have been consciously calculated. In the first *Federalist* paper, Hamilton appeared to throw it in as an afterthought. Jay, however, picked it up and made it almost the central theme of the second paper and used it again in the third. Hamilton then made it central in the fifth and sixth, used it quite a bit in the seventh and thirteenth, and mentioned it again in the fifty-ninth.

The literary structure suggests to me that Hamilton and Jay were deliberately seeking to instill self-doubt in those potential Antifederalist voters who might be using the standard of minimax regret.[23] This interpretation is supported by both eighteenth- and twentieth-century evidence. At least one Antifederalist writer accused Publius of attempting to frighten voters by falsely attributing plans for separate confederacies to Antifederalists. Centinel (probably Samuel Bryan), in refutation of Federalist arguments, wrote,

> The evils of anarchy have been portrayed with all the imagery of language, in glowing colours of elegance; . . . .The other spectre . . . raised to terrify and alarm the people out of the exercise of their judgment on this great occasion, is the dread of our splitting into separate confederacies or republics that might become rival powers and consequently liable to mutual wars. . . . This is an event still more improbable than the foregoing. . . . This hobgoblin appears to have sprung from the deranged brain of *Publius*, a New-York writer, who, mistaking sound for argument, has with Herculean labour accumulated myriads of unmeaning sentences, and *mechanically* endeavored to force conviction by a torrent of misplaced words. (CC 453)

Centinel's charge that Publius sought to frighten voters with an "improbable" expectation is, in my opinion, good evidence that at least one contemporary opponent recognized — and resented — Publius's rhetorical strategy of manipulating the calculation of minimax regret. In this century, Jackson Turner Main has investigated the objective validity of Publius's theme and finds that almost all references to separate confederacies in 1787–88 — whether approving or disapproving — were by Federalists.[24] So Antifederalists simply did not admit to Publius's charge that they intended to destroy the Union — except, rhetorically, Centinel himself in the essay just cited, in which he said that, even if rejection resulted in separate confederacies, "occasional wars" would be "infinitely preferable" to the "fangs of despotism" under the Constitution.

RISK AND CAMPAIGN RHETORIC

The main lesson to be taken from the analysis in the previous sections is that, in theory, rhetors are able to change voters' actions by structuring

23. Of course, it is anachronistic to attribute knowledge of utility theory to eighteenth-century rhetors and voters. Utility theory, however, is simply a way to describe human action, and the action so described can occur in any era. Presumably Hamilton and Jay thought of this tactic as a way to stymie some wavering Antifederalists, forcing them to reconsider their positions.

24. *The Antifederalists: Critics of the Constitution* (1961; repr. New York: W. W. Norton, 1974), 249.

and restructuring the terms of debate. Furthermore, in the concrete example discussed, it is known that one campaigner, Centinel, believed that his opponent, Publius, was doing exactly that. And the circumstances also suggest that Publius — as Hamilton and Jay passed the ball to each other — was quite conscious of the rhetorical effect of his theme.

The experiments and theorizing of Allais and Ellsberg demonstrate that risk aversion is a deep-seated feature of some persons' psyches. And the systematic efforts by Slovic and Lichtenstein, Tversky and Kahneman, Plott and Grether, Einhorn and Hogarth, and many others to reveal this feature in a wide variety of circumstances demonstrate that experimenters can produce inconsistent choices in the laboratory. The immediate inference is, then, that what experimenters can do in private rhetors can do in public. Laboratory manipulation of subjects' choices is a model for campaign manipulation of voters' choices.

It seems to me that an important element of campaigning consists of exploiting voters' attitudes toward risk. In this section, therefore, I will set forth a model of the actions of campaigners in the manipulation of these attitudes.

Because campaigners want to influence voters, the first consideration is the voters themselves. How do they behave in choosing among risky alternatives? Are they expected utility maximizers, expected regret minimizers, minimizers of maximum regret, or what?

Most of the experiments intended to detect violations of the axioms of expected utility show that a substantial number of people, typically a majority and often a large majority, do choose as if they maximize expected utility. What is found in the laboratory is probably also found in the less structured part of nature. Hence, a substantial body of voters also are probably expected utility maximizers. These are, I assume, those voters who have no doubts about where their interests lie and how they are going to vote. They are not tempted to avoid risk or to minimize maximum regret because they know, for certain, the outcome that benefits them. These are the voters for whom b is large or $c < 0$. (The term c can be negative when voters enjoy voting, as in fulfilling a duty. Hence the expected value of voting, $(b - cn) / n$, is guaranteed positive.)

What kind of appeal would a rational rhetor, one who wants to persuade voters, offer to such people? First, the rhetor would not waste much time on them. They are the core of either side, committed friends or obdurate enemies, and they are not susceptible to persuasion. Because they are thus rhetorically irrelevant, the utility-maximizing rhetor ignores them. If the rhetor should, however, decide to address them, the rhetor would observe that the main variable element in their calculation is b, the difference for them between the success of their favored candidate and the success of their disfavored one. That number may be increased either by an increased evaluation of the gain from winning or a decreased evaluation of the loss (that is, negative gain) from losing. While rhetors might thus strengthen the resolve of their supporters through either positive or negative arguments, rhetors can, as I will soon show, weaken the resolve of their opponents mainly by negative arguments. Public speech necessarily reaches both friends and enemies alike. So public speech, even for friends, would be mainly negative because negative appeals reach both audiences, whereas positive appeal is likely to reach only the irrelevant audience already committed to the rhetor.

Turning now to the minimizers of maximum regret, we need first to know who they are. Two kinds of voters stand out as possibilities: conscientious but ignorant voters might carefully avoid the worst, while the disengaged and indifferent might easily be misled. The disengaged, very much like the takers of paper-and-pencil tests, are easy to manipulate, as Tversky and Kahneman have shown, once the rhetor can get their attention. In a direct political study Michael MacKuen has demonstrated that editorial opinion much more easily influences disengaged citizens than it does politically involved citizens.[25] Unfortunately for rhetors, however, it also turns out to be much more difficult to get the disengaged to read or listen. The trick, therefore, is to get attention, and horror stories — the extreme negative appeals — help do that.

Conscientious but wholly uninformed voters, on the other hand, are perhaps already activated or at least easy to activate, but they need a survey of disasters to avoid. Such voters are like the self-interested but uninformed moralist behind John Rawls's veil of ignorance. Such persons, true minimizers of maximum regret, want to choose so as to avoid the worst for themselves. Not knowing their future location in society, which may indeed be the very worst, they choose so as to improve the lot of the worst off. Rawls assumes that serious but ignorant choosers would surely behave in this way.[26] Norman Frolich, Joseph Oppenheimer, and Cheryl Eavey challenge his belief by a contradictory laboratory demonstration, but their demonstration is far from conclusive because it is unlikely they were able to induce truly serious behavior in the laboratory.[27] So even though they find very little minimax regret choice, there may be much of it in the less

25. "Exposure to Information, Belief Integration, and Individual Responsiveness to Agenda Change," *American Political Science Review* 78 (1984): 372–91.

26. *A Theory of Justice* (Cambridge: Belknap Press of the Harvard University Press, 1971).

27. "Laboratory Results on Rawls' Distributive Justice," *British Journal of Political Science* 17 (1987): 1.

structured world outside the laboratory. The serious but ignorant chooser is also like James Scott's peasant, who chooses only to avoid crop disaster, not to maximize crop returns.[28]

In any event, for both indifferent citizens and uninformed citizens, the rational rhetor's appropriate strategy is to emphasize negative appeals. Emphasis on prospective disasters encourages the indifferent citizen to think about the choice to be made. Emphasis on the very worst disaster encourages the serious but uninformed voter to choose by the criterion of minimax regret. Because negative appeals are also appropriate for utility maximizing voters, it follows that rational rhetors would construct campaigns with mostly negative appeals.

A MODEL OF CAMPAIGN STRATEGY

Suppose that a campaigner is sensitive to the considerations just outlined, although, of course, without verbalizing them in this way. What strategy might the campaigner then adopt?

First, I think that campaigner would encourage voters to place the opponents' program to the left of zero on the horizontal axis and below zero on the vertical axis, as in figure 5.4, thus locating that program in the third, or negative, quadrant. This location means that the voters regard the program as having negative value (relative to the other programs) and that they believe it gives them negative utility. At the very minimum, the rhetor's advantage is that expected utility maximizers who move the opponent's program to the negative quadrant increase the difference between the programs. It is always possible that such an increase in the value of b will render positive a previously negative term $(b - cn)$. This would turn the rhetor's nonvoting supporters into voters.

Second, the good reason that the campaigner would give for thus locating the opponents' program is that this program leads to disaster. It does not matter if the disaster is, objectively, so unlikely as to be absurd. As Einhorn and Hogarth showed (see figure 5.5), voters may well give low-probability events a much higher subjective probability. And if intrinsically absurd predictions thereby appear to be reasonable possibilities, then the opponents' program is anchored firmly in the third quadrant.

The third element of the campaigner's strategy requires me to distinguish between the roles of the supporter and the opponent of the status

28. *The Moral Economy of the Peasant: Rebellion and Subsistence in Southeast Asia* (New Haven: Yale University Press, 1976). Scott concludes that such behavior is typical of very poor peasants, but Samuel Popkin indirectly challenges this view: see Samuel L. Popkin, *The Rational Peasant: The Political Economy of Rural Society in Vietnam* (Berkeley: University of California Press, 1979).

quo. The supporter often has nothing to defend positively. The status quo is visible to all and not subject to transformation by rhetorical reinterpretation. Supporters thus may devote almost all of their effort to locating the reformers negatively. The opponent of the status quo (that is, the reformer) is, however, offering an alternative program that is not completely understood and is vulnerable, therefore, to deliberate distortion by the supporters of the status quo. So the opponent has two tasks: to locate the status quo in the third quadrant and to defend the reform against attack. Although the reformer's campaign may be mostly negative, it must perforce contain some positive elements.

How might voters respond to campaigns structured in this way? As I have already shown, this strategy provides minimizers of maximum regret with a maximum to avoid and it provides already convinced expected utility maximizers with a large difference between candidates. But the most relevant category, rhetorically speaking, contains informed but uncertain expected utility maximizers. They are the potential marginal voters whom the rhetorician may be able to convince. So it is important to understand how they might respond.

Putting aside the voters whose choice is certain and those who are to be frightened with potential regrets, let us consider those who believe that some reform is desirable, but who are uncertain about the kind or quantity of reform. In the context of 1787, these are the persons who might decide to be either Federalists or Antifederalists.

How might Antifederalists appeal to them? Following the strategy of locating the Constitution at the extreme left of the horizontal axis, it becomes point I_1 in figure 5.6. Because the uncertain believe that the Articles, that is, the status quo, are not entirely adequate — otherwise they would be certainly Antifederalist — they place the Articles to the left of zero, at I_0. Finally, I locate their ideal point at zero, which is I_2. (Think of I_2 as a promise by Antifederalists of a second convention or conditional ratification.) We can then calculate the value of a lottery, I', on the following combination: $I' = pI_1 - (1-p)\ I_2$. Following Ellsberg and Einhorn and Hogarth, who assert that objectively small probabilities are overestimated, I have located I' as if $p > \frac{1}{2}$. According to Markowitz, Tversky and Kahneman, and Fishburn and Kochenberger, most people are risk acceptant in the third quadrant. [[Actually, the literature cited posits this risk acceptance in the third quadrant as defined when the origin is the status quo, rather than the *ideal point* as in Figure 5.6. However, owing to the steeper utility curve to the left of the origin (again, the status quo), the general result that Riker seeks should still hold in many cases.]] Tversky and Kahneman add that the utility curve is much closer to vertical in the third quadrant than in the first. So I have drawn it sharply convex in the third

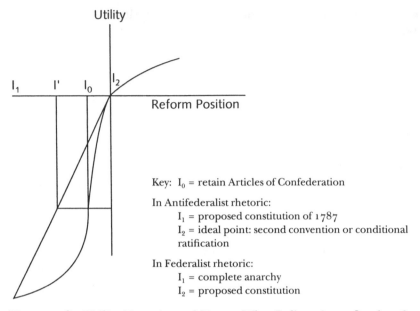

Key: I_0 = retain Articles of Confederation

In Antifederalist rhetoric:
    I_1 = proposed constitution of 1787
    I_2 = ideal point: second convention or conditional
    ratification

In Federalist rhetoric:
    I_1 = complete anarchy
    I_2 = proposed constitution

Figure 5.6   Utility Function of Voters Who Believe in 1787 that Some Constitutional Reform Is Desirable

quadrant. For convenience, I have drawn $I' = U(I_0)$, so that the expected utility of the lottery is the same as the utility of the status quo. Because the lottery carries some chance of improvement over the status quo, however, risk-acceptant voters can vote for Antifederalists who promise to repair the worst features of the Articles.

Federalists, on the other hand, appeal to the same voters by establishing complete anarchy as I_1, the Constitution as I_2, and the Articles at I_0. Then, by the same process, the uncertain voter can vote for the Federalists' promises, taking the risk of voting for the Constitution rather than enduring the status quo.

A TEST OF THE MODEL

Whether the above strategy of negative campaigning is rational or not depends upon whether the voters respond as expected. This question cannot be answered directly for campaigns in which all the voters are dead or have forgotten the campaign. But we can observe whether the campaigners did or did not adopt the strategy just outlined and, assuming that they were intelligent and sensitive people, we can infer from their successes or failures whether or not they correctly interpreted the voters. If users of the negative strategy are in some way successful, then we can infer that many voters minimize maximum regret or respond to uncertainty in the way described.

Many recent writers have commented on an apparent increase in negative campaigning.[29] Although the evidence offered here suggests that negativity has characterized campaigns from the very beginning, it still helps confirm the theory derived from an early campaign that other observers report similar evidence from recent campaigns. Lynda Kaid and Anne Johnston are the most convincing because they analyzed all the data from a part of each of eighteen national campaigns from 1960 to 1988 and found a far larger number of ad hominem attacks than I did. Had they used the same definition of negativity as I, doubtless the total amount of negativity in 1788 and 1988 would have been about the same, that is, averaging well over half. Unfortunately, these data do not definitively associate negativity with campaigners' plans, although Montague Kern and Kaid and Johnston both assert that the motivation for producing negative material is that rhetors wish to induce fear of bad outcomes. Hence presumably they wish to influence those who can be influenced by fear, namely, undecided and uninformed voters, in the way described in the preceding section.

That most campaigns have a large component of negativity is not, of course, a test because evidence that negativity exists does not confirm the details of the theory. But we have some confirmation if we can see that rhetors chose issues with a view toward producing effects in the way the theory specifies. So I examine briefly four campaigns.

Antifederalists built their campaign almost entirely around the prediction that the Constitution would destroy liberty, perhaps the worst disaster that Americans of 1787 could imagine. So their strategy was appropriately negative, although they hinted at more modest reform. Furthermore, the predicted disaster was, as we know from hindsight, an extremely remote possibility. The Constitution was adopted and liberty survived and flourished without serious threat. Apparently, however, the negative emphasis significantly influenced the voters. Turnout was higher than ever before in the United States and approached the level of turnout today. Initially, there seemed to be universal enthusiasm for the Constitution and few hostile writings appeared until mid-October. In the end, however, the Antifederalist delegates got about half of the vote, maybe even a bit more than

29. For example, Montague Kern, *Thirty-Second Politics: Political Advertising in the Eighties* (New York: Praeger, 1989); Lynda Lee Kaid and Anne Johnston, "Negative versus Positive Television Advertising in U.S. Presidential Campaigns, 1960–1988," *Journal of Communications* 41 (Summer 1991): 53–68; and Kathleen Hall Jamieson, *Dirty Politics: Deception, Distraction, and Democracy* (New York: Oxford University Press, 1992). All four of these studies argue that negative advertising has increased, although Jamieson cites anecdotal evidence from the nineteenth century, and Kaid and Johnston report on a systematic survey over the previous thirty years that showed the most negativity in 1964.

half.[30] So I conclude that negative Antifederalist rhetoric did in fact persuade many. This is evidence, in my opinion, that the campaigners of 1787 were correct in their beliefs about voters.

We get the same kind of evidence from Federalist campaigners. Aside from their defense of the Constitution, their main theme was the negative prediction that the Articles, if retained, would bring on military and commercial disaster. The probability of this event was, in my opinion, no higher than the Antifederalist prediction. In 1787, commerce was recovering, and the British threat was not compelling. Ultimately, in 1812, the Revolution did reopen, though not in the way the Federalists feared. It is difficult to believe, therefore, that without consolidation disaster was imminent. It is also difficult to believe that the Constitution was necessary for a modest amount of consolidation. Since many Antifederalists acknowledged the desirability of modest reform, reform of some sort was probably inevitable, Constitution or no Constitution. Nevertheless, the Federalists' negative campaign surely boosted turnout, and, given their negativity, they did retain about half of the voters — enough to win. I believe that, without their persistent negativity, they would have lost. If so, their campaign is further evidence that the campaigners of 1787 correctly interpreted voters.

Interestingly, the contemporary campaign for the Equal Rights Amendment (ERA) displayed many of the same characteristics.[31] The opponents of the status quo, like the proto-Federalists of the 1780s, conducted a long campaign stressing the economic and social disabilities of women. Jane Mansbridge describes this strategy as the theme of "fifty-nine cents," the supposed earnings of women for each dollar earned by men. Of course, the dire prediction that this ratio would continue indefinitely without the ERA was an extremely low-probability event. In fact, women's wages rose somewhat during the campaign (1970–82) for adoption of the amendment. Although we have no way of estimating the weight of various themes of the campaign, it seems obvious from Mansbridge's account that, like the Federalists, the women's rights leaders did defend the proposal against attack but devoted the most attention to the prediction of deep social and economic disabilities without it. Similarly, the opponents of the ERA, like the Antifederalists, conducted an almost entirely negative campaign. They predicted that the proposed reform would encourage "unisex toilets" (which became a joke and was abandoned as a theme), combat service for women (initially introduced and defended by supporters but exploited by oppo-

30. Main, *Anti-Federalists*.

31. Jane J. Mansbridge, *Why We Lost the ERA* (Chicago: University of Chicago Press, 1986).

nents), and, generally, the defeminization of American women. These, too, were mostly low-probability events. Because the amendment did not pass, we have no evidence from nature, but we can be sure, I believe, that deeply ingrained cultural inclinations are unlikely to be affected by constitutional provision.

Thus, on a contemporary campaign about an issue, a campaign similar in form to, but of longer duration than, the campaign for ratification, we observe campaigners adopting the same kind of rhetorical stance as the campaigners of 1787. Presumably in this recent campaign the rhetors observed in voters the same susceptibility to an overemphasis on and over-estimation of disasters. The success of the negative campaign by the supporters of the ERA to get the amendment through Congress and then the success of the extremely negative campaign by the opponents of the ERA confirms the rhetor's judgment and suggests that this susceptibility and overestimation is in fact characteristic of many voters.

Of course, these two issues turned out differently in the sense that the reformers won the first and lost the second. But that difference says nothing about the appropriateness of the choices on rhetorical strategy. As I will show later, the outcomes differed because the reformers differed in their choices of heresthetical strategy.

The behavior and political success of the rhetoricians in these two campaigns, conducted nearly two hundred years apart, are strong evidence that some voters minimize maximum regret and some are risk acceptant. Hence it is in fact rational to adopt a negative strategy. We do not know what proportion of voters are so inclined; it might be the vast majority or it might be a strategically placed few. I am inclined somewhat toward the latter estimate. Many voters know for certain how they will vote before a campaign starts and hence behave simply as expected utility maximizers. In many campaigns they may well be the majority. Others — the indifferent and uninformed, who minimize maximum regret, or the uncertain expected utility maximizers — may, however, be strategically located in all campaigns. As undecided voters, they are the ones whom campaigners can persuade. If they are indifferent citizens, they are the ones whom campaigners can activate. The indifferent may be small in number — as small, for example, as 5 percent — yet because they are positioned in the middle of the spectrum, it may be worth campaigners' while to appeal mainly to them. Consequently, even though minimizers of maximum regret or uncertain utility maximizers may be few, it may be entirely rational for campaigners to appeal to them as if they were in the majority. Clearly the campaigners both of 1787 and of 1970–82 thought that such voters were distributed so as to make it rational to campaign negatively. They were probably correct. The campaigners were acting on the following rhetorical principle, which I offer as a generalization to be tested on other campaigns:

Persuasion of Uncertain Voters
Given potential marginal voters who are uncertain or indifferent, rhetors emphasize extreme and objectively improbable dangers in the opponents' program.

6

Rhetorical Interaction in the Campaigns

I N THE PREVIOUS CHAPTERS I analyzed the content of the rhetoric of two campaigns separately, as if two sets of rhetors were independently addressing separate classes of voters. This form of presentation suggests a scenario of simple proselytizing, wherein sly, sophisticated rhetors convert shy, naive voters. This is a deceptive model, however, because actually the two campaigns were concurrent in time and entwined with each other in audience and content. Although victory would ultimately come to the side that most successfully impressed and manipulated the voters and delegates, it is descriptively inaccurate to attribute the outcome, as some scholars do and as I have perhaps previously done, to the inherent quality of the arguments.

Thus Herbert Storing, after reviewing the debate, asks, "Why did the Antifederalists lose?"[1] The negative cast of Storing's question probably results from Storing's acceptance of Jackson Turner Main's (possibly dubious) calculation that the Antifederalists likely got more votes for delegates than did the Federalists.[2] Hence for Main and Storing the puzzle was negative: "Why did the Antifederalists lose?" rather than the more natural and obvious puzzle: "Why did the Federalists win?" Storing answers that Antifederalists lost "not merely because they were less clever arguers or less skillful politicians but because they had the weaker argument." I agree that the Antifederalists had the weaker argument, but this is not a conclusive answer. One wonders why, if they had the weaker argument, they got about the same number of votes. Of course, what constitutes a weaker or stronger argument depends as much on the auditors' or readers' predispositions as

1. *The Complete Anti-Federalist*, 6 vols. (Chicago: University of Chicago Press, 1981), vol. 1, *What the Anti-Federalists Were For*, 71.

2. *The Antifederalists: Critics of the Constitution* (1961; rept. New York: W. W. Norton, 1974), 249.

it does on an objective evaluation of the debate. So to say that Federalists had the better argument reveals more about Storing (and about me!) than it does about the correct answer to the question concerning winning and losing.

As we know from social choice theory, all public opinion is flux. As elaborated in chapter 9, a *cycle of preference* is said to exist when there is no equilibrium of social choice, that is, for any issue position a majority of people prefer some other position. Cycles of preference are always possible and often ubiquitous.[3] The fact that voters mostly agree with one side's argument does *not* imply that they select its policy alternative. Rather the selection of one alternative in the cycle depends on a variety of both rhetorical and nonrhetorical features of the decision process.

It is not appropriate to elaborate social choice theory here, but I should point out one fundamental meaning of cycles for Federalist victory. The way parties interactively develop issues has a lot to do with which alternative ultimately wins. Of course, ratification must also have depended on a variety of heresthetical manipulations, for example, agenda control, that directed the selection of the Federalist-preferred alternative from the cycle.[4] But I will leave discussion of those devices for later. Here I concentrate on the sifting of issues in rhetorical interaction because the issues thus selected set the scene for heresthetical manipulations.

INTERACTIVE DEBATE

Campaigns are not like school debates or courtroom disputes. In debates and courtrooms, judges keep the disputants focused on the predetermined subject by scoring the arguments or by accepting only relevant ones. In trial courts, judges exercise even more control, limiting and even directing the presentation. As a consequence, disputants in these settings directly engage each other in argument, rebuttal, and surrebuttal or in complaints and answers followed by replications, rejoinders, and surre-joinders. As the vocabulary suggests, these disputes must therefore follow fairly rigid rules of relevance.

Campaigns are quite different because there is no judge. Each disputant decides what is relevant, what ought to be responded to, and what themes to emphasize. Today campaigners sometimes complain that the themes of the other side are "not the issue," as if there were a judge to decide what the real issue is. But of course there are no judges, and what-

3. A fuller explanation can be found, for example, in William H. Riker, *Liberalism against Populism*, chap. 5.
4. *Heresthetic* is defined and discussed in chapter 1.

ever a campaigner successfully emphasizes is, willy-nilly, an issue. In 1787–88 the writers, at least those in my sample, did not complain about false issues. Their silence implies recognition of the essential anarchy of the campaign forum.

In the unstructured situation of a campaign, what might we expect rational campaigners to do? In 1787–88 the disputants were for the most part attempting to estimate the consequences of consolidation or, alternatively, of maintaining the status quo. These were fundamental features of political organization, so the campaigners could reasonably attribute a wide array of potential consequences to the alternative outcomes. From this array, each rhetor was entirely free to choose which consequences to emphasize. Federalists and Antifederalists chose quite different things: Federalists emphasized the crisis of the times, Antifederalists the threat to liberty in the Constitution (see tables 4.1 and 4.2). Each side presumably believed that these disparate themes would work to their advantage. Surely neither side chose to emphasize themes that advantaged the other.

The result of this method of choosing issues was that rhetors in the two groups did not, by and large, discuss the same things. But of course they were conscious of each others' claims, and in many ways phrased their arguments in order to undercut the opponents' positions. So while we have two campaigns with different themes, we also have responses and deprecations. In some degree, which I shall try to assess, these interactions affected both the course of debate and, possibly, the outcomes.

The most direct sort of response is criticism of the words and actions of an opponent. In the national campaigns studied here, as distinct from local campaigns, by far the largest amount of direct criticism centers around the works and words of prominent public figures who wrote something for or against the Constitution under their own names. The bulk of the writing in both campaigns was pseudonymous: such names as Publius (The Federalist), Federal Farmer, Centinel, Landholder, and others were used. But several of the framers—Washington, Franklin, Wilson, Randolph, Elbridge Gerry, George Mason, Luther Martin, Robert Yates, John Lansing, Hugh Williamson, William Pierce—did write under their own names, and some of these writings were widely discussed, especially those printed early in the campaign. They were also lightning rods for criticism, and, to interpret the significance of the direct interaction, I will discuss several instances: those concerning Washington, Wilson, Gerry, and Mason.[5]

5. I have selected these four figures partly because their writings are among the most important in my sample, that is, they appear in table 6.1, which lists the number of printings of the most widely disseminated items in Kaminski and Saladino, *Commentaries on the Constitu-*

Table 6.1   Frequency of Printing of Widely Disseminated Items in
Commentaries on the Constitution, I–IV

Citation	Content	Times Printed
1. CC 76	The Constitution, with letter of transmittal to Congress	76
2. CC 96 A,B	Report of Washington's accident (with comments on his destiny)	73
3. CC 508 A,B	Massachusetts' Proposed Amendments	60
4. CC 386 A	Washington to Carter (endorsing the Constitution)	51
5. CC 638A	Washington to Gibbs (praising Massachusetts' ratification)	50
6. CC 339	Sullivan's speech to New Hampshire General Court praising the Constitution	50
7. CC 101, para. 6	*Pennsylvania Gazette* (Washington for President)	45
8. CC II, 456	Squib *Pennsylvania Gazette* (False report of Washington to represent Fairfax in Virginia Ratifying Convention)	45
9. CC 227 A	Gerry's Objections to the Constitution	42
10. CC III 565	Squib *Massachusetts Gazette* (Georgia's Ratification)	42
11. CC 77	Franklin's speech to the Federal Convention	40
12. CC 289	Wilson's speech to the Pennsylvania Convention (all versions)	40
13. CC 233A	Washington's comment (spurious) on signing the Constitution	39
14. CC 101, para. 3	Constitution wisest, etc., of any government	38
15. CC 134	Wilson's speech in the State House Yard	38
16. CC 407	An Old Man (Federalist description of Carlisle riot)	38
17. CC 566A	Hancock's speech to the Massachusetts General Court	36
18. CC 529A	Calculation of Delegates' support for Constitution	35
19. CC III, p. 559	Squib *Pennsylvania Herald* (West Indians attracted to U.S. by the Constitution)	34
20. CC 156A	Middle States Baptist Convention's endorsement of the Constitution	33
21. CC III, p. 558	Squib, *Pennsylvania Packet* (New Jersey ratification unanimous)	32
22. CC 552A	Francis Hopkinson, "A Yankee," poem celebrating Massachusetts ratification	32
23. CC 290B	Jay's endorsement of the Constitution	31
24. CC 125A	Statement of the Sixteen Seceding Pennsylvania Assemblymen	30
25. CC 150	"Federal Constitution," rejoinder to the Seceders	30
26. CC 276	Mason's Objections	30
27. CC 439	Clinton's Speech to the New York Legislature	30

WASHINGTON'S ENDORSEMENT

I start with Washington not because he wrote the most elaborate or provocative commentary but because his endorsement of the Constitution was one of the most widely used Federalist arguments (see table 6.1, items 1, 2, 4, 5, 7, 8, and 13). That Washington endorsed the Constitution must have been a widely known fact. His letter transmitting the Constitution from the federal convention to the Congress contained the first statement of what became typical Federalist arguments on the inadequacy of the Articles, on the consequent necessity of Union and consolidation, and on the desirability of ratification. His strongest remarks were probably that "the greatest interest of every true American" was "the consolidation of our Union, in which is involved our prosperity, felicity, safety, perhaps our national existence." The 423 words of this letter, appended to the Constitution, were printed at least 76 times (table 6.1, item 1, CC 76). I did not include this letter in my count of the campaigns, but it amounts to 32,148 weighted words, which, moreover, were disseminated early enough to impress nearly everyone.

Federalists used this endorsement immediately and extensively. One of the first newspaper discussions of the Constitution prophesied that Washington would be the first president (table 6.1, item 7, CC 101, 45 printings). Also the reports of Washington's accident on his trip home from the Philadelphia convention emphasized that his life was saved for the sake of his future leadership (table 6.1, item 2, CC 96B, 73 printings).

On 1 October a Boston newspaper praised the Constitution and said, "Its acceptance, will enroll the names of the WASHINGTONS and FRANKLINS, of the present age, with those of the SOLONS and NUMAS of antiquity. . . . Illustrious CHIEFTAIN! immortal SAGE — ye will have the plaudit of the world for having twice saved your country!" (CC 120, 7 printings). After some Antifederalist criticism of the Constitution had begun to appear, Federalists used Washington's endorsement to dispel fears: "It is ushered to us under the respectable and illustrious signature of GEORGE WASHINGTON. . . . [T]o suppose that any act of his, could . . . injure a people whose freedom he has already established, . . . would be a piece of base ingratitude, that no *honest* American can possibly be guilty of" (CC 220, 7

tion, vols. 1–4. For that table, note that the theoretical maximum of printings is just over one hundred, i.e., ninety-seven newspapers, three magazines, and several pamphlet editions. So the table, containing items ranging from thirty to seventy-six printings, consists of those attaining from, roughly, one-third to three-fourths of the theoretical maximum. Since there were more Federalist papers than Antifederalist ones, most of the widely disseminated items are Federalist. The only Antifederalist material included is Gerry's objections to the Constitution, Mason's objections, the statement of the sixteen seceding assemblymen in Pennsylvania, and Clinton's speech to the New York legislature.

printings). Soon Federalist editors transformed Washington's endorsement into a threat, attributing to him the following (uncharacteristic and of course spurious) utterance as he signed the Constitution: *"Should the states reject this excellent Constitution, the probability is, an opportunity will never again offer to cancel another in peace — the next will be drawn in blood"* (table 6.1, item 13, CC 233A, 39 printings, drawn from Curtius III). Other Federalist editors contrasted Washington and Franklin with the nonsigners: "Are the gentlemen who have withheld their assent from the Federal Constitution, superiour to Washington or Franklin . . . — men whose names . . . are known throughout the world. . . . [T]he good and great of every nation have been lavish in their panegyricks. . . — a French philosopher [Mirabeau], speaking of our illustrious Fabius, enraptured bids us to 'Begin with the infant in the cradle: Let the first word he lisps be WASHINGTON'" (CC 251, 11 printings).

Federalists' use of Washington's endorsement posed a difficult problem for Antifederalists. Most of them responded simply by ignoring the subject. A few attempted to divert attention, usually by pointing out that "great names" ought not to be decisive — a muted and indirect attack. Thus Cato I: "The wisest and best men may err, and their errors, if adopted, may be fatal to the community" (CC 103, 6 printings). Old Whig (possibly George Bryan) began his third essay with " 'Great men are not always wise.' They have their seasons of inattention" (CC 181, 2 printings). Early in his second essay, Centinel (probably Samuel Bryan, son of George Bryan), much more vituperative than Old Whig, more widely disseminated, and much more resented by Federalists, remarked, "What astonishing infatuation! to stake their [the people's] happiness on the wisdom and integrity of any set of men" (CC 190, 11 printings). Or again, Brutus, Junior, possibly the same author as Federal Farmer, noted in his first letter, "It is an invidious task, to call into question the character of individuals. . . . But when we are required implicitly to submit our opinions to those of others . . . [because] they are so wise and good as not to be able to err, . . . every honest man will justify a decent investigation" (CC 239, 2 printings). Altogether the be-suspicious-of-great-names argument accounted for 19,191 weighted words in 19 essays. By contrast, Federalist advice to follow the great names was at least 26,089 weighted words, entirely apart from Washington's and Franklin's own recommendations, which together were about 75,000 weighted words.[6] Although the argument from suspicion probably helped to dispel some of the framers' aura generally, it did not attack specifically the over-

6. Washington to Congress (CC 76): 32,148; Washington to Carter (CC 386A): 15,249; Washington to Gibbs (CC 638): 5,300; Franklin's speech to the convention (CC 77): 22,152.

whelming prestige of Washington. So Centinel carried the matter further. In his first essay he launched a direct assault: "The wealthy and ambitious... flatter themselves that they have lulled all distrust . . . by gaining the concurrence of the two men in whom America has the highest confidence [Washington and Franklin].... I would be very far from insinuating that the two illustrious personages... have not the welfare of their country at heart; but that the unsuspecting goodness and zeal of the one, has been imposed on, in a subject of which he must be necessarily inexperienced, from his other arduous engagements; and that the weakness and indecision attendant on old age [Franklin was eighty-one], has been practiced in the other" (CC 133, 19 printings, 5,440 weighted words). Centinel frequently repeated this argument (CC 190, CC 311, CC 410, CC 427, and CC 470); but the only other writers who used the argument that Washington was misled were those, like Centinel, in the coterie of Ebenezer Oswald of the *Philadelphia Independent Gazetteer,* namely, An Officer of the Late Continental Army (CC 231 and RCS: Penn., 210–16), Philadelphiensis IX (CC 507), and an unsigned note in the *Gazetteer* (CC 290A).

Although Centinel's disparagement of Washington's judgment garnered 12,162 weighted words — mostly from Centinel's own letters, the first two of which, probably owing to other arguments, were printed 19 and 11 times — it did not catch on. And for good reason: it excited substantial revulsion. In the next issue after Centinel I, Oswald printed (CC 158) a complaint about Centinel's "abuse." Similarly, Uncas (CC 247) remarked of Centinel's "insult" that "a *Bear* with a *sore head* will growl in the *serenest weather,*" while a New Haven writer (CC 283A) denounced Centinel for saying "General WASHINGTON is a Fool from habit and Dr. FRANKLIN a Fool from age." In each case the writer began a general attack on Centinel by assailing his disparagement of Washington, which suggests that all three of them believed that the presumed insult was Centinel's most vulnerable spot. That Antifederalists outside of Oswald's circle did not pick up Centinel's argument suggests that they, too, believed this.

The arguments against great names and against Washington as being misled were not successful, and most Antifederalists simply ignored Washington's initial endorsement, which, after all, might be interpreted as an official act rather than a personal opinion. But in December Washington wrote a personal letter (CC 386A) that made his endorsement unequivocal; printed 51 times in January, February, and March, the letter probably became universally known: "There is *no Alternative* between the *Adoption* of it [the Constitution] and *Anarchy*" (7,395 weighted words) and "General Government . . . is *really at an End*" (4,386 weighted words). Again, most Antifederalists ignored the letter as, presumably, unanswerable. But in

Massachusetts, where the state ratifying convention was in progress (it ran from 9 January to 7 February), the Antifederalists seemed to think it sufficiently dangerous to require a response. Some writers denied the letter's authenticity (CC 386C, 386H), while others (CC 386C, 386F), misreading one phrase, branded Washington a potential man on horseback. Washington had said that no one state or minority of states could dictate a constitution (read: the retention of the Articles) except by the "ultima ratio." An American (CC 386F) misinterpreted this to mean that "the General has declared, that this Constitution shall be supported by the ULTIMO [sic] RATIO, that is by force." Of course, Federalists quickly corrected the misreading (CC 386E, 386G), and there the matter apparently came to rest because these articles were seldom reprinted either inside or outside Massachusetts. Furthermore, Washington wrote still another endorsement of the Constitution (CC 638A) in the form of a letter (29 February) congratulating the Massachusetts Antifederalists for their "conciliatory behaviour" in acquiescing to the state's ratification and prophesying that this ratification would be "greatly influential in obtaining a favourable determination" in the remaining states. As Kaminski and Saladino observe, the reaction to this letter was "minimal" (CC 638), and it was printed 51 times in all but two states.

Washington's endorsement appears to have been persuasive. Of course, we do not know if there were people who voted for ratification purely because of the endorsement. But, then, we are equally ignorant about similar puzzles in contemporary campaigns, simply because we do not know much about individual choices. We do, however, have systematic knowledge of the editors' behavior in 1787–88, which gives us some evidence about the persuasiveness of the endorsement.

Federalist editors showed that they thought Washington's approbation persuasive by extensively reprinting his letters (items 4 and 5 in table 6.1). Seventy-six out of ninety-seven editors in the country printed the Constitution with his official letter to Congress appended, but they also printed his two nonofficial letters 51 and 50 times, which is close to the maximum in table 6.1. They also widely disseminated newspaper accounts of his actions (items 2, 7, 8, and 13).

Antifederalist editors displayed a similar conviction of the persuasiveness of the endorsement by treating it as unanswerable. Because the be-suspicious-of-great-names rejoinder was self-defeating and shunned by all but the Oswald circle and because Washington's letters occasioned little response, Antifederalist editors must have given up on refutation and conceded, albeit reluctantly. This seems reasonable. Citizens were accustomed to recognizing and accepting Washington's leadership, and this custom would not change because of a few editorial criticisms.

WILSON'S SPEECH

Although Antifederalists could not effectively oppose Washington's endorsement, they could and did rebut other Federalist writers. Antifederalists directed their most intense and most effective attack on James Wilson, even though Publius produced a much larger volume of Federalist argument. Indeed, the first seventy-four *Federalist* papers, which are the ones in my sample, constituted 771,682 weighted words, about 24 percent of my Federalist campaign. Of course Publius achieved this by writing a lot. Most of the papers were printed only infrequently: only five were printed 10 to 16 times; twenty-nine 5 to 9 times; and forty 3 or 4 times, including the book form that was too late to influence much of the campaign. Wilson wrote far less. But his speech of 6 October before the ratifying convention in the Pennsylvania State House Yard (CC 134) was the main rhetorical event of October. Editors printed it 38 times, producing 92,118 weighted words, about 3 percent of my Federalist sample. Probably because of the interest generated by the 6 October speech, editors then printed his speech of 24 November to the Pennsylvania convention (CC 289) 40 times. It is difficult to measure its weighted words, but because it was quite long it constituted a maximum of 386,720, or about 12 percent. Since, however, much of this weight came later in the campaign, the response to it was fairly muted.

The 6 October speech generated an intense Antifederal response. To demonstrate this I list here all those essays that responded directly, naming Wilson or referring to him clearly though obliquely. Several writers attempted a systematic refutation, point by point: Democratic Federalist (CC 167), Old Whig II (CC 170), Republican I (CC 196), and Cincinnatus (Arthur Lee) I, II, III, IV, and V (CC 222, 241, 265, 287, and 307). Others devoted more than half of more general essays to rejoinders to Wilson: Old Whig III (CC 181), Centinel II (CC 190), and Brutus II (CC 221). Still others responded with several paragraphs: Timolean (CC 223), Brutus, Junior (CC 239), and Federal Farmer (CC 242) as well as many, not counted here, who referred to Wilson in passing.

Altogether these direct responses sum to 109,813 weighted words, about 6 percent of the Antifederal campaign. Considering that the speech of 6 October was only 3 percent of its campaign (double the size of the Antifederalist campaign) and that the Antifederal response is thus propor-

Table 6.2   Extentions of Wilson's Arguments and Responses to Them

	Weighted Words	
Wilson's Argument	Antifederalists: Extensions of Responses to Wilson's Arguments	Federalists: Extensions of Wilson's Arguments
1. It is proper to omit rights in a government of delegated powers	91,863	31,125
2. The Constitution does not abolish trial by jury in civil cases because state codes provide for it	50,429	25,929
3. The Constitution provides for a standing army for national safety	71,369	105,696
4. The Senate cannot be aristocratic because it can act only with the House and President	19,674	39,330
5. The Constitution does not reduce states to mere corporations because they fill national offices	149,075	181,650
6. For national safety, the Constitution provides for direct taxes with civilian collection, though the impost will be the main national tax	101,923	91,578
7. State office holders oppose the Constitution out of private interest	3,603	28,988
TOTAL	487,938	504,296
Percent of Campaign	28%	16%

tionately four times as large as Wilson's speech, Antifederal editors must have believed they had a great advantage in attacking him. Furthermore, the themes developed in this attack ultimately become a very considerable part of the Antifederalist campaign. In table 6.2, I list Wilson's propositions, along with the volume of Antifederal responses and Federal volume of extensions of Wilson's arguments.

Ultimately, the Antifederalists' responses to Wilson's arguments account for over one-fourth of their campaign (see table 6.2). On the other

Table 6.3   Relative Weight of Wilsonian Arguments and Responses
Thereto

Subject	Federal Volume/Antifederal Volume
1. bill of rights	31,125/91,863 = .33
2. civil juries	25,929/50,429 = .51
3. standing army	105,696/71,369 = 1.48
4. Senate	39,330/19,674 = 1.99
5. states' role	181,650/149,075 = 1.21
6. direct taxes	91,578/101,923 = .89
7. state office holders	28,988/3,603 = 8.04

hand, Federalists' elaboration of Wilson's arguments account for less than one-sixth of their campaign. Antifederal editors thought Wilson was vulnerable and indeed that all Federalists were vulnerable when they reiterated Wilson's points. Furthermore, though constrained to defend themselves by continuing to make arguments similar to Wilson's, Federalists obviously had less enthusiasm, as if they too sensed the vulnerability. If both sides were right about vulnerability, we can learn a lot about the interaction of the two campaigns by investigating this apparent Federal weakness.

Table 6.3 reveals just where the Federalists' vulnerability lay, that is, just where Antifederalists were far more eager than Federalists to discuss the subject. In volume of weighted words, the total Federalist campaign is just about double the volume of the Antifederalist campaign: 3,204,819 Federalist + 1,742,434 Antifederalist = 4,947,253 total weighted words; the Federalists produced 65 percent of the total and the Antifederalists 35 percent. Hence it is expected that, if the editors on the two sides concurred on the importance and value of developing or attacking Wilsonian arguments, the Federalists would produce about twice the volume of the Antifederalists. That one side produces more or less of the expected volume indicates that this side senses an advantage or disadvantage.

The relative volume on these arguments is set forth in table 6.3. Most of the ratios are easy to understand. On the fourth argument (Senate), volume is as expected: a ratio of about 2 to 1. Presumably Antifederalists hoped they could make "aristocracy" an issue, while Federalists believed that even the dullest voter would understand an upper house, which existed in most states. On the third (standing army) and fifth (states' role) arguments, volume is only moderately disproportionate. The issue of a standing army is something of an intellectual tie. Conventionally Americans opposed it but perhaps also thought it was a military necessity in a hostile world. Similarly, the Antifederalists were entirely correct that the Constitution diminished the states' role, but Federalists could also show that to call them "mere corporations" was a demagogic exaggeration. The Antifederalist volume on the sixth argument (taxes) is relatively quite large, but that is to be expected. Supporters of the status quo (Antifederalists here) usually denounce the cost of reform, whereas reformers (here Federalists) usually ignore cost increases if they can. On the seventh argument (state officials), the Federalists obviously sensed a great advantage, though the argument is not very large in absolute terms. This sense of advantage is easy to understand. In Philadelphia and New York, where the state officials employed in the metropolis typically belonged to the faction with few urban supporters, Federalist editors could believably attribute greed for retaining a metropolitan job to Antifederal officeholders like George Bryan in Pennsylvania and John Lamb in New York.

The truly striking ratios are the first (bill of rights) and second (civil juries). Here the Antifederalist advantage and Federalist disadvantage are abundantly clear.

Wilson's argument on a bill of rights was, in his own words (CC 134), that in establishing state governments "everything which is not reserved is given," but in establishing the federal government "everything which is not given, is reserved. This distinction being recognized, will furnish an answer to those who think the omission of a bill of rights, a defect in the proposed constitution: for it would have been superfluous and absurd to have stipulated with a federal body of our own creation, that we should enjoy those privileges, of which we are not divested either by the intention or the act, that has brought that body into existence." No one can deny that Wilson here created a neat and memorable formula — "not reserved is given, not given is reserved" — a formula worthy indeed of a Philadelphia lawyer, which is exactly what Wilson was.

Wilson did not, however, invent this argument. It was accepted by the framers in the convention and subsequently accepted in Congress at the time it sent the Constitution to the states. The first person recorded as uttering it was Roger Sherman, the Connecticut "Countryman" of the ratification campaign. According to Madison's *Notes*, on 12 September in the federal convention George Mason (Vir.) proposed a bill of rights, saying it might be prepared in a few hours. Elbridge Gerry (Mass.) then moved for a committee to do so. Madison recorded, "Mr. Sherman was for securing the rights of the people where requisite. The State Declarations of Rights are not repealed by this Constitution; and being in force are sufficient." Mason then responded, "The Laws of the U.S. are to be paramount to State Bills of Rights." The convention then rejected Gerry's motion, zero to ten (Farrand 1937, 2:587–88). As Mason implied, the time constraint was more of an issue than Sherman's argument—though the joint sponsorship of Mason and Gerry would probably have doomed any motion at this point in the convention. Two days later, Gerry, this time with Charles Pinckney (S.C.), tried to insert a declaration for liberty of the press. Again Sherman was the spokesman of the opposition, and this time he made his argument clearer by saying of the notion, "It is unnecessary— the power of Congress does not extend to the Press." This motion was then rejected by a much closer margin, five to six, which ought to have warned the framers of the tone of the forthcoming ratification debates (Farrand 1937, 2:617–18).

It does not seem likely, however, that Sherman was the sole inventor of the argument. Pierce (Ga.), who left the convention before the end of July, set forth a primitive version of it in a letter of 28 September (CC 634): "The defined powers of each department of the government, and the restraints that naturally follow, will be sufficient to prevent the invasion of . . . those rights. Where then can be the necessity for a Bill of Rights?" Pierce thus has the core of the all-not-given-is-reserved argument, and he may have learned it before Sherman's recorded utterance.

Or Pierce may have learned it in New York, where he was on 28 September, because the previous day Nathaniel Gorham (Mass.), a framer who was also a member of Congress, used it in the congressional debate over the transmission of the Constitution to the states. According to Melancton Smith's (N.Y.) notes, Gorham argued there was "no necessity of a Bill of rights, because a Bill of rights in state Govts. was intended to retain certain powers, as ye Legis. had unlimd. powers—" (CC 95).

Except for Mason's remark about the supremacy clause, both the convention and Congress accepted the Sherman-Gorham-Pierce rationale without question. It can thus be regarded as the settled Federalist response to the charge of omission of a bill of rights. It was left to Wilson, however, to encapsulate the argument in a memorable formula.

Unfortunately for the Federalists, the improved argument was not much help and may have caused much harm. Only a few Federalists used it, mainly perhaps because only a few Federalists talked about a bill of rights anyway.[7]

---

7. Wilson's argument involved only 24,417 weighted words, of which 20,805 were by Wilson himself. Non-Wilsonian defenses added another 6,708 words. So Wilson's defense in one speech is much more than half of the total Federalist discussion of the issue. Publius, by far the most voluminous Federalist, delayed discussion of a bill of rights until the next to last paper (the eighty-fourth)—not in my sample—and then barely alluded to Wilson's argument.

I think the Federalists were afraid of Wilson's formula. One Federalist sympathizer, A True Friend (CC 326), referred to Wilson's argument as "*not sufficient* to *calm the inquietude* of a *whole nation*" and proposed a bill of rights as a compromise. (See also a private letter, CC 249.) Of those Federalists who did use Wilson's argument, only five used it unequivocally. An American Citizen IV (Tench Coxe, CC 183B), writing at Wilson's request, wrote one brief paragraph on this theme; Anti Cincinnatus (CC 354), writing against Cincinnatus I, followed Wilson closely and more extensively but inelegantly; Williamson (N.C.), a framer, used Wilson's formula briefly in a speech in North Carolina on 8 November (not published until 25 February, CC 560); Marcus (James Iredell, CC 548) used Wilson in a point-by-point refutation of Mason's objections, identifying it from "Mr. Wilson's celebrated speech"; and Aristides (Alexander Contee Hanson, CC 490) set forth Wilson's argument fully.

These few passages make up the entire Federalist use of the most famous argument in the "celebrated speech." By contrast, the Antifederalists had a field day. I have already listed the writers who attacked Wilson, most of them on his first argument, among others, because it was made to order for their purposes. One can sense their delight as they speak of his "flimsy sophistry," denounce his "specious" argument, and sneer at his formula for having "more the quaintness of a conundrum than the dignity of an argument." They devised several telling responses. Like Mason's riposte to Sherman, they pointed to the necessary and proper clause, the supremacy clause, the federal court system, and so forth to show that congressional power could override popular liberties and should therefore be restrained by a bill of rights. Cincinnatus and several others argued that the states making a federal constitution were just like citizens making a state constitution, so if a bill of rights was appropriate in the latter, then it was equally so in the former. But the Antifederalists' neatest argument, one that matches Wilson's formula in cleverness, observed that the Constitution itself listed a number of prohibitions on Congress (for example, no bill of attainder, no title of nobility, and so on). Thus, as Brutus II said, "If everything which is not given is reserved, what propriety is there in these exceptions?" (CC 222) Or as Republican I said of titles of nobility, "Is this power *expressly* given to Congress? if it is not, then the exception must be to guard against an incidental or implied power" (CC 196). Thus they proved, out of the Constitution itself, the falsity of Wilson's formula. It cannot be that everything not given is reserved.

In a sense Wilson got what he deserved: a sophistical claim invites a sophistical rejoinder. Not surprisingly, therefore, the Federalists left this particular field of battle quite shaken up, and, as noted, stayed well away from it thereafter.

The same thing happened in the argument over civil juries. Wilson had argued that, because the practice of the states varied widely on the use of juries in civil cases, the framers thought it best not to impose a national rule, knowing, of course, that the states would continue to follow their established practices. Unfortunately for Wilson, however, the guarantee of juries in criminal cases attracted attention to the absence of a guarantee for civil cases. Cincinnatus II (CC 241) observed that the "reservation of trial by jury in criminal, is an exclusion of it in civil cases. Why else should it be mentioned at all?" Cincinnatus's inference is logically false — as he himself elsewhere said, civil juries are "not secured" rather than "excluded" — but "exclusion" was, perhaps, rhetorically effective. The Antifederalists had a much better theoretical argument, namely, that federal appellate jurisdiction on law and fact denied the finality of juries' factual determinations and thus threatened juries in a systematic way (Democratic Federalist, CC 167). These arguments are a bit sophistical, but the Antifederalists also had a practical argument, that the federal court system jeopardized juries of the vicinage. As Federal Farmer IV (CC 242) pointed out, the difficulty — and here he rebuked cruder thinkers — was not so much the loss of juries of neighbors, for "in this enlightened country men may be probably impartially tried by those who do not live very near them," but rather that "the common people can establish facts with much more ease with oral than written evidence." Considering that in a rural society civil disputes often concern land ownership, the prospect of generating effective written testimony must have seemed daunting to owners of small holdings. Hence Federal Farmer's argument must have seemed quite realistic. Altogether, then, Wilson's argument on juries apparently seemed to both sides to be much less impressive than the Antifederalist critique. So the Federalists left the field.

Wilson's speech of 6 October did the Federalists more harm than good. With all the publicity, Wilson became a whipping boy for the Antifederalist campaign. In the Carlisle (Pa.) riot that followed the Pennsylvania ratification, the rioters burned him in effigy. As the Pennsylvania Antifederalists became increasingly vituperative, Centinel began referring to "James, the Caledonian, lieutenant general of the myrmidons of power, under Robert, the cofferer [Robert Morris]" (CC 443); other Antifederalists published spurious letters by James the Caledonian in which Wilson appeared utterly Machiavellian (CC 570; squibs: CC 2:552, 560); and Centinel (CC 565) interpreted the ex post facto clause as a device to allow Morris and Wilson to escape punishment for defaulting on debts to the United States.

What happened to the reputation of one man is not, however, so important as what happened to the Federalist cause. Wilson's speech gave Antifederalists the opportunity to systematize and make memorable their attacks on the absence of a bill of rights and civil juries and on taxes and standing armies. The Antifederalists owed much of the coherence of their campaign to the chance that Wilson gave them to answer his defenses. It may very well be that their emphasis on liberty (instead of consolidation) was brought about by their response to this speech. Main and Storing both believe that Antifederalists were truly interested in attacking consolidation, while I have already shown that they mainly attacked the Constitution as a threat to liberty. Perhaps the Antifederalists went in this direction because of the opportunity Wilson afforded them.

MASON, GERRY, AND LANDHOLDER

The objections by Mason and Gerry served the same function in the Antifederalist campaign that Washington's persona and letters served in the Federalist campaign. Mason and Gerry were well-known delegates to the convention whose opinions the Antifederal editors presumably believed would be influential. Because both delegates refused to sign the Constitution and wrote clear and unequivocal objections early in the campaign, they became central figures in it.

Other nonsigners had much less influence, even though they too wrote out objections. Edmund Randolph (Va.) wrote a long but late-appearing piece (CC 385, 2 January, 135,562 weighted words) in which, however, he equivocated, saying that if prior amendments proved impossible, he would support the Constitution. Consequently, Federalists used him as much as Antifederalists, and it is hard to tell how to assign his work to one side or the other. In the middle of the winter Robert Yates and John Lansing (N.Y.), who left the convention on 10 July, and Luther Martin (Md.), who left on 4 September, published their objections (Yates and Lansing [CC 447, 14 January, 15,400 weighted words] and Martin, *Genuine Information* [CC 389, 401, 414, 425, 441, 451, 459, 467, 484, 493, 502, 516, 28 December to 8 February, 201,905 weighted words]). The prolix Martin's commentary was almost the equal in volume to Centinel's, whose volume was 268,597 weighted words.

Mason's and Gerry's commentaries, 17,875 and 18,174 weighted words, respectively, were each about 1 percent of the Antifederal campaign. They had little to say about personalities or tactics or the campaign strategies, and they ignored peripheral issues as well as a few major ones (for example, taxes). Otherwise, however, they touched on most of the important substantive Antifederalist ideological themes, themes that, taken together in all writers, amounted to 714,840 weighted words, or about 41 percent of the Antifederal campaign total. So they can be regarded as epitomes of their campaign. Furthermore, the Federalist response is also an epitome of that part of the Federalist campaign. Marcus (James Iredell, CC 548, 571, 596, 616, 630), whose lengthy point-by-point response to Mason was 40,735 weighted words, about 1 percent of the Federalist campaign, nevertheless touched on themes that accounted for 767,990 weighted words, or 24 percent of the Federalist campaign in my sample.

On the level of political ideas, therefore, Mason and Gerry are unremarkable because they mirror a large part of the ideological element of the campaign. On the personal level, however, they stand out because they occasioned fairly vicious criticism. Of course publicists on both sides attacked the rhetors and leaders of the other, especially in Pennsylvania, where the campaign was notably virulent: Federalists like Benjamin Rush and Francis Hopkinson were attacked, as were Antifederalists like George Bryan (thought to be Centinel, though apparently Centinel was his son Samuel) and Benjamin Workman (Philadelphiensis). But Federalists sprayed special venom on Mason and Gerry, almost as much as Antifederalists sprayed on Wilson.

The main critic of both Mason and Gerry was Landholder (Oliver Ellsworth, a framer from Connecticut). His fourth (CC 295, 26 November, 17,875 weighted words) and fifth (CC 316, 3 December, 21,461 words) papers attacked Gerry, his sixth (CC 335, 10 December, 43,729 words) attacked Mason, and his eighth (CC 371, 24 December, 25,418 words) attacked both as well as Luther Martin. Altogether these four Landholder papers accounted for 108,483 weighted words, or about 3 percent of the Federalist campaign. These papers circulated mainly in New England and New York and may well have neutralized the effect of Mason and even Gerry.

Although less intellectual than Publius or Wilson, Landholder was a very important writer. After reading the fourth and sixth papers, Rufus King, a framer and one of the two or three main leaders of the ratification campaign in Massachusetts, believed that " 'the Landholder' will do more service our [the Federal] way, than the elaborate works of Publius" (CC 368). The most practical recognition of Landholder's merit came as imitation: When Luther Martin (CC:460, 18 January) defended Gerry against Landholder VIII, an unidentified framer, whom Kaminski and Saladino believe was Daniel St. Thomas Jenifer (a framer from Maryland), responded under Landholder's pen name, attacking Martin and Gerry (CC 580, 29 February).

Landholder tried to trivialize Gerry and Mason. Of course, he attacked their arguments whenever these seemed vulnerable. To Mason's com-

plaints that the president lacked a council and the Senate seemed aristocratic, he responded that the states found governors' councils useless and
that the Senate was not at all like the House of Lords. Furthermore, he
said, the danger "is not aristocracy or monarchy, but anarchy" (CC 335).
To Gerry's complaints about "inadequate representation" and the powers
of Congress, Landholder responded that federal representation was much
like Connecticut's and that Congress needed broad powers to defend freedom. But these substantive rejoinders do not convey the flavor of Landholder's prose. His main thrust was to show that, however much Mason
and Gerry purported to fear for the common good, they actually wanted
instead to satisfy the crassest of private and provincial interest.

As Landholder proceeded from his fourth to eighth papers, his por-
trayal of their supposed deceit moved from indirect insinuation to direct
charges of greed. Initially, he simply suggested that Gerry was personally
interested in "state dignities and emoluments" and that he was a "cun-
ning" politician "of metaphysical nicety." In the sixth paper, however,
Landholder, probably less inhibited in denouncing a Virginian than a New
Englander, launched a powerful attack on Mason's private pecuniary motives. Editors showed their appreciation by printing this paper 23 times,
double the 11 printings of the fourth and fifth papers. Thus encouraged,
Landholder blasted Gerry even more in the eighth paper.

In both cases Landholder developed his allegations by pointing out
that both framers had cooperated fully in writing the Constitution, presumably because they were actuated by concern for the public good. Then,
suddenly, at the end of the convention, they turned against the Constitution as, presumably, they realized it would hurt their private or provincial
interests. Mason had, Landholder said, "zealously supported" the proceedings, and as for Gerry, during "almost the whole time . . . no man was
more . . . conciliating." So there is a real puzzle why these enthusiastic
framers turned sour in the end.[8] Having posed the puzzle, Landowner
resolved it by offering a believable and discreditable reason why these two

8. Landholder was, we now know, entirely correct in identifying the puzzle. Although
Mason was often cited in the campaign for his dramatic pronouncement that "he would
sooner chop off his right hand than put it to the Constitution," this was still the same Mason
who in the middle of the convention said "he would bury his bones in the city [i.e., Phila-
delphia] rather than expose his Country to the Consequences of a dissolution of the Convention without any thing being done." Max Farrand, Records of the Federal Convention of 1787, 4
vols. (New Haven: Yale University Press, 1964), 1:533, 2:479. Similarly, it was Gerry's and
Strong's pivotal votes on July 14 — contrary to Massachusetts' superficial interests as defined
by King and Gorham — for equal representation in the Senate that saved the convention from
collapse and made a Constitution possible. In the summer, then, both men did indeed seem
actuated by national goals, not provincial or personal interests.

framers switched. He pointed out that Mason had moved to require a two-thirds majority in Congress to pass a navigation act (that is, an act to cartelize the shipping trade, potentially prohibiting foreign carriers from transporting cargoes of American origin). Mason may have believed that an American shipping cartel would aid eastern carriers at the expense of southern planters, and a two-thirds rule would make that kind of sectional legislation difficult. When the motion failed, Mason turned against the Constitution, and this was one of his objections. Landholder's clinching argument was that northern editors omitted this objection in order to conceal the fact that "Mason preferred the subjects of every foreign power to the subjects of the United States who live in New England."[9]

Landholder's other charge against Mason related to an even more direct and even more discreditable pecuniary interest. Mason objected that the Constitution restrained Congress for twenty years from prohibiting the importation of slaves. Although this objection to the delay sounds humane, Landholder pointed out that slaves increased in population numbers naturally, and owners in Virginia sold the surplus to the South in competition with the imports from Africa. Mason, as the owner "of three hundred slaves," wished to minimize competition: "Perhaps Col. Mason may suppose it more humane to breed than import slaves . . . but his objections are not on the side of freedom, nor in compassion to the human race who are slaves, but that *such importation render the United States weaker, more vulnerable, and less capable of defenses*" (CC 335). Landholder concluded, "A man governed by such narrow views and local prejudices, can never be trusted." No doubt many readers in New England and the middle states agreed.

Having discredited Mason, Landholder devoted his eighth paper to doing the same to Gerry, who, he said, turned against the Constitution because of the failure of his motion for the redemption of the Continental money: "As Mr. Gerry was supposed to be possessed of large quantities of this species of paper, his motion appeared to be founded in . . . barefaced selfishness."[10]

9. Landholder was entirely correct that Mason rejected the Constitution because of this provincial economic interest. In 1792, Jefferson, visiting Mason's home, summarized for posterity Mason's reminiscences about the convention: "The constn as agreed to till a fortnight before the Convention rose was such a one as he wd. have set his hand & heart to . . . [including] a vote of ⅔ in the legislature . . . on navigation. . . . [T]hose 2 states [South Carolina and Georgia] struck a bargain with the 3.N.Engld. states, if they would join to admit slaves for some years, the 2 . . . states wd join in changing the clause which required ⅔. . . . [I]t was done . . . & from that moment the two S. states and the 3 Northern ones joind Pen. Jers. & Del. & made the majority 8 to 3 against us" (Farrand, *Records*, 4:367).

10. Landholder was probably less accurate on Gerry than on Mason. Gerry responded

Having founded opposition to Mason and Gerry in private interests, Landholder concluded his eighth paper with a systematic attribution of private interest to other opponents. Thus, he said, Massachusetts Antifederalists were Shaysites, New York Antifederalists wanted to keep the state impost, which produced about fifty thousand pounds annually on goods bound for Connecticut, Massachusetts, and New Jersey, and Virginia Antifederalists reflected the Lee faction's (Richard Henry and Arthur) "implacable hatred" of Washington.

CONCLUSIONS

[[Both rhetoric and heresthetic contribute in important ways to how campaigns unfold and how campaigns are won. It is important, however, not to confuse the two. Heresthetic matters for the manner in which alternatives are selected and set forward by individuals seeking advantage. Rhetoric matters in its own right for the ways in which arguments are presented and framed with respect to arguments raised by an opponent.

Subsequent chapters return to the problem of heresthetic. To demonstrate the importance of rhetoric, the discussion thus far has focused on the first national political campaign ever waged — not a campaign to elect individuals, but rather the 1787–1788 campaign for the ratification of the proposed Constitution. This was a national campaign, waged largely by the Federalists, addressing specific groups of voters. Recognizing the closeness of the campaign, the Antifederalists, who were less well organized, responded ably to the Federalist campaign.

A major finding, detailed in chapter 4, is that the rhetorical themes adopted by the Antifederalists were largely negative. As shown in chapter 5 there is a powerful rationale for selecting negative themes in a campaign. But campaigns do not take place in a vacuum. Campaigners take into account one another's actions and respond in kind. In chapter 6 we have

---

(CC 419, 5 January, with a specific denial, but pseudo-Landholder nevertheless repeated it (CC¡580, 29 February, Daniel of St. Thomas Jenifer [?]). According to Madison's *Notes*, Gerry, like most framers, supported the provision (Article VI, section 1) declaring valid the prior debts of the United States. But there is no evidence that he made a special motion on the redemption of Continental money, although he did urge that Congress be specifically obligated to pay prior public debts. There are three possibilities: (1) Ellsworth (Landholder) and pseudo-Landholder (surely a framer, possibly Jenifer) heard Gerry make a special issue of Continental money, but Madison did not record it (Madison's *Notes* sometimes differ substantially from those of other careful note takers); (2) Ellsworth and pseudo-Landholder (Jenifer?) misinterpreted Gerry's concerns about prior debts as a plea for payment of Continental money; or (3) Gerry did not mention Continental money and Landholder fabricated the charge, which pseudo-Landholder repeated.

seen how campaigners, using rhetoric, chose different strategies and elaborated different themes in response to their opponents, an analysis that uncovered a number of patterns. The Federalists adopted a theme emphasizing the current crisis in government while the Antifederalists emphasized the proposed Constitution's threat to liberty. Each campaign thought its theme ran to its advantage, and neither side often challenged the other. In addition, the Federalists stressed the support of patriots like Washington for the proposed Constitution. When it became obvious they could make no headway on this theme, the Antifederalists quickly retreated, abandoning the issue to the Federalists.]]

III

General Principles of
Rhetorical Interaction

7

Toward a Theory of Rhetoric in Campaigns

HE EXAMINATION in chapter 6 of several concrete themes in the
ratification campaigns suggests the presence of interesting patterns in the rhetorical strategies of the two sides. I want now to
construct a model that suggests two general principles of rhetorical behavior and then in the next chapter to survey the main themes of
the two campaigns to confirm that the overall patterns of the arguments
used in the campaigns follow these principles.

A MODEL OF RHETORICAL STRATEGY[1]

In order to locate these examples of rhetorical interaction within an abstract framework for analysis, I construct a model of the main decision,

1. [[Professor Riker did not have an opportunity to revise this section, and as it stands it
does not appear to us sufficiently to motivate the conclusions presented at the end of this
section, namely, the Dominance Principle and the Dispersion Principle. In particular, the
connection among positions, arguments, and costs and benefits is rather underdeveloped.
We present the section as Riker left it, except for some small revisions to render the notation
consistent. Moreover, there are two additional arguments that would tend to support the two
principles.

First, in most campaign rhetoric it seems reasonable to expect that the marginal effect on
voter opinion of resource expenditures on a given rhetorical issue would be higher for one
side than for the other. Consider an issue represented in Riker's model below by a collection
of "dimensions" $d_1, \ldots, d_r$. If side 1 in a campaign is more successful with this issue than side
2, then it is only rational for side 2 to ignore that issue and instead expend its resources on
another issue, if available, on which side 2's marginal effect on voter opinion is higher. Thus
we should seldom see both sides emphasizing the same issue; this is precisely the Dominance
Principle. Furthermore, given limited resources, there may be some third issue on which
both side 1 and side 2 have lower marginal values than on other issues. In such a case, neither
side would devote resources to the third issue. Such an occurrence would correspond to the
Dispersion Principle.

Second, David Austen-Smith demonstrates a result closely analogous to the Dominance
Principle in his article "Information Acquisition and Orthogonal Argument," (in William

99

typically a binary vote on some pair of alternatives, one of which is identified as a^+, the other as a^-. (Here I use a^+ for ratification of the Constitution and a^- for rejection.)

In this model there is a set of N voters, $i \in N$, $i = 1,2,\ldots n$. There are also rhetors for each side who state positions and utter arguments to attract voters to their sides. The positions are alternatives, x_j, $j = 1,2,\ldots$, that are identified relative to one or more dimensions, $d_1,\ldots,d_K$, where $K \leq m$ and R^m defines the alternative space.

For example, on the subject of the provision of a military system, some relevant dimensions are, among others,

- size: the number of troops
- specialization: the degree of professionalization ranging from a militia of citizen soldiers to an entirely full-time army
- permanence: the period of time for which the military is mobilized from semiannual musters to a standing army
- centralization: the degree of control of the military forces by national rules, officers, and so forth.

The actual x_j chosen for the Constitution was as follows: on size, the existing state militia plus a national army of unspecified size; on specialization, unspecialized militia plus national professionals; on permanence, state organization and training of the militia according to national rules, along with a national standing army; and on centralization, a state militia nationally armed and subject to national takeover but trained by locally chosen officers, plus a national army. Of course, many other x_j might have been chosen, from a small, unspecialized, temporary local militia to, exclusively, a large, professional, standing national army.

A justification of x_j is an argument, σ_h, $h = 1, 2, \ldots$, to persuade voters that x_j is a desirable alternative. (To justify the military provisions of the Constitution, $\sigma_h x_j$ might, relative to the dimensions of permanence and centralization, defend the divided control of the militia as a means to provide a large army without depriving states of their military forces, and so on.)

A particular position x_j is thus tied to a cluster of dimensions, $d_1, \ldots, d_r$,[2] by the arguments, σ_h, used to justify x_j. Identifying such clusters as d,

---

Barnett, Melvin Hinich, and Norman Schofield, eds., *Political Economy: Institutions, Information, Competition, and Representation* [New York: Cambridge University Press, 1993]). There he demonstrates that, at least under certain conditions, two rational lobbyists will avoid emphasizing the same issue in attempting to convince a decision-maker of their opposing positions.]]

    2. A subset of $d_1, \ldots, d_K$.

where $d = (d_1, \ldots, d_r)$, there is a set of voters $C(d)$ for whom d is salient in the sense that d is used in the voters' choices between a^+ and a^-. For some particular d', *salience* means that a voter in $C(d')$

1. prefers some $x_j(d')$ to any $x_h(d')$ with $h \neq j$, and
2. uses $x_j(d')$, among other things, to choose between a^+ and a^-.

This means that the voter thinks there is a "best argument" in d' and that he uses it, with others, to decide how to vote. Although $C(d)$ may be a singleton, it may also contain most voters. Typically a voter belongs to more than one set $C(d)$, but the human attention span limits the number of a voter's memberships in various $C(d)$, perhaps to "the magic number 7 ± 2."[3]

A voter's choice, si, between a^+ and a^- is an operation on the preferred xj for all $C(d)$ to which i belongs. Thus,

1. for all d' such that $i \in C(d')$, i prefers $x_j(d')$ to $x_h(d')$, for all $h \neq j$, and
2. $s_i(a', a\ ) = f(x_j(d_1), x_j(d_2), \ldots)$.

In general, no one knows just what the function f is or how it operates. Indeed, it may operate differently for each person, so one might properly write f_i instead of f.

The voter's calculus sets the rhetor's problem. To persuade voters to choose, say, a^+, a rhetor cannot simply extol a^+. Instead, the rhetor must set forth positions, x_j, defending them with those arguments, σ_h, that establish d such that $x_j(d)$ enter into f(.) in a way that influences $s_i(a^+, a^-) = a^+$. This is indeed a roundabout procedure, much complicated by the rhetor's uncertainty about how d affects preferences for x_i and how f (or f_i) operates. Consequently, the rhetor works by trial and error, testing by experience what positions on what clusters of dimensions encourage voters to choose a^+.

In undertaking persuasion by trial and error, the rhetor faces many costs. First, there are the costs of argument, which are in effect opportunity costs. Spending time and energy on one position and related arguments precludes spending time and energy on others, which might indeed be more profitable. Second, related to the opportunity costs are the costs of research, such as determining which $C(d)$ include many voters, selecting arguments, σ_h, that call forth those clusters, d, that favor the rhetor's cause, avoiding σ_h and d that give opponents an opening, and so on. Third, there are the mechanical costs of speaking, writing, printing, distributing, and so on.

3. [[George A. Miller, "The Magical Number Seven, Plus or Minus Two: Some Limits on Our Capacity for Processing Information," *Psychological Review* 63 (1956): 31–96.]]

Rhetors incur these costs whether they win or not, indeed whether or not they win a single voter. I assume these costs increase, after an initial investment in writing, linearly with the number of voters persuaded, so that for any $C(d)$ the costs of persuasion range from the cost of the initial investment to some maximum, when the rhetor persuades all the members of $C(d)$. The assumption of linearity means that the cost per person persuaded is constant. It is possible that the marginal cost of persuasion rises with the number persuaded, but I ignore that possibility because of the homogeneity of the persons in the set $C(d)$. They all think that the dimensions are salient; so an argument that is successful, with some probability, with one randomly chosen member should, with equal probability, be successful with another randomly chosen member, regardless of their positions in the queue of the persuaded.

On the other hand, the rhetor benefits from successful persuasion because the voters in $C(d)$ are thus partially encouraged to choose between a^+ and a^- in the way the rhetor wishes. I point out three features of the rhetor's benefits:

1. Benefits, like costs, increase linearly with the number persuaded. I reject the possibility of decreasing marginal benefits because the number in $C(d)$ is unknown, but probably fewer than half the voters. If $C(d)$ contained all voters, then the marginal value of additions would decrease after half were persuaded (in accordance with the Size Principle).[4] But if $C(d)$ contains an unknown but minority number, then each addition is as good as each other addition.

2. Benefits exceed costs if the rhetor is completely successful, that is, if the rhetor persuades all members of $C(d)$. I assume that rhetors are rational in the sense that they do not offer positions and arguments if they gain nothing by complete success. Hence benefits must exceed costs, at least when all members of $C(d)$ are persuaded.

3. Benefits accrue to rhetors only when they persuade more than half the members of $C(d)$. Given two sides, if rhetors on one side persuade fewer than half, then the other side must have the allegiance of more than half. Because a rhetor's costs are linearly increasing with each voter persuaded from first to last and because benefits do not accrue until the number of voters persuaded exceeds $.5|C(d)|$, costs initially exceed benefits. But because a rational rhetor's benefits exceed costs at the maximum persuaded, $|C(d)|$, benefits must exceed costs at some point t^+, where $.5|C(d)| < t^+ \leq |C(d)|$. These two features lead to the following observation:

4. See William H. Riker, *The Theory of Political Coalitions* (New Haven: Yale University Press, 1962), chaps. 2–4.

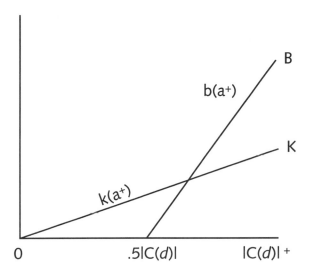

Figure 7.1   Benefits, b(a⁺), and Costs, k(a⁺), of Rhetoric in Favor of an Alternative, a, Involving Dimensions d, as a Function of the Number of Voters for Whom d is Salient, $|C(d)|$

Proposition: Benefits for rhetors on one side exceed costs at some point t⁺, where $.5|C(d)| < t^+ |C(d)|$.

A corollary is that the same holds true for the other side, using t⁻, where $0 \leq t^- < .5|C(d)|$. A second observation follows:

Proposition: In the range from t⁻ to t⁺, costs exceed benefits for rhetors on both sides.

The observations can be displayed graphically. In figure 7.1, the horizontal axis measures the number of i in $C(d)$ from 0 to $|C(d)|$. The vertical axis measures costs, k(a⁺), and benefits, b(a⁺). The linearly increasing line k(a⁺) indicates costs from (0, 0) to point K. The linearly increasing line from $(.5|C(d)|, 0)$ to point B indicates benefits, b(a⁺). The mirror image for k(a⁻) and b(a⁻) is figure 7.2, where the measurement on the horizontal axis goes from $|C(d)|$ at the left to zero at the right. The line k(a⁻) from (0, 0) to point K′ measures costs, and the line b(a⁻) from $.5|C(d)|$ to point B′ measures benefits. In figure 7.3, the diagrams of figure 7.1 and 7.2 are superimposed. Although $|C(d)|^+ = |C(d)|^-$, I label them differently to indicate the direction of the horizontal axis. Figure 7.3 also shows the points t⁺ and t⁻ where benefits exceed costs.

Two inferences follow from the propositions and from these figures. First, if a side persuades more than t⁺ (t⁻) members of $C(d)$, then that side profits from continued persuasion, while the other side does not. Hence, assuming rational rhetors, the successful side reiterates its arguments,

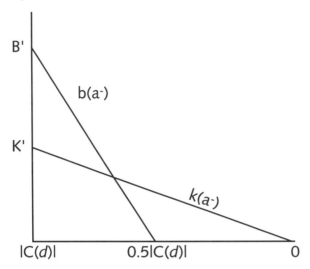

Figure 7.2 Benefits, b(a⁻), and Costs, k(a⁻), of Rhetoric Against an Alternative, a, Involving Dimensions d, as a Function of the Number of Voters for Whom d Is Salient, $|C(d)|$

while the unsuccessful side abandons its arguments. Thus, there are two equilibria: (1) o for a⁻ and $|C(d)|^+$ for a⁺ and (2) o for a⁺ and $|C(d)|^-$ for a⁻. I call this feature the Dominance Principle.

The second inference is that if neither side persuades as many as t⁺ (t⁻) members of $C(d)$, then neither profits. Again assuming rational rhetors, both sides abandon their arguments. Hence, there is one more equilibrium point, at o for a⁺ and simultaneously o for a⁻. I call this feature the Dispersion Principle.

The rhetorical interaction in the ratification campaign so far described illustrates these principles. The way the two sides used Washington's endorsement is an indisputable instance of the Dominance Principle. The Federalists made much of the endorsement throughout the campaign. The Antifederalists, after some feeble, initial attempts at refutation, simply ignored the issue, leaving the field free for Federalist domination. Presumably there was an equilibrium at $|C(d)|^+$. At least, nothing stood in the way of Federalists persuading all persons who took seriously the d_h clustered in this particular d.

Similarly, when Wilson exposed the Federalists to attack on the absence of a bill of rights and the issue of civil juries, the Antifederalists responded with enthusiasm, swiftly driving Federalists out of the field. Consequently, the Antifederalists dominated, so there was an equilibrium at $|C(d)|^-$; or at least nothing stood in the way of Antifederalists persuading everyone who took these d seriously.

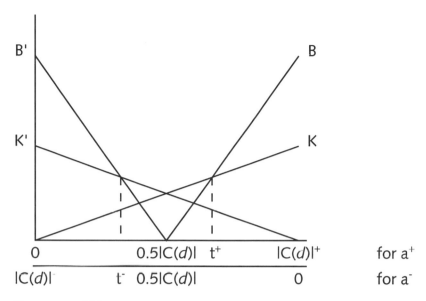

Figure 7.3   Values of the Number of Voters Susceptible to d for Which the Benefits of Rhetoric on d Exceed the Costs

The joint responses to Wilson's other arguments are instances of the Dispersion Principle, as I will later show when I discuss the temporal development of rhetorical themes. For now, however, I can display the motivation involved in the Dispersion Principle through the development of Landholder's letters. Landholder initially undertook to refute Mason and Gerry, but his efforts, while reprinted, were not definitive. Mason and Gerry had developed the main themes of their side so that Landholder's broad attack was diffuse and clearly did not result in a rhetorical victory. At best he achieved a rhetorical standoff, that is, some point between o and t^+. Then Landholder changed rhetorical tactics, attempting to trivialize his opponents' persona and interests rather than their arguments. Of course, we cannot know whether he succeeded with the voters, but he certainly did so with Federalist editors, who reprinted his new themes much more than his old ones; and he infuriated Luther Martin, who replied in Gerry's (but not Mason's) defense. Landholder's change of tactics reveals the motive involved in the Dispersion Principle. Failing on the d involved in his initial papers, he switched to a new d, for example, the private pecuniary interests of the opponents of the Constitution, the provincial economic interests of Virginians, and so forth.

The Dominance and Dispersion principles are closely related to each other, as figures 7.1, 7.2, and 7.3 display. Consequently, they can be stated in a single sentence:

> *When one side has an advantage on an issue, the other side ignores it; but when neither side has an advantage, both seek new and advantageous issues.*

Although the formulation of these principles is based on the study of direct interactions, the principles apply to the whole of the Federalist and the Antifederalist campaigns alike, as will be seen in chapter 8.

SOME CONTEMPORARY EVIDENCE ABOUT THE DOMINANCE AND DISPERSION PRINCIPLES

Are there theoretical principles of auditor behavior that could underpin my theory about what rhetors do? An experimental investigation by Richard Lau, Richard Smith, and Susan Fiske does suggest a rationale for these principles in terms of the information-processing capacities of the audience.[5]

The overall model for their investigation consists of an alternative space, an outcome space, and mappings from the former to the latter. Subjects are uncertain about what outcomes will result from their choices of various alternatives. Rhetors, in this case the experimenters, offer the subjects various interpretations of the consequence of choices. These interpretations are mappings of each alternative to an outcome. Auditors accept or reject these mappings as bases for their choices among alternatives. If auditors accept, they are said to be persuaded; otherwise not. We want to know what is involved in the auditors' acceptance of interpretations.[6]

Lau, Smith, and Fiske offer an elegant answer based on their investiga-

5. "Political Beliefs, Policy Interpretations, and Political Persuasion," *Journal of Politics* 53 (1991): 644–75.

6. As a bridge from the model to the ratification campaigns, consider how the elements of Lau, Smith, and Fiske's research might correspond. In my application the "alternatives" are ratifying, ratifying conditionally (in several ways), and rejecting the Constitution. The "outcomes" are states of the world produced by various choices of alternatives. Although the adversaries of 1787–88 agreed that ratification would lead to consolidation (and rejection to the status quo), there was uncertainty about what life after consolidation would be like. Consolidation might mean a free, secure, and prosperous nation or an unfree, insecure, and impoverished one. Similarly, the meaning of the status quo might be a decline into anarchy or stabilization and growth. In this situation, the rational rhetor seeks to offer interpretations of consolidation persuasive to a majority of voters. That is, the rhetor attempts to supply believable reasons $\sigma_h x_i$ that his mapping from alternatives to outcomes is correct. So the crucial question of a rhetor's mapping is whether a goodly number of auditors accept it as correct.

tion of auditors' processing of the messages of an interpretation. They assume that auditors are persons with preexisting knowledge and that this knowledge is organized in schemata which are used for processing interpretations. Auditors bring schemata — which I call d — into play by initially accepting or rejecting key features of interpretations through entry points, or "chronically accessible constructs." These entry points may be key words (for example, party, group, or class names), issue positions (for example, a desire for security against anarchy or foreign war, an attachment to liberty), or simply catchwords (for example, representation, separation of powers, liberty, anarchy).

The investigators show how the processing worked through an ingenious experiment in which they distinguished three cases:

1. rhetors present a single interpretation at least marginally acceptable to auditors;
2. rhetors present two interpretations, both marginally acceptable to auditors;
3. rhetors present two interpretations, only one of which is marginally acceptable to auditors.

In the experiment, a nonrandom sample of adult Pittsburgh citizens read arguments composed by the experimenters out of sentences from Pittsburgh newspapers, arguments about alternatives on potential local referenda on widely discussed public issues. The citizens then chose between the alternatives. The experimenters correctly predicted that, in case 1, the single interpretation and, in case 3, the single acceptable interpretation (but not the unacceptable one) would significantly affect the auditors' evaluations. In case 2, they correctly predicted that an interpretation would influence evaluations when its assertions about consequences of alternatives agreed with the auditors' general political beliefs.

Applying the Lau-Smith-Fiske discoveries about auditors to the rhetors' use of the Dominance Principle, let us assume that rhetors on both sides recognize that, for a great majority of auditors, a pair of interpretations lies in case 3. Then rhetors offering the unacceptable interpretation know that their effort is wasted. Appropriately, therefore, they abandon the presentation of their interpretation. On the other hand, the rhetors offering the acceptable interpretation are effectively in case 1, and so they have a motive to continue the presentation of their interpretation. This pair of actions by rhetors on the two sides is summarized by the Dominance Principle. For rhetors who want to win, this rhetorical situation is a rational response, once they discover that they are in case 3. So it is entirely to be expected that rhetors, given time to observe the consequences for auditors of the presentation of mappings, would preempt (or abandon) issues. As will be seen in later chapters, this is just what happened in 1787–88.

Applying the Lau-Smith-Fiske discoveries about auditors to rhetors' use of the Dispersion Principle, as in case 2, both groups of rhetors offer marginally acceptable interpretations. The success or failure of presentations thus depends on auditors' general political beliefs, which are auditors' tastes in the outcome space. So it behooves rhetors looking for an advantage to seek out other issues with new interpretations that can lead them into case 3 and thence to case 1. Action so taken is of course exactly in accord with the Dispersion Principle.

This rationale for the Dispersion Principle seems at odds with the median voter theorem that occupies such a large place in contemporary political science.[7] The conflict is, I believe, more apparent than real. To begin with, the median voter theorem has no time element. Action is assumed to be simultaneous and instantaneous. In the world of campaigning, however, the situations of the campaigners change. They have different amounts and kinds of resources. They have different tolerances for stalemate and different opportunities to introduce new subjects. In the temporal world, therefore, they do not typically waste resources fighting out the issues in exactly the same locations. If they arrive at a point near the median on some issue, they probably do not, of course, abandon it. But they do decrease the resources they put into maintaining that position, and they do divert resources to a search for new issues. Thus, both sides, having initially staked out positions in accordance with the median voter theorem or not, as the case may be, undertake to find new issues, gradually and approximately together ceasing to emphasize their initial positions as they take new positions on new issues. Indeed, within a temporally extended campaign, one should probably not expect even initial position taking at the median because rhetors, if they expect their opponents to have as strong a case as their own, know they will ultimately abandon their argument and need not waste resources hunting for the median. Hence follows the Dispersion Principle.

In addition, the median voter theorem applies to one-dimensional space. But a campaign space is multidimensional. The Dispersion Principle applies to a single dimension in this space. And there is no reason to expect a median location on a specific issue. Even if the outcome on the whole set of dimensions taken together is in some more or less central

7. Beginning with Duncan Black, *The Theory of Committees and Elections* (Cambridge: Cambridge University Press, 1958), and Anthony Downs, *An Economic Theory of Democracy* (New York: Harper and Row, 1957).

position in the space, it can easily be that the outcome is quite far from the medians on at least some of these dimensions.[8] So there is no obvious conflict between the theorem and the principle.

[[This model of rhetorical strategy, consistent both with goals and capabilities of rhetors and with those of their auditors, suggests the Dominance Principle and the Dispersion Principle as possible general laws about the nature of rhetorical campaigns. Chapter 8 demonstrates that the overall usage of arguments in the ratification campaigns, as described in chapter 6, comport with these Principles. The Principles also imply that the actors in a campaign will react to each other's rhetorical strategies in specific ways, and chapter 8 argues, in addition, that the dynamics of the ratification campaigns also conform to the Principles. The remainder of the book examines in much more detail the rhetorical and heresthetic decisions of particular actors in that campaign and how they reacted to each other. Examination at this level of detail shows clearly the relation between rhetorical and heresthetical strategies.]]

8. See, for example, the discussion of outcomes located in the "yolk" in Richard McKelvey, "Covering, Dominance, and Institution-Free Properties of Social Choice," *American Journal of Political Science* 30 (1986): 911–34.

8

Evidence about Dominance and Dispersion

T HE Dominance Principle and the Dispersion Principle refer to dynamic features of the campaigns. In order to visualize and study the changes subsumed by these principles, I have divided the campaign into stages and summed the weighted words, by stages, on the major issues. Unfortunately, this is a rather Procrustean procedure because issues change at different rates with different apogees. Hence the stages appropriate for one issue may not be appropriate for another. Nevertheless a division into stages demarcated by state ratifications, some of which changed the political situation dramatically, is likely to reveal significant variations on a number of themes. Thus tables 8.1 and 8.2 show three stages: (a) the period prior to Pennsylvania's ratification (December 15) (b) the period between Pennsylvania's ratification and Massachusetts's (February 6), and (c) the period between Massachusetts's ratification and March 31, when my sample ends.

The rationale for creating these stages is that the two ratifications were events that reoriented politics for the whole country. Pennsylvania's ratification, the first by a large state, gave both sides a good start. As expected, Federalists were excited by this sendoff, especially because they garnered a big majority. But Antifederalists also benefited in a backhanded way. They were able to explain the ratification away with the claim that the procedures were outrageously unfair, and this inspired their troops to greater effort. The Massachusetts ratification, the sixth and the first really difficult one, foreshadowed the ultimate outcome. Federalists were elated. They could easily visualize three more and thus victory, even without Virginia and New York. Antifederalists, however, were demoralized.

For purposes of analysis I have gathered in tables 8.1 and 8.2 the 178 categories discussed in chapter 4 into just about the same themes used there.

Table 8.1   Federalist Campaign Themes, By Stages in the Campaign

		Periods of the Federalist Campaign					
		Before Pennsylvania ratification		Pennsylvania ratification to Massachusetts ratification		After Massachusetts ratification	
	Themes	number of words	%	number of words	%	number of words	%
1	Ad hominem	130,491	8	107,842	10	79,393	15
	Crisis:						
2	in general	203,001	13	39,495	4	27,251	5
3	responses to crisis	189,750	12	138,656	13	7,346	1
4	foreign military crisis	132,180	8	96,363	9	49,715	9
5	economic crisis	52,083	3	70,163	7	36,736	7
6	constitutional	37,483	2	74,321	7	27,784	5
7	subtotal (2-6)	614,857	39	418,998	39	148,832	27
8	Populist legislature	117,077	7	43,678	4	22,473	4
	Positive defenses:						
9	on liberty	312,737	20	146,823	13	123,973	23
10	on consolidation	122,100	8	75,600	7	2,232	<1
11	miscellaneous	36,807	2	24,462	2	2,406	<1
12	subtotal (9-11)	471,644	30	240,885	23	128,611	24
13	Response to Federalists	12,755	1	14,353	1	7,602	1
14	Cheers	249,794	16	242,358	23	157,523	29
15	TOTAL	1,596,628	100%	1,068,114	100%	544,434	100%

Total of all three stages (continued columns):

	Themes	number of words	%
1	Ad hominem	317,726	10
2	in general	265,747	8
3	responses to crisis	335,752	10
4	foreign military crisis	278,258	9
5	economic crisis	158,982	5
6	constitutional	139,948	4
7	subtotal (2-6)	1,182,687	37
8	Populist legislature	183,228	6
9	on liberty	577,533	18
10	on consolidation	199,932	6
11	miscellaneous	63,675	2
12	subtotal (9-11)	841,140	26
13	Response to Federalists	34,720	1
14	Cheers	649,675	20
15	TOTAL	3,209,176	100%

* To arrive at the entries in tables 8.1 and 8.2, I summarized each essay in Kaminski and Saladino, *Commentaries on the Constitution* (1981, ff.) in sentences of unit meaning, counting words allocated to each unit and multiplying this number by the number of printings. I thus arrived at the "weighted words" of each summary sentence. Then I categorized the sentences into 178 categories of meaning (101 for Federalists and 77 for Antifederalists) and summed the weighted words of sentences in each category. In these tables I have further combined the categories into 15 for Federalists and 11 for Antifederalists. For more detail on the construction of categories and a list of the 178 categories, see chapter 4 and the Appendix.

Table 8.2 Antifederalist Campaign Themes, By Stages in the Campaign

| | Stages of the Antifederalist Campaign | | | | | | | | |
| | Before Pennsylvania ratification | | Pennsylvania ratification to Massachusetts ratification | | After Massachusetts ratification | | Total of all three stages | |
Themes	number of words	%	number of words	%	number of words	%	number of words	%
1 Ad hominem	69,086	8	60,448	9	61,549	33	191,083	11
2 Tactics	119,651	13	21,343	3	17,380	9	158,374	9
3 Miscellaneous	17,686	2	16,018	2	– –	—	33,704	2
4 Subtotal (1-3)	206,423	23	97,809	15	78,929	42	383,161	22
Threats to liberty								
5 in general	98,854	11	130,373	20	15,493	8	244,720	14
6 to civil liberty	140,018	16	53,481	8	57,696	31	251,195	15
7 from government structures	156,694	18	79,925	12	9,888	5	246,507	14
8 from federal powers	58,880	7	62,116	9	5,800	3	126,796	7
9 subtotal (5-8)	454,446	51	325,895	49	88,877	47	869,218	50
10 Consolidation	161,939	18	187,594	28	13,534	7	363,067	21
11 Positive positions	67,917	8	53,020	8	6,015	3	126,952	7
12 TOTAL	890,725	100%	664,318	100%	187,391	100%	1,742,398	100%

DOMINANCE IN THE MAIN THEME: FEDERALISTS

The attention each side paid to its main theme was remarkably stable. In all three periods the Antifederalists devoted about half their rhetoric to warning that the Constitution would, if adopted, endanger American liberty. Similarly, in the first two periods, the Federalists devoted about two-fifths of their rhetoric to warning that the national crisis endangered peace, prosperity, liberty, and national existence. In the third period they decreased their warning on crisis to just over one-fourth. Part of this decrease was artifactual: Whereas in the first two periods Publius mainly discussed crisis, in the last period (papers 52–75) he discussed institutions almost entirely, showing that they would enhance liberty, not endanger it. Because this emphasis accorded with his plan as set forth in the first paper, it is hard to think of this change — involving about 20 percent of the whole third-period campaign — as responding to any features of the campaign itself; except, of course, Publius could have changed his program had it seemed appropriate to do so. This artifact of Publius's plan accounts for about half of the decline in attention to crisis. The other half derives from Federalists' increased cheering for their success. This is the positive form of the emphasis on crisis, namely, crisis averted. So, with the exceptions noted for the third period — half reflecting campaign developments, half not — the Federalists too maintained their emphasis on their main theme.

Each side thus appeared to preempt a theme. But to show that the Dominance Principle applies fully, it must also be demonstrated that opponents ultimately ignored the issue.

It is clear that the Antifederalists gave up on the theme of crisis. It was a difficult issue for them. In 1786–87, the delegates to the Annapolis convention, the members of the state legislatures, especially the Virginia legislature, and finally the delegates to Congress had requested the states to send delegates to Philadelphia because of the widespread belief that the defects of the Articles of Confederation had brought on, at least, a constitutional crisis. Proto-Federalists, of course, believed that the crisis was also economic, military, and even moral. Legislation enacted in twelve state legislatures (all but Rhode Island) to select delegates acknowledged the crisis. All the Acts instructed the delegates to render the federal Constitution "adequate to the exigencies" of Union, but Virginia spoke of "extending the revision of our federal system to all its defects," and New Hampshire spoke of the "truly critical and alarming situation" (Farrand, 3:559–86). Even Antifederalists often acknowledged the crisis. In Pennsylvania, the Seceding Assemblymen (CC 125A), Old Whig (CC:202, 292), the Convention Minority (CC 353), and even, amazingly enough, Centinel (CC 311) and Philadelphiensis (CC 438); in New York, Brutus (CC 178) and

Table 8.3   Net Effect of Antifederal Denials of Crisis

	Period I		Period II		Period III		Total	
	volume in period	% of volume	volume in period	% of volume	volume in period	% of volume	volume	% of total
Denials of Crisis	13569	1.5	13447	2.0	805	0.4	27871	1.6
Acknowl-edgements of Crisis	10495	1.2	4498	0.7	232	0.1	15225	0.9
Net Denial	3074	0.3%	8949	1.3%	573	0.3%	12596	0.7%

Federal Farmer (CC 242); and elsewhere, again amazingly, Luther Martin (CC 425) and Columbian Patriot (Mercy Warren, CC 581) — all conceded that a crisis existed, although they often bracketed their concessions with remarks tending to minimize its significance.

In the face of so much official and journalistic acknowledgment, it was extremely difficult for Antifederalists to deny crisis. Some of them attempted to do so: Centinel (CC 133), Federal Farmer (CC 242), the Pennsylvania Minority (CC 353) — all of whom also affirmed the crisis — Gov. George Clinton of New York (CC 439), and others. Alfred (CC 345), writing in Oswald's *Philadelphia Independent Gazette,* composed the most elaborate denial, though not the most widely distributed one. He pointed out that European liberals praised American liberty under the state constitutions, that exports were flourishing and living was cheap, and that the rich hinterland awaited exploration. He blamed "our misfortunes" on "*manners*" or "our attachment to . . . foreign luxuries" and explained away the difficulties with foreign debt by civil lists that "*enormously* exceeded what they formerly were prior to the late revolution." He did not defuse the foreign dangers, but Federal Farmer (CC 242, also Brutus, Junior CC 239), among others, attempted to do so, saying, "We are in a state of perfect peace."

The net effect of Antifederal ambivalence on crisis is summarized in table 8.3. Although net denials increased in the second period, they declined in the third, and in any event the absolute amount is tiny compared with the Federalists' emphasis of 39 percent or 27 percent. So it seems clear that, given the Antifederalists' concession, the Dominance Principle applies to the Federalists' argument on crisis.

DOMINANCE IN THE MAIN THEME: ANTIFEDERALISTS AND THE THREAT TO LIBERTY FROM THE STRUCTURE OF GOVERNMENT

As for the Antifederalists' main theme of threats to liberty, the case is somewhat more complicated. They emphasized the theme itself about the same amount in each period, but they sharply varied the emphasis among subthemes — and the Federalists sharply varied their responses.

The Antifederalists' variation appears to be opportunistic and thus determined — as required in the Dominance and Dispersion principles — by the events of the campaign itself. For example, part of the shift is owing to the decrease in the second period in attention given to the two main subthemes of the first period. These initially dominant subthemes were the threat to liberty in the structure of the proposed Constitution (17 percent in the first period) and the absence of a bill of rights (16 percent in the first period). Both of these rhetorical lines are more or less obvious initial criticisms. However, in the second period, beginning with the Pennsylvania ratification, they emphasized themes that seem to derive from this very ratification. The Antifederalists thought the procedure for ratification was outrageously unfair, so they emphasized the potential for despotism. The third period began soon after the Post Office changed its method of delivery in such a way that Antifederalist editors failed to receive newspapers from other states, and they interpreted the delays as deliberate sabotage of their campaign material and concrete evidence of the potential for despotism. The Federalists both responded and failed to respond to these shifts in emphasis in ways that show the application here of both the Dominance Principle and the Dispersion Principle.

Though the persistence of the Antifederalist emphasis on liberty reflects the Dominance Principle, the internal shifts in emphasis reflect the Dispersion Principle as well. Thus from the first period to the second there is a striking decline, as previously noted, in the emphasis on threats to liberty from the proposed governmental structure — from 18 percent of the volume in period I to 12 percent in period II. A good part of that decline results from a standoff in period I, so that Antifederalists sought out other issues, entirely in keeping with the Dispersion Principle. In the transition from period II to III, the Antifederalists substantially gave up, dropping on this theme from 12 percent of the volume in II to 5 percent in III. They did, however, keep the issue of the federal judiciary, which, in fact, they preempted. The fact that on this one issue they followed the Dominance Principle seems to me to indicate that it was no accident that they followed the Dispersion Principle on the others. When one side abandons a contested issue, it is always possible for the other side to dominate it, and that is what happened here.

Both sides initially wrote quite a bit about five issues on the theme of governmental structure; but the Antifederalists wrote much less about them in the second period and abandoned them in the third:

1. that the proposed system would violate the principle of the separation of powers, with the Federalist response that separation ensured liberty;

2. that the president would have too much power, with the Federalist response that he should be energetic and yet restrained in the ways provided;

3. that the Senate would be too powerful, with the response that its power would be shared;

4. that a unicameral legislature would be more liberal than a bicameral one (this came almost entirely from Centinel, CC 133, and was uniquely an issue in Pennsylvania because of its radically majoritarian unicameral legislature, much admired by the state Constitutionalists, who became the Antifederalists, and much despised by the Republicans, who became the Federalists);

5. that Congress would be too small and would lack rotation and annual elections, with the Federalist response that Congress was structured to guarantee liberty.

The relative volume on these five issues is displayed in table 8.4. In reading this table, one must recall that Federalist volume is about double Antifederalist volume, so the expected ratio of Federalist to Antifederalist volume on an issue is 2.0, but, as before, a ratio of 1.0 suggests a standoff in obtaining the public's attention.

Table 8.4 reveals that, in the first period, the ratio is greater than 1.0 on the first three issues. Although it is less than 1.0 on two other issues, it rises for these issues to greater than 1.0 in the second period. So by February, there is something of a standoff. Furthermore, on *each of* these issues the Antifederal volume falls by more than the expected amount. As shown in table 8.2, the total Antifederal volume falls by only one-fourth from period I to period II, but on these five issues the Antifederal volume falls by much greater amounts, as shown in table 8.5.

Thus, Antifederal writers and editors were abandoning these apparent standoffs from mid-December on. On the other hand, the Federalists, whose total volume declined by one-third from period I to period II (see table 8.1), did not so clearly abandon the standoffs. They abandoned issues 2, 3, and 4 of table 8.4, but on the first issue their volume declines only by the expected amount, and on the last issue their volume actually rises. This presages what happened in the third period, in which the Anti-

Table 8.4   Ratios, by Periods, of Federalist to Antifederalist Volume on Five Issues of Liberty and Governmental Structure

	Period I	Period II	Period III	Total
1. Violation of the separation of powers				
Federalist	36367	24410	12561	77338
	—— =1.52	—— =2.04	—— = ∞	—— =2.04
Antifederalist	23915	11962	0	35877
2. President too powerful				
Federalist	42429	2420	48898	93747
	—— =1.43	—— = .20	—— = ∞	—— =2.25
Antifederalist	29719	11890	0	41609
3. Senate too powerful				
Federalist	12578	0	11811	24389
	—— =1.01	—— = 0	—— = ∞	—— =1.50
Antifederalist	12477	3836	0	16313
4. Unicameral legislature				
Federalist	9470	1630	8433	19533
	—— = .57	—— =1.34	—— = ∞	—— =1.10
Antifederalist	16600	1218	0	17818
5. Congress poorly structured				
Federalist	23569	23803	29127	76499
	—— = .73	—— =1.25	—— = ∞	—— =1.49
Antifederalist	32367	18975	0	51342

federalists are silent on all five issues and the Federalists increase their volume mightily on four of the five. Of course, most of the Federalist increase is from Publius, but I do not believe it should be discounted simply for that reason. He could have muted his discussion of institutions, but he did not. Evidently he sensed the Federalist advantage. Thus, the Antifederalists, who initiated the issue of the structural threat to liberty, discovered a standoff and went on to other themes in accord with the Dispersion Principle, while Federalists, who gradually realized their advantage here, seized it in accord with the Dominance Principle.

Table 8.5   Decline in Antifederalist Volume from Period I to Period II for
the Five Issues of Liberty and Governmental Structure

1. Period I   23915   Violation of the separation of powers
    Period II   11962
    Decline   11953   or 50%

2. Period I   29719   President too powerful
    Period II   11890
    Decline   17829   or 60%

3. Period I   12477   Senate too powerful
    Period II   3836
    Decline   8641   or 69%

4. Period I   16600   Unicameral legislature
    Period II   1218
    Decline   15382   or 93%

5. Period I   32367   Congress poorly structured
    Period II   18975
    Decline   13392   or 41%

Note: The expected decline for each issue, based on overall rates, is 25%.

The interpretation of table 8.4 and five issues of structure and liberty could be duplicated on several other lesser issues, but on the issue of judiciary, another structural issue, the story is quite different: the Antifederalists dominated it. Their volume was much higher than Federalist volume in all three periods, as set forth in table 8.6. Although Antifederal volume declined over time, its decline on this issue was less than would be expected from the decline in total Antifederal volume. Furthermore, the Federal response is a whisper. Had my sample included Publius's discussion of the judiciary, Federalist volume in the third period would have been larger, but not by any means large enough to declare a tie. So, on this one issue of structure, the debate displays the Dominance Principle, and this fact increases one's confidence in the attribution of the Dispersion Principle on the other issues.

Why were the Antifederalists able to preempt on the proposition that the federal judiciary, especially as empowered by the supremacy clause, would absorb and dominate state courts and thereby cause injustice by the complexity of law and the remoteness of courts? Other structural issues were a standoff or were dominated by Federalists. But not this one. Why?

Although the federal government of the Articles had a legislature and a rudimentary executive, it had nothing like a judiciary. Citizens were

Table 8.6   Ratios of Volume, by Period, on the Judiciary and Liberty

	Period I	Period II	Period III	Total
Federalist	14460	4253	4572	23285
	—— = .40	—— = .15	—— = .33	—— = .30
Antifederalist	36450	28489	13886	78825

Decreases in Antifederal Volume

Period I	36450		Period II	28489	
Period II	28489		Period III	13886	
Decline	7961	or 22%	Decline	14603	or 51%
Expected Decline		25%			72%

already accustomed to some national legislation, and they could easily imagine a new federal government with a legislature and an executive modeled on those of the states. Indeed, even if the Constitution had been rejected, the states would probably have enhanced federal powers to tax, legislate, and even execute because moderate Antifederalists seemed willing to accept these reforms. So it seems likely that neither side could win the dispute about the effects of the revised legislature and executive on liberty. But the constitutional provisions on the judiciary centralized a heretofore exclusively local part of government. Furthermore, it was just the part that nationalists, eager to enforce the peace treaty, wanted to take out of the hands of the local judges and juries, who had often been unwilling to enforce the payment of debts to British subjects or to restore improperly seized property. This Federalist predisposition made Antifederalists nervous, even after ratification. It is no accident, I believe, that the first structural feature of the Constitution to be repaired was the judiciary (Eleventh Amendment). The politically delicate nature of the judiciary explains why, in accord with the Dominance Principle, the Antifederalists continued to emphasize the judicial threat to liberty. Indeed, the entire 9,888 words on threats from structure in the third period (table 8.2, line 7, column 3) concern the judiciary. Conversely, in accord with the Dispersion Principle, the Antifederalists, faced with standoffs, changed the subject on all the other issues in the structural subtheme.

DOMINANCE IN THE MAIN THEME: ANTIFEDERALISTS AND THE THREAT TO LIBERTY FROM FEDERAL POWERS

Volume on the Antifederalist subtheme of the threat to liberty from federal powers (table 8.2, line 8) increased modestly (5 percent) from period

I to period II (as against an expected decline of 25 percent) and then from period II to period III declined sharply (91 percent), far beyond expectations (72 percent). This pattern is quite different from that of the issue of the threat to liberty from governmental structure and deserves explanation.

In part the issues on federal powers do display the same pattern as the issues on structure. The Antifederalist assertions that the powers of Congress were too broad and that the proposed government would increase taxes are similar to the arguments on structure and might have been classified with them. Because the Federalist responses on federal powers are wholly tied into their assertions about crisis, however, it is impossible to calculate ratios of volume for the two sides. Still, on these two issues Antifederalist volume declines 60 percent from period I to period II (as against an expected 25 percent) and 67 percent from II to III (close to the 72 percent expected). So the pattern is about the same as in table 8.4.

But when we look at other issues in this subtheme a different pattern emerges, one that combines features from tables 8.4 and 8.6. The Antifederalists interpreted the military clauses of the Constitution as provision for a standing army, and Federalists on the whole did not disagree. The Antifederalists argued heatedly that standing armies threatened liberty and that the Federalists' espousal revealed sinister intentions. The Federalists responded that standing armies were necessary and would be politically controlled. The ratios of volume on those issues are set forth in table 8.7.

The pattern in this table is odd. In period I there is a definite standoff. Federal volume is about double Antifederal volume, which means that each side devoted about 2½ percent of its entire argument to standing armies. One expects, therefore, that one or the other or both of the sides would have abandoned the issue in accord with the Dispersion Principle. Instead, both sides intensified their arguments, the Federalists by 40 percent (when a decline of 33 percent was expected) and the Antifederalists by 129 percent (when a decline of 25 percent was expected). How can we explain this unanticipated behavior?

Conventionally in America, citizens despised the idea of standing armies, and Antifederalists appropriated this emotion. Philadelphiensis prophesied that the despotism would be supported by a standing army composed of "profligate idle ruffians," cruel to fellow citizens but "a body of mean cowards" when "facing a foreign foe" (CC 320). According to the Pennsylvania Minority, the framers knew "Congress under this constitution will not possess the confidence of the people" and so they "made a provision for . . . a permanent STANDING ARMY" (CC 353). But Federalists thought that a standing army was also a good argument on their side. Publius, especially, repeatedly argued for "national forces" necessary for

Table 8.7   Ratios of Volume, by Period, on Standing Armies

	Period I	Period II	Period III	Total
Federalist	41842	58503	5351	105696
	$\dfrac{}{}$ =2.04	$\dfrac{}{}$ =1.25	$\dfrac{}{}$ =1.39	$\dfrac{}{}$ =1.48
Antifederalist	20522	46986	3861	71369

	Period I to Period II volume of change		Period II to Period III volume of change	
	actual	*expected*	*actual*	*expected*
Federalist	+ 40%	− 33%	− 91%	− 49%
Antifederalist	+ 129%	− 25%	− 92%	− 72%

the "common defense" (*Federalist* 23, 24, and 26; CC 352, 355, and 366) and emphasized the dangers on borders with Britain, Spain, and Indians (*Federalist* 25, CC 364). But so convinced were Antifederalists of the persuasiveness of their position that they rejoiced that Publius and others had been trapped. An editorialist in the Philadelphia *Freeman's Journal* (CC 409) crowed that "the last numbers of *Publius* have done still more" to defeat the Constitution in New York because his "attempts to prove the expediency of supporting a *standing army* in time of peace have been so futile, that even the friends of the new plan are offended with them" (see also Brutus, CC 455, 475). But it seems that the Antifederalist writers and editors were wrong because Federalists too increased their volume greatly (though not as much as Antifederalists) from period I to period II.

This Antifederal misconception explains the odd pattern. In spite of the standoff in period I (which should have warned both, but especially the weaker Antifederalists, to try another issue), the Antifederalists, ideologically disposed to believe it was persuasive, stepped up their volume by a huge amount. The Federalists responded appropriately. By the third period, however, the Antifederalists had apparently shaken off their ideological blinders. So both sides knew they could not dominate. In belated accordance with the Dispersion Principle, therefore, both sides almost abandoned the issue, both cutting their volume by 90 percent or more.

DOMINANCE IN THE MAIN THEME:
ANTIFEDERALISTS AND THE THREAT TO CIVIL LIBERTY

The two remaining themes (lines 5 and 6 of table 8.2) seem closely related. As the subtheme of threats to civil liberties (line 6) declines in period II, the theme of general threats to liberty (line 5) rises; then in period III the reverse occurs. How can this inverse relation between these two subthemes be explained?

It is almost entirely an artifact of my classification. The themes allocated to line 5 are Antifederal claims that the Constitution endangers liberty by creating an aristocratic, despotic government. In period I the illustration of this general claim is the absence of a bill of rights, which I allocated to line 6. In the next two periods the Antifederalists opportunistically derived illustrations from the events of the campaign. Because I assigned the illustrations in period II to line 5 and those in period III to line 6, lines 5 and 6 ought properly to be combined for all three periods.

In period II, the Antifederalists drew their main illustration from the Pennsylvania campaign: (a) Federalist haste, which Antifederalists interpreted as evidence of the Federalists' despotic intentions, and (b) the large size of the United States, which the minority in Pennsylvania (CC 353), followed by Luther Martin (CC 425, 502), Centinel (CC 453, 501), and others, asserted would more readily admit despotism than would small, loosely confederated states.[1] Because these themes involved claims of despotism, I allocated them to line 5. In period III, however, the Antifederalists drew their main evidence of the potential for despotism from the collapse of postal delivery, especially north of Philadelphia. Postmaster General Ebenezer Hazard changed the method of intercity newspaper delivery from the more expensive stagecoaches to postriders, who often sold or destroyed the papers. By February most northern editors were frantic about the failure of deliveries, which the Antifederalists blamed on the postmaster, whom they interpreted as muzzling their campaign and the freedom of the press.[2]

Viewing lines 5 and 6 as closely related in content and therefore as appropriately combined reveals that the Dominance Principle is at work on these themes. These lines together are by far the most important Antifederalist argument: In period I, they are 27 percent of the whole Antifederal campaign; in period II, they are 28 percent; and in period III, 39 percent. The ratio of Federalist to Antifederalist words on this subject is remarkably low. Instead of the expected ratio of 2.0, the actual ratios are 0.24, 0.12, and 0.21.

---

1. This theme was initially developed in period I by the New York writers (Cato III, CC:195; Federal Farmer, CC:242), but the Pennsylvania writers greatly increased the volume and intensity of this theme in the next period.

2. Hazard's planning for the change had apparently begun the previous spring, so it is difficult to blame him for the problem. Presumably, he was only trying to save the post office money. But it may be, of course, that he did not respond as promptly as he might have when the problem appeared.

Table 8.8   Ratios of Volume, by Period, on Consolidation

	Period I	Period II	Period III	Total
Federalist	360,358	323,039	38,893	722,490
	——— =2.2	——— =1.7	——— =2.9	——— =2.0
Antifederalist	161,939	187,594	13,534	363,067

Volume of Change

	Period I to Period II		Period II to Period III	
	Actual	*Expected*	*Actual*	*Expected*
Federalist	− 10%	− 33%	− 88%	− 49%
Antifederalist	+ 16%	− 25%	− 93%	− 72%

The danger of despotism and the loss of civil liberties are thus a mostly unchallenged theme throughout the campaign, which is exactly an instance of the Dominance Principle at work.

DOMINANCE AND THE THEME OF CONSOLIDATION

For each side, then, the Dominance and Dispersion principles apply to the main themes of crisis and liberty, respectively. Among Antifederalists, however, there is a significant secondary issue, namely, the threat of consolidation.

The Antifederalists discussed this theme in just those categories listed under consolidation in table 8.2. The Constitution, they said, would by consolidation destroy the states (and liberty) as well as bring on civil war (#5006 and #5039). For evidence they pointed to the text of the Constitution itself: provisions for a federal judiciary (#26201) and a congressional treaty-making authority (#45001) empowered through the supremacy clause; federal authority over taxation empowered through the necessary and proper clause (#43002); and Congress's substantive authority over interstate commerce (#46002), empowered through constitutional decree. Such consolidation was, they said, impractical over a large territory and thus incompatible with a free government (#5010), and it could not be justified with a claim of crisis because there was no crisis (#13002). They argued that the consolidation would be illegal because the convention had been called only to amend the Articles, not to consolidate the states (#5020 and #14004). Moreover, consolidation would be unfair because there had been few Antifederal delegates at the convention (#14101), yet the proposed Constitution would for all practical purposes be unamendable (#30001). Ideally, they pointed out, the states should be juridically equal (#20501), and the minor provision on senatorial election did not go nearly far enough to preserve states' independence (#5004).

The Federalist discussion of consolidation was carried on in a variety of categories, some summarized on line 10 of table 8.1 and some summarized elsewhere. Bringing these categories together, one finds that the Federalist argument on consolidation ran about as follows: The Constitution does not fully consolidate but is both federal and national (#5052 and 5053), and furthermore such compound government is well adapted for a large territory (#53157 and 53257). Nevertheless, the Articles of Confederation were, they asserted, inadequate constitutionally (#11058) and militarily (#11060), and this federal weakness justified consolidation (#5082) to surmount provincialism (#12151), to provide for defense (#12350) and military strength (#51052), and to save the nation from crisis (#13052) by providing energetic government (#21350). Indeed, the choice before the nation was, they said, stable government or anarchy (#97054), and the Antifederal alarm about consolidation was sophistical (#5051), especially because legislation for states (as against individuals), as necessary under the Articles, weakened federations (#53152).

The volume by each side on consolidation looks very much like the pattern of debate on the standing army. As table 8.8 shows, the ratios of volume by periods vary around 2.0, which is what I have defined as a standoff, with each side devoting about 22 percent of its total volume to this subject. By the Dispersion Principle, a standoff should lead both sides to abandon the subject; but, until the third period, neither did so. They began in period I with a standoff ratio of volumes of 2.2. Then from period I to period II the Antifederalists increased their volume by 16 percent, as against an expected decrease of 25 percent. Similarly, the Federalists actually decreased by only 10 percent, though their expected decrease was 33 percent. The result was again a standoff in period II at a ratio of 1.7. Finally, however, in the third period both sides came fairly close to abandoning the subject in accordance with the Dispersion Principle. Federalists decreased by 88 percent (as against an expected decrease of 49 percent) and Antifederalists by 93 percent (as against an expected decrease of 72 percent). So in the end there was still a standoff at a ratio of 2.8, but both sides had decreased their volume on consolidation from near 20 percent of their total words to near 7 percent.

The reason for the reluctance of both sides to abandon this unfruitful subject lies, I think, in the intentions of the Antifederalists. They increased their volume greatly in the second period (though they would be expected to lower it if the proportion of words devoted to each subject remained constant). Furthermore, they did so from a lower base — in the first period their volume on consolidation was only about 15 percent of their total volume, while the Federalists' proportion of volume was about 22 percent. So the Antifederalists proceeded from behind to relative leadership on this issue. What explains this surprising intensification?

Students of Antifederalist thought like Main and Storing assert, as I pointed out in chapter 4, that the Antifederalists' primary concern was to prevent consolidation. Against this assertion, I showed that whatever their concerns, Antifederalists wrote much more about threats to liberty. We all three, however, could be correct. Because the Antifederal arguments about consolidation are somewhat self-serving, as Wilson and Publius were quick to point out, Antifederalists had a rhetorically appropriate motive to mask their deepest private concerns with heavy emphasis on their public concern about liberty. Under this interpretation, Main and Storing can be correct about motives and I about behavior. Still, if consolidation so deeply worried Antifederalists, it is understandable that they would wish to display its supposed evils, even in spite of the implicit warning in period I that there was a standoff on the issue. Assuming, then, that Main and Storing are right about the Antifederal motives, their intensification in period II is an instance of emotion temporarily triumphant over reason.

When Antifederalists intensified, however, the Federalists had a motive to do so as well. If the Dominance Principle were to apply here, then the Federalists would concede. But they presumably realized that their arguments on consolidation were just as good as their opponents'. So they kept up their discussion even though they did not intensify it. Consequently, there was a standoff again in period II.

A standoff is, by the Dispersion Principle, inherently unstable. As figure 7.3 (p. 105) indicates, there is no equilibrium between t^- and t^+ on the horizontal axis. Rational rhetors, recognizing that debate is wasteful, have a motive to abandon the subject. And in the real world, even the most ideologically committed will likely observe after four months the futility of arguing to a standoff. So at the end of period II, both sides abandon the subject, finally in accordance with the Dispersion Principle.

IV

The Heresthetic of the
Ratification Campaigns

9

The Agenda for Ratification

R HETORIC ALONE does not win elections. Rhetors persuade some people, but it is difficult to imagine mass conversions among adults with settled opinions. And if conversions are few in number, then they only occasionally affect outcomes, except when the two sides are almost evenly supported. But if rhetors do not usually win by persuasion, what do they accomplish through all their effort? The answer, as I tried to show in the previous chapters, is that they selectively activate voters' memories and concerns. Ordinarily a single human being can simultaneously evaluate only a few issues and alternatives. I think most rhetors intuitively understand this limitation and seek, therefore, not to persuade, but to call into voters' consciousness those themes that will incline them, so rhetors hope, to the rhetors' sides. As I showed in chapters 4 and 5, rhetors on one side seek to structure marginal voters' decision making so that they accept the risk offered by that side in order to avoid the presumably worse outcome offered by the other side. At the same time, as I showed in chapters 6, 7, and 8, rhetors organize their arguments around these themes and ignore issues raised by the other side. Both of these rhetorical efforts are aimed at changing an auditor's calculations of advantage rather than simple conversion. Thinking of an auditor's decisions as made in n-dimensional space, the rhetor seeks to change not the auditor's position on a particular dimension, but rather the mix of dimensions deemed relevant.

But the rhetor also has another purpose: The set of relevant dimensions is the setting for the agenda. Indeed, the dimensions to some degree form and constrain the agenda. Thus, successful rhetoric can shape the agenda, and to the degree that rhetors can shape the agenda, they can arrange the decision-making process so that their alternative is greatly advantaged.

The reason that setting the agenda is so important politically is that, in settings that lack institutional structure, typically no alternative has a majority over each of the others. As a consequence, the sequence and methods by which alternatives are considered are at least as important for the outcome as the tastes of the voters are. This proposition, which is the primary discovery of twentieth-century political theory, has seldom been used to interpret historical events. It does, however, enable us to attain a deeper understanding of political life, and so I use it here to interpret the campaigns and decisions of 1787–88.

The initial content of recent political theory is the potential existence, given appropriate distributions of tastes, of the paradox of voting, namely, that with pairwise, simple majority voting on three or more alternatives, no alternative is able to defeat all others. Stated another way, each alternative may lose to some other; or still another way, alternatives may be in a cycle so that a beats b, b beats c, and c beats a. This paradox, first observed by the Marquis de Condorcet in 1784 and brought into scholarly consciousness by Duncan Black, is not an artifact of the method of voting but, as Kenneth Arrow showed, a feature of the distribution of tastes among voters.[1] Cyclical distributions may occur under any fair method of amalgamating individual preferences into social choices.

If this possibility were seldom realized, then it would not be of much practical consequence. But in fact it is highly probable, given an institution-free environment. To see just how probable, let us, following Black, define an equilibrium under majority voting as an alternative that beats each other alternative in a head-to-head vote. (Such a winner is an equilibrium because some majority of voters will reject any alternative to it, and, once it is reached, no majority of voters will wish to depart from it.) When voters judge alternatives by one criterion (for example, on one issue dimension), an equilibrium exists by Black's median voter theorem if, for all voters, each voter's ideal point (that is, most desired alternative) can be placed on the dimension so that, for any pair of alternatives, a voter prefers the alternative closer to his or her ideal point. Of course, if the alternatives are equidistant, the voter is indifferent as to one or the other. For decisions by large electorates, it is frequently possible to relax Black's sufficient condition from "if, for all voters, . . . " to "if, for a large majority of voters, . . ."[2] (These conditions for equilibrium do not imply that voters agree — they

1. Duncan Black, "On the Rationale of Group Decision Making," *Journal of Political Economy* 56 (1948): 23–34; Duncan Black, *The Theory of Committees and Elections* (Cambridge: Cambridge University Press, 1958); Kenneth Arrow, *Social Choice and Individual Values*, 2d ed. (New Haven: Yale University Press, 1963).

2. Richard Niemi, "Majority Decision-Making with Partial Unidimensionality," *American Political Science Review* 63 (1969): 489–97.

may disagree extremely — but rather imply merely that all or most voters rate alternatives by the same standard.)

Consequently, on one dimension, real world equilibria seem probable. But if there are two or more dimensions — like crisis and liberty in 1787, for example — then an equilibrium exists if, for $(2k + 1)$ voters, the ideal points of $2k$ voters can be matched in pairs — for example, 1st and $(k + 1)$th, 2d and $(k + 2)$th, . . . , kth and 2kth — so that, for each pair, the contract curve between them passes through the ideal point of the $(2k + 1)$th voter.[3] (The definition is similar for an even number.) Clearly, the condition for a Plott equilibrium, a unique central point, is difficult to satisfy in the real world. Just how difficult is shown by the fact that, if the condition is not met precisely, then a cycle must exist and must include all possible alternatives.[4] This draconian result is mitigated somewhat — but not very much — by the fact that there is a central area of unknown size in the alternative space to which movement through cycles is constrained if voting is sophisticated.[5]

What typically prevents cycles in the real world is the existence of institutions that force participants to modify their opinions, to bunch them up, and, usually, to agree, more or less unconsciously, on a single dimension. But, of course, in an institution-free setting or a setting in which existing institutions work awkwardly — and the process of adopting a constitution is surely such a setting — there is very little to force convergence to an equilibrium of tastes.

The practical consequence of the existence of a cycle of tastes is that there are many potential majorities, at least one for each alternative in the cycle. In my opinion, there is no acceptable theory of justice from which one can infer that any one of these potential majorities is superior to another. Even if one could so infer, no institutional arrangement could guarantee the selection of the putatively superior majority. This means, first of all, that preexisting institutional bias and current political maneuver have as much to do with the social choice as do the tastes and values of the populace. In the real world where social decisions are necessary, some one of the numerous potential majorities must be realized; but which one

3. Charles Plott, "A Notion of Equilibrium and Its Possibility under Majority Rule," *American Economic Review* 57 (1967): 787–806. [[A contract curve is the curve between the two voters' ideal points such that, for any point not on the curve, there is a point on the curve that is better for both voters.]]

4. Richard McKelvey, "General Conditions for Global Intransitivities in Formal Voting Models," *Econometrica* 47 (1979): 1085–1112.

5. John Ferejohn, Richard D. McKelvey, and Edward W. Packel, "Limiting Distributions for Continuous State Markow Voting Models," *Social Choice and Welfare* 1 (1984): 45–68; Richard D. McKelvey, "Covering, Dominance, and Institution-Free Properties of Social Choice," *American Journal of Political Science* 30 (1986): 283–314.

is decided by the political contest over the agenda. This is why rhetorical dispute on the structure of the agenda is so intense.

Another important consequence of a cycle of tastes is that, whatever alternative is adopted by a majority, there is some other majority that prefers another alternative. Of course, the "other" majority may not know about its potential existence. When *a* is adopted in a vote against *b*, the fact that *c* could beat *a* has not been tested. Hence the supporters of *c* cannot be sure of their potential majority. But they can sometimes be almost sure. And when they are almost sure, they are likely to feel terribly aggrieved. Hence one evidence of the existence of a cycle is the depth of resentment by those losers who believe they could have been winners. The passionate hatred displayed by writers like Centinel, Philadelphiensis, and Columbian Patriot and by politicians like Patrick Henry *after* they had lost on ratification is an indication of their conviction that the Constitution could have been ratified conditional on the inclusion of specified amendments rather than, as actually happened, merely with recommended amendments.

CYCLES OF VALUES DURING THE CAMPAIGN

It seems pretty clear that cycles existed in 1787–88. It is almost always in the interest of those who think they are at a disadvantage to introduce new alternatives. When they do so, they open up an opportunity for a cycle. To see how easily this can happen, I offer a wholly imaginary example based on the development of issues in the first two weeks or so after the Convention transmitted the proposed Constitution to the Congress of the Articles of Confederation. Suppose a public opinion survey had been possible then and imagine its outcome to be as follows:

35% preferred *R*(atification) to *D*(efeat)
30% preferred *D* to *R*
35% were undecided between *R* and *D*.

If we ignore the undecideds, *R* would beat *D*. But after obtaining some information, the undecideds would begin making up their minds, and at the same time, as actually happened, an opponent (Richard Henry Lee) would call for an *S*(econd Convention). As a result, the voters would now face three alternatives, and the three groups would divide up into six. Imagine those in favor of ratification would divide as follows: 25 percent with preference ordering *RSD* and 10 percent with *SRD*, where *RSD* is the position of Federalists determined to win and *SRD* the position of Federalists who generously wish to allow more Antifederalist participation. Imagine also that the undecideds would go mostly to Antifederalists: 30 percent with ordering *DRS* and 5 percent with *RDS*, which would accord with the common observation today that the "don't knows" are mostly against the incumbent—here presumably the Philadelphia convention. Imagine finally that the opponents of ratification would divide thus: 10 percent with ordering *DSR* and 20 percent with *SDR*, where the *DSR*s would seek to defeat the Constitution out of hand, while the *SDR*s would strategically prefer the delaying tactic of a second convention. All this would result in the following set of tastes:

	R vs. S		R vs. D		S vs. D	
RSD	25		25		25	
RDS	5		5			5
DRS	30			30		30
DSR		10		10		10
SRD		10	10		10	
SDR		20		20	20	
	60	40	40	60	55	45

so that *D* beats *R*, *R* beats *S*, and *S* beats *D*. This is not, I admit, a particularly realistic reconstruction—the real world was surely more complicated. But it does indicate how easily and quickly the introduction of just one more alternative can complicate decision making.

During the campaign over ratification there were, at the very least, six alternatives offered and discussed:

1. Unconditional Ratification.

2. Ratification with Recommended Amendments. Actually, this is a whole series of positions ranging from the four fairly innocuous amendments recommended by the South Carolina convention (states to decide time, manner, and places of federal elections; states to retain all powers not expressly relinquished; no direct taxes, but if imposts and excises are inadequate, Congress to make requisitions on states; and Article VI to be amended from "no religious test . . . required" to "no other religious test . . . required") to the New York recommendations of a bill of rights with twenty-four items followed by thirty-two proposed amendments.

3. Ratification Conditional on Amendments. This also is a whole series of positions depending upon which conditions might be imposed. Because no conditions were in fact either proposed or imposed, it is not possible to specify exactly the range of possibilities.

4. Ratification Conditional on Amendments Coordinately Imposed by Several States. Again a series of possibilities.

5. Second Convention. Finally, this too is a series of possibilities.
6. Unconditional Rejection.

But even this list of potential alternatives does not capture the full range of opinion and possible action. Writing to Jefferson on 9 December 1787, Madison described the parties as he saw them in Virginia at that point:

> My information leads me to suppose there must be three parties in Virginia. The first for adopting without amendments. This includes Genl. W — and ye other deputies who signed the Constitution. . . . At the head of the 2d party which urges amendments are the Govr. [Edmund Randolph] & Mr. Mason. These do not object to the substance of the Governt. but contend for a few additional Guards in favor of the Rights of the States and of the people. I am not able to enumerate the[se] characters . . . , as distinguished from those of the third class, at the head of which is Mr. Henry. This class concurs at present with the patrons of Amendments, but will probably contend for such as strike at the essence of the System.[6]

Henry's party represents still another alternative between Second Convention and Unconditional Rejection. Madison's categorization is reasonable for Virginia in December, but it does not at all cover the full range of opinion during 1787–88 in all states. His second category was even then breaking apart into Randolph, who would eventually vote for ratification with recommended amendments, and Mason, who, although never as hostile as Henry, would vote against the Constitution even with recommended amendments.

One way to visualize the wide range of opinion is to locate groups of opinion-makers in the areas of a two-dimensional space determined by the issues of crisis and liberty, which, as I have already shown, were the main issues raised in the campaigns.[7] In figure 9.1 the horizontal axis measures the degree of emphasis on liberty, with indifference to the subject at the right and extreme emphasis on it at the left. The vertical axis measures the

6. Robert A. Rutland, ed., *The Papers of James Madison* (Chicago: University of Chicago Press, 1977), 10:312.

7. [[This manner of representing opinion leaders is bolstered by another analysis using recorded roll call votes in the Continental Congress. Jillson and Wilson find a good deal of separation among delegates to the Congress. In particular, their figure 8.12 from 1787 demonstrates the manner in which Federalists and Antifederalists were opposed in the Congress. Additional empirical analysis shows similar splits for other years. Calvin Jillson and Rick K. Wilson, *Congressional Dynamics: Structure, Coordination, and Choice in the First American Congress, 1774–1789* (Stanford: Stanford University Press, 1994).]]

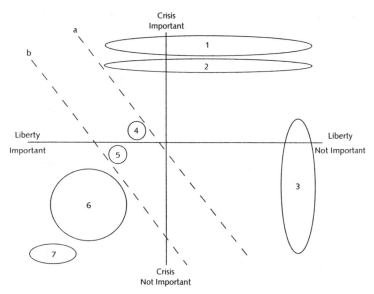

line a: the Constitution as proposed
line b: the Constitution as adopted

Group 1: Original Federalists
Group 2: Compromisers

Group 3: Bargainers
Group 4: Amendment Recommenders
Group 5: Reluctant Recommenders
Group 6: Conditional Ratifiers
Group 7: Extreme Antifederalists

Figure 9.1   Spatial Model of the Ratification Campaign: Locations of Ideal Points of Various Groups, and Lines Separating Supporters from Opponents of the Constitution

degrees of emphasis on crisis, with indifference at the bottom and extreme emphasis at the top. Within that space are the following sets of opinion leaders:

Group 1: Original Federalists, those for whom the depth of the crisis implied the necessity of immediate and extreme centralization and for whom the issue of liberty was, by comparison, trivial, though some would of course welcome appropriate protections for liberty. At the extreme right end in this group are people like Hamilton and Fisher Ames (Mass.) and at the left end of the group, that is, slightly left of center, are people like Madison. Some members of the group are hard to place on the liberty scale: Wilson (Penn.) made the most democratic remarks of anyone in the convention, in sharp contrast to people like the Antifederalist Gerry (Mass.), who was quite hostile to and afraid of democratic processes. On the other hand, Wilson argued strongly against a bill of rights. There is a similar problem with Gouverneur Morris (N.Y.), who along with Rufus

King (Mass.) spoke most forcefully against slavery and who, like Wilson, strongly advocated democratic procedures, but who was also proudly an aristocrat. Nevertheless, Wilson and Morris are at the very top of the vertical scale.

Group 2: Compromisers, those who were completely satisfied with the Connecticut compromise — for example, Sherman, Ellsworth, and William Johnson of Connecticut, Caleb Strong (Mass.) and Franklin (Penn.). Both Strong and Franklin had initially opposed compromise but decided it was better than failure. This would appear to make them more conscious of crisis than group 1. But in fact the people of group 1 were so certain the crisis was compelling that they believed the small states would not dare to go it alone. Franklin probably belongs at the left end of the group on the liberty dimension — about like Madison — and Johnson at the right end — about like Hamilton.

Group 3: Bargainers, those who were sufficiently indifferent to crisis as to threaten (with, apparently, complete sincerity) to disrupt the convention rather than concede their special privileges and who never showed any interest in the liberty dimension. This group contains two subgroups: (3a), those who insisted on equal representation for small states, for example, William Paterson (N.J.) and Gunning Bedford (Del.); and (3b), those who insisted on protection for slavery, for example, Charles Cotesworth Pinckney (S.C.), John Rutledge (S.C.), Abraham Baldwin (Ga.), and William Davie (N.C.). What brings 3a and 3b together, despite the difference of their special interests, is the fact that, being unconcerned about crisis, they were willing to scuttle the convention if they did not get their way and that they displayed no concern at all about liberty. They do vary among themselves, however, on the crisis dimension. Some were quite nationalistic once their interests were protected (for example, Rutledge) and helped to write the whole Constitution, while others lapsed into silence (for example, Davie and Bedford) or went home (for example, Paterson) once their interests were satisfied. None of the people in this group, either during the convention or during ratification, had anything to say about liberty and, of course, the Southerners' special interest was the antithesis of liberty.

Group 4: Amendment Recommenders, those who hesitated about the Constitution but who thought it reasonable once the notion of recommended amendments surfaced. They were concerned about crisis but hesitated because of liberty. The idea of recommending moderate amendments resolved their problem. John Hancock (Mass.) is the prime example.

Group 5: Reluctant Recommenders, those who initially supported conditional amendments out of concern for liberty, but who, owing to the development of politics in their state conventions, came to support ratification with recommendations. This category includes people like Samuel Adams (Mass.), Melancton Smith (N.Y.), and Randolph (Va.).

Group 6: Conditional Ratifiers, those who insisted on a bill of rights and structural reforms and were willing to ignore the crisis in order to get their way. This is exactly Madison's second group, those who wanted reasonable amendments. They were sufficiently concerned about crisis to cooperate actively in framing the Constitution, but in the end liberty meant more to them than crisis. As Madison indicated, Mason led this party in Virginia, and his counterpart in Massachusetts was Gerry.

Group 7: Extreme Antifederalists, those who were completely unconcerned about crisis, were hostile to any diminution of state power, and took up the cause of liberty as their main rallying cry. This group includes leaders like Luther Martin (Md.), Henry (Va.), Willie Jones (N.C.), and Robert Yates (N.Y.).[8]

The location of the seven groups in figure 9.1 allows us to interpret, on a very broad scale, the main developments in the framing and ratification of the Constitution. At the convention, people in group 1, who had led the movement for a convention and who made up about 38 percent of the delegates, proposed the agenda, namely, the Virginia Plan. Group 2, small but crucial, consisted of about 7 percent; group 3a about 18 percent; and group 3b about 29 percent. Group 4 was unrepresented. Group 5 constituted about 2 percent, group 6 about 3 percent, and group 7 about 7 percent. Group 1 obviously could not have framed a Constitution alone. During the long struggle on representation through most of the first half of the convention, group 2 forced groups 1 and 3a together with the compromise of equality in the Senate and proportionality in the House. Even the 63 percent thus brought together was not enough when the method of ratification (9/13) required almost 70 percent.[9] Having learned from experience, groups 1 and 2 attracted group 3b with the compromise on the slave trade, the provision for counting 3/5ths of the slaves for representation, and the fugitive slave provision. Thus, the Constitution as proposed separated the political groups by a diagonal line running from the

8. [[This alignment of delegates is similar to that employed by others who have studied the Constitutional Convention. For a summary of voting alignments and an extensive analysis of the roll calls, see Calvin C. Jillson, *Constitution Making: Conflict and Consensus in the Federal Convention of 1787* (New York: Agathon Press, 1988), esp. chap. 2.]]

9. [[Of course the Constitutional Convention used the unit rule, in which each state delegation cast a single vote. Depending on the voting distribution within those delegations, the percentage of individual delegates' votes required for passage could vary.]]

northwest to the southeast (line a in figure 9.1), placing all the first quadrant and the upper halves of the second and fourth quadrants on the side of the Constitution.

As it turned out, however, this was not quite enough to gain ratification. To carry Massachusetts, it was necessary for groups 4 and 5 to join. Once they had done so by the device of recommended amendments (by moving to line b in figure 9.1), the Constitution attracted majorities in eleven of thirteen states. Eleven states is more than a minimally winning coalition, but in four states the margin was close. Consequently, the adopted Constitution differed from the proposed Constitution by the expectation that some unspecified recommended amendments would subsequently be adopted.

Viewing the politics of 1787–88 in this way makes it possible to resolve some traditional questions while raising others not heretofore apparent. One traditional question is why the Federalists ultimately won when, presumably, they received fewer votes in the elections of the ratifying conventions than did Antifederalists. Another is how group 1 came to be initially the largest single group in the convention. One hitherto unapparent question concerns how the nationalists, group 1, were able to dominate the agenda all the way from the selection of delegates for the Philadelphia convention on through eleven state ratifying conventions, and another concerns the way the line dividing pro and con voters can be moved about rhetorically and heresthetically. To the elucidation of some of these questions I now turn.

10

Nationalist Domination in the Congresses of the 1780s

THE MOST IMPORTANT fact about the whole process of framing and ratifying the Constitution is that the initiative and hence the control of the agenda was, for most of the time, in the hands of the nationalists, those identified in the previous chapter as group 1. In some states and at some times the initiative fell into the hands of members of groups 2, 3, and even 4, but even when this happened group 1 benefited by compromising or by absorbing some members of other groups into itself. How did this initiative come about and how was it sustained? In the next several chapters I will attempt to answer this question.

The politics of the mid-1780s were in deadlock. At the beginning of the decade those nationalists who favored a strong central government gained control of Congress at the same time as the Articles of Confederation came into operation. (For this discussion, I call this group nationalists because although they disagreed on many subjects in many ways, they agreed on the desirability of a strong national government.) Under Robert Morris (Penn.), who was the nationalists' ideological leader and the new superintendent of finance, nationalists began a series of reforms intended both to repair the financial devastation of the Revolution and to strengthen the federal government: the assumption of state war debt, the acquisition of western lands from the states, and a national impost (that is, tariff) to be nationally collected. The federal government did assume a good portion of the war debt, the claiming states did transfer the western lands north of the Ohio to the federal government, but, as noted in chapter 2, the impost failed. And as it failed the nationalist program withered. The states treated the proposed impost as an amendment to the Articles of Confederation, reasonably so because the impost as a tax on individual transactions side-stepped the Articles' system of federal requisitions from state governments. Because the impost was an amendment, it could be defeated by one state's veto, and Rhode Island did indeed veto the impost of 1781. Nationalists then devised a new financial plan, the so-called impost of 1783, which New York vetoed. In 1784 Congress, now less nationalist in tone, accepted Morris's resignation and replaced him with a three-member Board of Treasury, which ultimately included two intense opponents of Morris and all his works.[1] Some states also began to reclaim their debts in order to pay off their own citizen debtholders. Thus, the only part of the nationalists' program that succeeded was the federalization of western lands. The states did abandon claims to the northwest, and, at the very time that nationalists in Philadelphia were writing the new Constitution, other nationalists in New York were composing the Northwest Ordinance of 1787, a constitution for the new territory.

NATIONALISTS IN CONGRESS

The fact that nationalists were unable to carry through their program does not mean, however, that they were insignificant in Congress. It is true that after Morris's nationalist program failed the issues in Congress became increasingly regional.[2] But throughout the regional controversies, people with nationalist tastes still dominated Congress. Except possibly for the year 1784, people who later favored the Constitution controlled a majority of the state delegations.

I have identified the attitudes toward ratification of most members of Congress who actually attended from 1783 to 1787. My assumption that in earlier years the supporters of the Constitution in 1787–88 were sympathetic to nationalism, while the opponents were earlier and consistently provincials, allowed me to estimate the distribution of ideologies in Congress and to show the degree of nationalist sympathies. (Although my assumption may not be entirely correct because a few congressmen like Rufus King [Mass.] may have shifted position, it still seems adequate for the rough estimates I intend to make.)

The congressmen easiest to identify were those who voted or announced for or against the Constitution at some point—in the conven-

1. Some writers interpret the composition of the board as a slap at Morris. The fact is, however, that Congress first elected six others before ending up with the perennial candidate Arthur Lee only because, as Monroe said, "We can get none better," and even though Lee's retirement from the public service would "be advantageous to the publick." Edmund C. Burnett, ed., *Letters of Members of the Continental Congress* (1936; rept. Gloucester: Peter Smith, 1963), 8:92, 7:633.

2. Calvin Jillson and Rick K. Wilson, *Congressional Dynamics: Structure, Coordination, and Choice in the First American Congress, 1774–1789* (Stanford: Stanford University Press, 1994), chap. 8.

Table 10.1   The Distribution of Ideology in Congressional Delegations, 1783-87

	Number of Delegations with			
	Nationalist Majorities	Provincial Majorities	Ties Between Nationalists & Provincials	Uncertain Majorities
1783*	8	3	1	0
1784	5	1	4	3
1785	8	3	1	1
1786	8-½	2-½	1	1
1787	10-½	1-½	1	0

*Georgia had no delegation in 1783.

In the delegations indicated by half values, those in attendance during one-half of the year were of one opinion, while those in attendance in the other half were of the contrary opinion.

tion, in Congress, or in a state ratifying convention. A few such cases are ambiguous: for example, Melancton Smith and Zephaniah Platt, Clintonian Antifederalists who wrote and worked against the Constitution nevertheless voted for it in the New York convention, lest New York be left out of the Union; Nathan Dane (Mass.) and Abraham Clark (N.J.) voted in Congress to transmit the Constitution to the states but then expressed themselves strongly against it. To avoid overcounting those with nationalist sympathies, I treated all ambiguous cases as provincials. The congressmen whose positions were more difficult to identify were those who simply expressed private opinions. A few were impossible to identify, either because they had died by 1787 or because they were not prominent enough to inspire a written record. Altogether I was able to identify the attitudes toward the Constitution of about 87 percent of the congressmen for the 1783–87 period.

These data on individual attitudes reveal the effective distribution of attitudes toward centralization in Congress. As shown in table 10.1, the majority of delegations for every year except possibly 1784 were nationalist in tone.

This tabulation, which politicians of the 1780s must have carried in their heads, is a fairly good prediction of the course of politics in 1787 and later. It suggests an enduring and increasing nationalist majority. Of the sixty-four delegations for the period 1783–87, forty, or more than 60 percent, were clearly nationalist, while only eleven, about 17 percent, were clearly provincial. And in the crucial year of 1787, about 80 percent of the

Table 10.2   The Distribution of Ideology in the Delegations of the Three Largest States, 1783-87

	Massachusetts	Pennsylvania	Virginia
1783	Provincial	Nationalist	Provincial
1784	Tied	Nationalist	Provincial
1785	Tied	Uncertain	Provincial
1786	Nationalist	½ – ½	Tied
1787	½ – ½	Nationalist	Nationalist

delegations had clear nationalist majorities, while only about 12 percent were clearly provincial. To avoid overemphasizing nationalist strength, I separated out Massachusetts, Pennsylvania, and Virginia, the three largest states, and thus those whose politicians were most likely to think they could go it alone. In table 10.2, I show that in these states the provincials were stronger: about one-third of the large state delegations and indeed about 45 percent of all provincial delegations in the five-year period. Nationalists were weaker in these states than in the Congress as a whole (only just over half), but they dominated in all three in the fall of 1787. This difference between the large and small states probably accounts for the fact that most of our contemporary historians interpret the Congress of the mid-1780s as provincialist. Some of the most prominent men from the most prominent states were indeed provincial. But the Congress as a whole was distinctly nationalist in four of the five years.

It is easy to see why the nationalists of 1787 sensed that they were on an upswing—at least after 1784. By 1787 they dominated most delegations, even those from the large states. In hindsight, we can see the upswing even more clearly. Nationalists and protonationalists dominated the federal government for the whole twenty-year period from 1781, when Robert Morris became the financier, to 1801, when John Adams left the presidency. From our vantage point, the nationalist majorities of the 1780s were part of a long-term swing in opinion culminating in the adoption of the Constitution and the creation under Washington and Hamilton of a strong federal government.[3]

3. Many historians of American party politics begin their interpretation with the rise of the Jeffersonian Republicans. They forget that the Republicans were the response to the Federalists' initial domination, which really began in 1780 or 1781. In my interpretation of American political parties, the Whigs of the Revolution were a party that effectively wiped out its opponents, driving them out of the country or into total silence. The Whigs themselves split into national and provincial wings. The national dominated from 1780 to 1800, the provincial from 1801 to 1858, the national again after 1858, although with the final national-

The nationalists of 1787 would not have been far wrong if they had used the data of table 10.1 to predict the outcome of the struggle over ratification. The states that ratified quickly or easily also regularly sent delegations with nationalist majorities to Congress:

Delaware, four out of five times with one provincialist;
Pennsylvania, three and a half out of five times, with one uncertain;
New Jersey, four out of five times, with one tied;
Georgia, three out of four with one uncertain;
Connecticut, four out of five with one tied;
Maryland, four out of five with one tied;
South Carolina, five out of five.

On the other hand, most of the states in which ratification was slow and difficult signaled as much by their more provincialist delegations:

Rhode Island never sent a delegation with a nationalist majority, although three times it sent tied delegations;
Massachusetts sent only one and a half clearly nationalist delegations, with two tied and one provincialist;
New York sent only one nationalist delegation, with three provincial and one uncertain;
Virginia also sent only one nationalist delegation with three provincial majorities and one tied.

Only two states gave incorrect signals: North Carolina and New Hampshire each sent four nationalist delegations with one uncertain. These incorrect signals, especially in North Carolina, resulted from the fact that the legislatures elected many more delegates than attended. Consequently, the delegations in these two states were partially self selected. Presumably those who felt financially free to attend and chose to do so were merchants and professional men from coastal cities (for example, Portsmouth, Edenton) and hence more likely to be nationalist in ideology.

Given these signals — mostly correct ones as it turned out — a nationalist delegate to the Philadelphia convention might easily have mused, "We have nine states for sure. Although we will probably lose New York and Rhode Island, we have an even chance for Massachusetts and Virginia. By the arithmetic of probability we will win one of these latter two for ten in all. So the provision in the proposed Constitution to start up after nine ratifications will be easy to satisfy."

---

ist victory in the Civil War, the issues changed as greatly as they had in 1780 and the years following.

These facts about the delegations account for several important features of the politics of 1787:

First, the nationalists believed that they had been unfairly deprived of the chance to govern. They could confidently point to their majorities in Congress (from 1781 to 1787 except for 1784) as evidence that they represented a majority of the society. (Of course, the filter effect, by which state legislatures made like-minded appointments, exaggerated the nationalists' significance, but they never mentioned this fact.) At the same time they could argue that the unanimity requirement — giving each state legislature a veto on national reform — placed an insuperable obstacle in their way. (The nationalists typically blamed unanimity; but as Calvin Jillson and Rick Wilson demonstrate, the whole institutional structure of Congress — extraordinary majority requirements, weak president, ad hoc committees, term limits, and so on — prevented action and encouraged Congress to waste time on regional disputes.)[4] In modern terms, the nationalists could claim that the veto and all the other institutional decentralization prevented a potential majoritarian equilibrium for national taxes and imposed instead an unpopular equilibrium of the status quo, certainly an antirepublican result.[5]

Of course, their belief that the Constitution (that is, the Articles) frustrated them led the nationalists to propose constitutional reform. One can see the effect in Rufus King's letters: On 5 May 1786 he confidently wrote to John Adams that the last state, New York, would soon and finally accede to the impost proposal of 1783, thus solving the immediate constitutional problem of the Articles.[6] On 14 May 1786, he wrote in complete disillusionment to Elbridge Gerry about the conditions New York attached to its agreement and described the confederacy as being deranged.[7] On 11 June 1786, writing to Jonathan Jackson, he called the situation of the confederacy critical.[8] On 17 September 1786, just after the Annapolis convention failed, he wrote to Gov. James Bowdoin (Mass.), "Foreign nations had been notified of this convention, the Friends to a good federal government . . . looked to it with anxiety and hope; the History of it, will not be more agreeable to the former, than it must be seriously painful to the latter."[9] Therefore he looked forward eagerly to the Philadelphia convention. On 11 February 1787, he wrote desperately but hopefully to Gerry,

4. *Congressional Dynamics*, Conclusion.

5. Evelyn C. Fink and William H. Riker, "The Strategy of Ratification," in Bernard Grofman and Donald Wittman, eds., *The Federalist Papers and the New Institutionalism* (New York: Agathon Press, 1989), 220–56.

6. Burnett, *Letters of Members of the Continental Congress*, 8:355.

7. Ibid., 8:360.

8. Ibid., 8:389.

9. Ibid., 8:469.

"Events are hurrying to a crisis; prudent and sagacious men should be ready to seize the most favorable circumstances to establish a more permanent and vigorous government. I hope you will be at leisure to attend the convention. Madison is here. I presume he will be preparing himself for the convention; you know he is a delegate from Virginia; he professes great expectation as to the good effects of the measure."[10] Thus did the frustration over unanimity lead to eagerness for constitutional reform.

Furthermore, even those who later turned out to be Antifederalists recognized the need for reform. Although James Monroe voted against ratification in the Virginia convention in 1788, as a Virginia congressman in 1785 he actually proposed and worked hard for strengthening the powers of Congress as listed in Article IX, paragraph 1, of the Articles of Confederation.[11] And Nathan Dane, who ran unsuccessfully as an Antifederalist for the Massachusetts ratifying convention, nevertheless as a congressman in 1786 wrote to Sam Adams, "We are at a loss to govern our commerce, and how to call forth our resources for federal purposes." Recalling that, when the Articles were written, most states rejected federal control of trade, he went on, "Experience has faithfully taught us that we were then mistaken, and we may venter [venture] to affirm that more than ¾ of the Community have changed their opinions, since far more than 8/10 of the Union have adopted the impost system, and 9 states have granted to Cong. Com'l. powers as fully as they recom'd it be done."[12]

If, after observing the effects of the unanimity rule and other institutional defects, even subsequent Antifederalists were convinced of the need for reform, imagine how much more emphasis nationalists laid on this theme.

A second consequence of the striking contrast between nationalists' electoral success and their constitutionally induced inability to carry out their program was the boldness of nationalists at the Philadelphia convention. During the spring of 1787, James Madison, sitting in a Congress that could seldom act because so few members attended, devised extremely bold plans for reform. In a succession of letters to Jefferson (19 March 1787), Gov. Edmund Randolph (8 April 1787), and Washington (16 April 1787), he developed what subsequently became the Virginia Plan, which the Philadelphia convention adopted as its agenda.[13] The most notable feature of this plan is that it almost eliminated state government influence over the national government. Thus, it provided that the people elect the

10. Ibid., 8:539.
11. Ibid., 8:88, 143.
12. Ibid., 8:305.
13. Robert A. Rutland, ed., *The Papers of James Madison* (Chicago: University of Chicago Press, 1975), 9:317, 369, 382.

lower house; that the lower house elect the upper house, although from nominees selected by state legislatures; that the two houses elect the executive and judiciary; that the legislature have substantially unlimited authority; and that state conventions (that is, temporary bodies) rather than state legislatures ratify the new constitution. Having thus eliminated almost any possibility of state control of the national government, the Virginia Plan then provided substantial national control of state governments through a national (legislative) veto on state laws (analogous, so Madison thought, to the Privy Council's imperial veto over colonial laws) and through a national guarantee of republican government for the states (that is, a potential for active interference in state government).

As it turned out, the Philadelphia convention modified the Virginia Plan to retain some national role for the states. Still, the Constitution was, as I have shown in an essay entitled "The Invention of Centralized Federalism,"[14] closer to centralized government than any federation theretofore designed.

Had they lacked the sense that the country was basically nationalist, as revealed in the composition of congressional delegations in the mid-1780s, Madison and his friends would not, I believe, have dared the centralization that they attempted and almost achieved. In that way the nationalistic delegations in Congress were a necessary condition for the particular Constitution written in 1787.

A third important consequence of the contrast between nationalist electoral success and legislative failure is that the framers were rather more confident than they should have been about the ratification of their extremely centralized design for government. Two states (North Carolina and New Hampshire) gave false signals by sending nationalist delegates when the population itself was more provincial in spirit. And the same institutional arrangements that led to this extreme distortion induced a more moderate distortion in other states. Delegates consisted always of persons willing to leave their own business to attend Congress, and the persons who were willing and eager to do so were, on the whole, people who believed in the nationalist cause. The ideological composition of the congressional delegations thus implied greater popular nationalist sentiment than actually existed, which is why the ratification issue turned out to be so intense.

The frustration of the electorally successful but legislatively impotent nationalists set the scene for the nationalists' success and boldness at Philadelphia.

14. In *The Development of American Federalism* (Boston: Kluwer, 1987), 17–42.

11

Nationalist Domination of the Selection of Delegates to the Philadelphia Convention

A MOST STRIKING FEATURE of the Philadelphia convention is the ideological homogeneity of the delegates. Overwhelmingly they became Federalists. Jackson Turner Main has estimated that the votes cast for delegates to state ratifying conventions indicate that slightly more than half the voters were at that later date Antifederalists. Because he probably counted those who voted in groups 4 and 5 in figure 9.1 (p. 135) as Antifederalists, this may be an exaggeration of Antifederal strength.[1] A more cautious method is to count as Antifederalist only the district majorities whose representatives ultimately voted against the Constitution (that is, groups 6 and 7 in figure 9.1). By this method about 50 percent were Federalists and only about 46 percent were Antifederalists.[2]

But regardless of the estimate used, the Antifederalists surely were a larger segment of the society than their representation in the convention. Of the fifty-five delegates, forty-eight, or about 87 percent, signed or supported the Constitution (that is, groups 1–3 of figure 9.1). One additional delegate, Edmund Randolph (Va.), refused to sign but voted for the Constitution in the Virginia convention (that is, group 5 of figure 9.1). This left only six true Antifederalists (groups 6–7 of figure 9.1), or about 11 percent.

Furthermore, these six Antifederalists had less influence in the convention than even their small number suggests. Robert Yates (N.Y.) and John Lansing (N.Y.) went home early in July, even before the delegates reached the Connecticut compromise, and thus were absent throughout the time

1. *The Antifederalists: Critics of the Constitution* (1961; rept. New York: W. W. Norton, 1974), 249.
2. Evelyn C. Fink and William H. Riker, "The Strategy of Ratification," in Bernard Grofman and Donald Wittman, eds., *The Federalist Papers and the New Institutionalism* (New York: Agathon Press, 1989), 225.

that the convention modified the Virginia Plan. John Francis Mercer (Md.) showed up for several days in mid-August, found that no one paid much attention to him, and quickly went home without contributing anything to the outcome. Of the three Antifederalists who were present most of the time, George Mason (Va.) initially favored centralization and did not seriously criticize the content of the Constitution until near the end, when he lost on navigation laws. Up to that point he cooperated fully with the nationalists. Similarly, Gerry (Mass.) appeared to cooperate constructively in the same endeavor, although Gerry's animosity was, I believe, revealed somewhat earlier. Consequently, only Luther Martin (Md.) stayed at the convention most of the summer and consistently criticized the direction in which the delegates were moving. Mason and Gerry belong to group 6, while Martin belongs to group 7. (The mostly absent Yates, Lansing, and Mercer also belong to 7.)

In terms of contribution to debate, only three persons, roughly 5 percent, represented groups 6 and 7 of figure 9.1 at the convention, whereas in the society they constituted perhaps 46 to 52 percent. The ideological homogeneity of the convention is astonishing.

WHY NATIONALIST DELEGATES PREDOMINATED IN THE CONVENTION

How did such homogeneity come about? The immediate answer is clear: The same legislatures that elected delegates to Congress also elected delegates to the convention. In Congress there were ten delegations with majorities of later Federalists, one with a majority of later Antifederalists, one (Mass.) with a Federalist majority spring and fall but an Antifederalist majority in the summer, and one tied. In the convention there were eleven delegations with majorities of later Federalists (Massachusetts sent a tied delegation to Congress, but a proto-Federalist delegation to the convention), one with a proto-Antifederalist majority (N.Y.), and Rhode Island sent no delegation to the convention. Thus the convention was even slightly more nationalist than Congress.

In most states the legislatures were, of course, divided on local and national issues. But when the legislatures served as electoral colleges for Congress and the convention, only the preferences of the majority counted. Consequently, the legislatures acted as ideological filters, straining out provincialists and allowing only (or mostly) nationalists to go on to Congress and the convention.

The deeper question about the homogeneity of the convention then is, Why did the state legislatures of 1787 have strong nationalist majorities? Most historians of the era emphasize two events in 1786 as contributors to that nationalism: (a) Shays' Rebellion in Massachusetts, which, as it turned out, the state government easily put down but which initially surprised everyone because it did not fit the expectations of republican theory; and (b) the Jay-Gardoqui negotiations, which led to a proposal to open Spanish ports to American ships but to close the mouth of the Mississippi to American traffic. Shays' Rebellion affected all New England because its discontent spread north to New Hampshire and south to eastern Connecticut and Rhode Island, where indeed the spirit of Shays' was the majority. The Jay-Gardoqui negotiations infuriated the South, which saw the old southwest as its natural extension, its children's fortunes. So two parts of the country simultaneously sought constitutional reform, thus temporarily at least producing large nationalist majorities in all states but New York and Rhode Island.

Federal Farmer, the main Antifederal writer comparable in rhetorical and intellectual sophistication to Publius, believed the nationalism of the Constitution came about because so few provincialists were in the convention, and he blamed this on the fact that some notable provincial leaders, though elected, refused to attend:

> Tho' they [the states] chose men principally connected with commerce and the judicial department, yet they appointed many good republican characters — had they all attended we should now see, I am persuaded, a better system presented. The non-attendance of eight or nine men, who were appointed members of the convention, I shall ever consider as a very unfortunate event to the United States. — Had they attended, I am pretty clear that the result of the convention would not have had that strong tendency to aristocracy now discernable in every part of the plan. (CC 242, p. 23)

Perhaps. One can see why people like Patrick Henry (Va.), Willie Jones (N.C.), and Richard Henry Lee (Va.) did not attend. As Henry said, "I smelt a Rat," that is, he looked on the convention as a nationalist propaganda device that he certainly did not wish to support because he confidently expected to be able to veto its potentially undesirable results in one or more state legislatures. This is undoubtedly why, for example, Yates and Lansing went home when things did not go their way. Why should they, by their presence, give respect to a body whose proposals they would subsequently disown and veto? So it is easy to understand why some provincial leaders refused to attend.

But did their nonattendance make as much difference as Federal Farmer believed? It is doubtful. The elected delegates from New Hampshire, Massachusetts, Maryland, and Georgia who did not attend were later Federalists who would simply have strengthened the nationalist cause.

Nonattendees from other states who were later Antifederalists would simply have been submerged in their nationalist delegations, which is probably why they did not choose to attend. Some of those whom Federal Farmer had in mind were, in fact, so easily moved by the atmosphere around them that they voted for the Constitution in their state ratifying conventions. They were in group 4 or 5 of figure 9.1: Erastus Wolcott (Conn.) and Henry Laurens (S.C.). Another person whom Federal Farmer may have counted on was Abraham Clark (N.J.). But Clark moved in Congress (as against a group 6 or 7 Antifederalist, Richard Henry Lee) to pass the Constitution on to the states. He did not work for ratification, but he was eager to explain that he did not oppose it either (CC 95, note 5). Thus, Clark also was in group 4 or 5, not 6. The clearest cases of what Federal Farmer had in mind were Patrick Henry (Va.), Richard Henry Lee (Va.), and Willie Jones (N.C.). Had Henry and Lee attended, the Virginia delegation would have consisted of Washington, Madison, Randolph, Mason, George Wythe, Lee, and Henry. Because Randolph and Mason initially supported the Virginia Plan and even kept on supporting it after the Connecticut compromise (on representation in the Senate), Lee and Henry could at most have contributed a bit more to compromises in Virginia's interest. But perhaps not even that. Wythe went home to his dying wife after just a few days and did not come back after her death. But in a delegation containing Lee and Henry, perhaps he would have returned. Finally, Jones in North Carolina would have been only one provincialist voice among four nationalists. So except for the Virginia delegation, the absent delegates probably made little difference.

Thus, I think Federal Farmer was wrong in believing that a few more persons in groups 5, 6, and 7 of figure 9.1 would have made a great difference. People in group 1 had the greatest weight. They could, by reason of their preponderance, seize the initiative, and they did so.

NATIONALIST DOMINATION OF THE CONVENTION AGENDA

Nationalist delegates, of course, succeeded in dominating the convention. I have already described the extreme nationalism of the Virginia Plan, which served as the agenda for the whole convention. The plan organized the writing of the Constitution through the following procedure:

Step 1: After organizational preliminaries, Randolph introduced the Virginia Plan, which the convention referred to a Committee of the Whole House (fifty-five members), where it was read for amendments and then reported back to the convention floor.

Interlude: William Paterson introduced the New Jersey Plan, which the convention referred to the Committee of the Whole, where it was rejected in favor of the Virginia Plan as amended in the committee.

Step 2: The convention went through the Report of the Committee of the Whole, which was substantially the Virginia Plan, adopting and amending its resolutions. It then referred the report as amended to the five-member Committee of Detail, which composed a draft constitution out of the amended report.

Step 3: The convention read and amended the Report of the Committee of Detail and referred the amended report to the Committee of Style.

Step 4: The convention read and (briefly) amended the Report of the Committee of Style and then adopted the amended report as the proposed Constitution to be submitted to Congress and state ratifying conventions.

Essentially, then, the work of the convention consisted of four successive revisions of the Virginia Plan. Although the convention changed it in many ways, the Constitution at the end was recognizably the descendant of the Virginia Plan. This extremely nationalistic plan was in effect the agenda for the convention.

Furthermore, at crucial points in the procedure when the agenda, not the substance, was at stake, the convention appointed committees that were overwhelmingly drawn from group 1 of figure 9.1. The Committee of Detail consisted of two persons from group 1 (Nathaniel Gorham [Mass.] and Wilson [Penn.]), one from group 2 (Oliver Ellsworth [Conn.]), one from group 3 (John Rutledge [S.C.]), and one from group 4 (Randolph [Va.]), although he was still in his nationalistic phase. The Committee of Style had four persons from group 1 (King [Mass.], Hamilton [N.Y.], Gouverneur Morris [N.Y.], and Madison himself) and one from group 2 (William Johnson [Conn.]). Although these committees could not revise substantive decisions made on the floor, they could, of course, compose many sentences in a nationalistic mode.

Consider the history of the preamble, which the convention did not discuss extensively, but which Antifederalists often denounced during the campaign. The Antifederalists were right to do so, from their point of view, because it ignores the states and assigns all the functions of government to the United States. It begins, "We the People of the United States," and, ignoring the existence of states, it proceeds with a list of purposes: "to form a more perfect Union, establish Justice, insure domestic Tranquility, provide for the common defense, promote the general Welfare, and secure the Blessings of Liberty to ourselves and our Posterity." There is not much left for states to do.

This grand and sonorous preamble appeared in its first, rather pedestrian form in the Virginia Plan, as the first resolution: "Resolved that the Articles of Confederation ought to be so corrected & enlarged as to accomplish the objects proposed by their institution; namely 'common defense, security of liberty, and general welfare.' "[3] It came out of the Committee of Detail (where it was presumably the work mainly of Wilson, Randolph, and Rutledge) in the following form: "We the people of the States of New Hampshire, Massachusetts, . . . and Georgia do ordain, declare, and establish the following Constitution for the Government of Ourselves and our Posterity." Finally, it came out of the Committee of Style (where, according to Madison's later recollection, its final form was mainly the work of Gouverneur Morris).[4] References to the Articles and to the list of states disappeared. In their place is the magnificent list of purposes, which embed all important political action in the federal government.

The only discussion on the floor of themes related to the preamble concerned the addition and later the deletion of the word *national*. All the rest was the work of small committees, and highly nationalistic committees at that. Thus did the nationalists use their votes to dominate the agenda and, wherever possible, to direct the substantive content of the Constitution.

A related example of nationalistic domination is the first debate of the convention, in which Hamilton and Gouverneur Morris successfully maneuvered the convention in a highly nationalist direction. They obtained a revision of the Virginia Plan to describe it as *national* and *supreme*. In some ways this was one of the most important decisions of the convention because it established at the very beginning that the convention would create a highly centralized government. A large number of delegates came to Philadelphia with the intention simply of revising the Articles. This group included all the Connecticut and some Massachusetts delegates, Yates and Lansing of New York, probably most of the New Jersey, Delaware, and Maryland delegates, and also probably the North and South Carolina and Georgia delegates. Madison and, through his influence, the rest of the Virginia delegation, the Pennsylvanians, and Hamilton of New York came with much bolder plans. Gouverneur Morris, by his maneuver on May 30, committed the convention to his extreme plans. Once committed, delegates like Roger Sherman, George Read, Charles Cotesworth Pinckney, and Pierce Butler, all in groups 2 and 3, accepted the goals of members of group 1. So this very close decision on May 30 is a fine example of a

3. Max Farrand, ed., *Records of the Federal Convention of 1787*, 4 vols. (New Haven: Yale University Press, 1964), 1:20.
4. Ibid., 3:499.

determined minority driving an uncertain and divided majority in the minority's direction.

The event was simple, though somewhat convoluted parliamentarily. The first resolution of the Virginia Plan, as cited above, proposed to correct and enlarge the Articles for "common defense, security of liberty, and general welfare." Call this motion *a*. Randolph moved to replace this with a three-part motion, which was "seconded" by Morris, according to the *Journal*, but which was "at the suggestion" of Morris, according to Madison. The crucial part of Randolph's revision was that "a *national* Government ought to be established consisting of a *supreme* Legislature, Executive, & Judiciary."[5] Call this motion *b*. Since *b* seemed to several speakers to be too strong, Read (Del.), seconded by Charles Pinckney (S.C.), moved a less extreme motion: "Resolved that in order to carry into execution the Design of the States in forming this Convention, and to accomplish the objects proposed by the Confederation a more effective Government consisting of a Legislative, Executive and Judiciary ought to be established."[6] Call this motion *c*.

These three motions can be easily arranged on one dimension:

least nationalistic		*most nationalistic*
a	*c*	*b*

Following customary procedure, the convention voted on the choice between *b* and *c*. The most nationalistic, *b*, won. But it was a close call, just about the closest possible because the change of just one vote could have altered the final outcome to, probably, *c*. It is an odd but understandable accident that Yates (N.Y.), provincial and later Antifederalist to the core, cast this one vote leading to the extremely nationalistic outcome.

The explanation of this oddity is, in my opinion, that Yates, a provincial figure both in ideology and experience, misread the debate and voted inappropriately. On the first division, *b* vs. *c*, the roll call was to postpone *b* for *c*:

b	*c*
(Nay)	(Yea)
N.Y.	Mass.
Penn.	Conn.
Va.	Del.
N.C.	S.C.

5. Ibid., 1:30–35.
6. Ibid., 2:30–35.

So the postponement motion lost on a tie, and *b* remained the motion on the floor. On the second division, *b* vs. *a*, the roll call was to postpone *a* for *b*:

b (Yea)	*a* (Nay)	*Divided*
Mass.	Conn.	
Penn.		NY (Hamilton Yea, for *b*)
Del.		(Yates Nay, for *a*)
Va.		
N.C.		
S.C.		

So the postponement motion won, and thus *b* won again. Having beaten both alternatives, *b* was the final winner. Reconstructing preferences from this roll call data, we see the following orders of alternatives:

> *bca* or *bac*: Penn., Va., N.C., Hamilton (that is, *b* is unequivocally best)
> *cba*: Mass., Del., S.C. (assuming these voters have a transitive order)
> *cab* or *acb*: Conn. (that is, *b* is unequivocally last).

Yates's preferences, as inferred from his votes, seem wrong. He was about the least nationalistic delegate present that day. I believe that actually his preferred order was *acb* and that he voted as he did in favor of *b* over *c* because he believed, mistakenly, that if *b* passed the convention as a whole would then prefer *a* to *b*. But only Connecticut preferred *a* to *b*, so *b* survived. How can one explain Yates's presumably out of place vote? Perhaps it was confusion because even in his notes he does not seem to be aware of his gaffe. But I think he was no fool. Instead, he mistakenly inferred from the debate that *b* was the least popular motion and that, if forced to choose between *b* and *a*, the convention would choose *a*, which was what Yates preferred. It was easy for him to make this mistake. He was not a national politician — indeed, he seemed a bit awed by the company and never spoke in the convention. He knew the debaters little or not at all, and he had only the evidence of the morning's debate to go on. That morning delegates from only two states (Randolph and Mason of Virginia and Morris of Pennsylvania) spoke in favor of *b*. The other speakers (from three states: King and Gerry of Massachusetts; Sherman of Connecticut; Butler, Charles Cotesworth Pinckney, and Charles Pinckney of South Carolina) were dubious about their authorization to depart from the Articles. So Yates inferred, in my opinion, that *b* could never win and voted in such a way that, if his belief had been correct, a victory would have resulted for *a*.

Moral: It is not safe to try heresthetical maneuvers when you have poor information about others' tastes.[7]

Subsequently, the convention eliminated the word *national* with no dissenting vote.[8] Apparently, the delegates believed the use of the word impolitic; and, because it was by then determined that a highly nationalistic government would be proposed, they no longer needed the word to guide discussion.

The extreme nationalists could dominate the agenda, but they could not dominate all outcomes. The delegates in group 1 of figure 9.1 were not a majority. To make a majority on some issues they had to concede to those in groups 2 and 3. The main example is their compromise with small-state delegates on the structure of the legislature. This was truly a compromise, made possible by the fact that the delegates of New Jersey, Delaware, and, ultimately, Connecticut were quite nationalistic on nearly every other issue. As Charles Pinckney (S.C.) accurately and acidly remarked, "Give N. Jersey an equal vote, and she will dismiss her scruples and concur in the Nat'l. system."[9] Madison explained in a footnote that the supporters of the New Jersey Plan (which, compared to the Virginia Plan, was a modest revision of the Articles) were divided into two camps: (a) New Jersey and Delaware, who simply wanted equal representation, and (b) New York and Connecticut, who wanted to retain the principle of the confederation.[10]

7. That Yates voted in this foolish way rests on Madison's report of the roll calls. Farrand thinks that Madison was mistaken in assigning the 4–4 tie vote to *b* and *c*. His main argument is that, since the secretary's records are confused for the first few votes, the 4–4 vote ought to be assigned to the previous day. I believe Farrand is wrong. On the previous day (29 May), Madison and the secretary agreed that there were nine states voting, which declined to eight on 30 May because New Jersey did not vote either on that day or on several later days. Presumably all or all but one of New Jersey's delegates were sick or at home, and one delegate alone could not vote. So I think a 4–4 tie must have occurred on 30 May because only eight states voted on this and on several subsequent days, while nine voted on 29 May. Farrand also thought that a tie vote would be remarked upon, as if ties were parliamentarily difficult. In support of this view Farrand cites the questioning of whether a 5–4 with 1 divided roll call could count as an affirmative (when less than half voted yea.) But note that questioning about this issue was not about a tie but rather about a majority. In ordinary procedure a tie always results in the victory of the status quo (here *b*), so *c* unequivocally lost, and no one needed to raise a question about it. On the later vote, about which the question was raised, there was less than an absolute majority (i.e., only 5 out of 10 votes) for the motion to change the status quo, so it was reasonable to question whether or not the motion with 5 votes could be a winner. Thus Farrand's second argument about this roll call also errs. I think that there is very little question that Madison figured the votes out correctly, and Farrand was wrong to edit him. In any event, motion *b* won, and this definitively set the convention down the path of extreme nationalism.

8. Farrand, *Records of the Federal Convention* 1:334–36.

9. Ibid., 1:255.

10. Ibid., 1:242.

(Ultimately, of course, Ellsworth and Sherman of Connecticut became ardent Federalists.) Because at least half the opposition to the Virginia Plan came from delegates interested simply in power (New Jersey and Delaware) rather than ideology, it was easy for nationalists to compromise with members of the first group by conceding some of the power they wanted. Then the nationalists did not need to compromise with the ideologues at all.

Consequently, the compromise leaned toward the nationalists' side. Let the extremes be (a) minimal reform: national commercial regulation, an improved method for Congress to collect requisitions from states, and no change in the structure of Congress; and (b) maximal reform: the Virginia Plan as initially introduced. Clearly the compromise drew from minimal reform the feature of state equality in one house while it drew from maximal reform the feature of proportional representation in the lower house. But the powers of Congress were greatly enlarged, and the upper house, with equal representation to satisfy New Jersey and Delaware, nevertheless was much more national in tone than the Congress of the Articles. The Senate was to have six-year (not annual) terms with an unlimited number of terms (not limited to three consecutive one-year terms) and no provision for recall to enforce state legislatures' instructions.[11] As it turned out, therefore, the Senate, while representing states equally, was a nationally oriented body from the beginning. Thus today it typically seems more nationalistic than the rather provincial House.

These examples of nationalist domination (the Virginia Plan and the procedure for revising it, the appointments for and work of the committees on framing, the initial adoption of the word *national,* and the nationalistic tone of the main compromise) all indicate that group 1 of figure 9.1 led the way. So it is not surprising that the Constitution was a sharp break with the past. Nationalists in 1781 and 1783 dared to propose only modest fiscal reform. But nationalists in 1787 proposed a strikingly centralized reform. No wonder the provincials — soon to be Antifederalists — were appalled and began to attack the Constitution almost as soon as it became public.

Because the provincials were taken by surprise, they had no plan of opposition. Nationalists did have a plan, which they developed during the convention. This gave them control of the agenda during most of the ratification campaign, and I think it goes far to explain why the Federalists won.

11. William H. Riker, "The Senate and American Federalism," *American Political Science Review* 49 (1955): 452–69. Reprinted in William H. Riker, *The Development of American Federalism* (Boston: Kluwer, 1987), 135–56.

THE NATIONALISTS' STRATEGY FOR RATIFICATION AS
DEVELOPED DURING THE CONVENTION

Suppose that voters choose one candidate of a pair by one method of counting votes and that the political authority decrees another method of counting. Will the same candidate win? Not necessarily. Indeed, if both candidates have substantial support, it is easy to find a method that will change the winner.

Now, suppose in addition that the political authority itself has an interest in which candidate wins — perhaps, for example, the members of the dominant faction fear they will not themselves win. As politicians, presumably one of their main goals is winning. So might not the members of this faction change the method in order to help themselves out? Of course. But they may be constrained by considerations of morality. They may believe that changing the rules in midgame is cheating, or, at least, they may believe the voters will think so and will punish them as cheaters. So, if the members of the dominant faction want to change the rules and yet not be punished, they must find some moral justification for the change. On the whole, this is not a difficult task.

What is the fairest way to count votes? It's impossible to say for sure. Although one method may satisfy more standards of fairness than another, there is no uniquely fairest way. Every method fails to satisfy some easily justifiable criterion of fairness that other methods satisfy. So for any method currently in use, there is some other method that is fairer by some moral standard.[12] As might be expected, therefore, legislatures frequently change methods to the advantage of some temporary majority. For example, they change the method of counting or the rule of eligibility of voters (that is, which votes will be counted) or how much votes will count or what geographic areas will be used for subtotals.

The Constitution itself, for example, changed the weight of votes in two ways. First, it provided that the votes of individual voters in large states would weigh the same as those of voters in small states for the House of Representatives — a dramatic change from the Articles, under which small-state voters weighed vastly more. At the same time it ensured that small-state voters would continue to weigh more in the Senate. Second, it provided that the votes of southern whites would weigh more than the votes of northern citizens because three-fifths of the slaves, who were prohibited

12. William H. Riker, *Liberalism against Populism: A Confrontation between the Theory of Democracy and the Theory of Social Choice* (1983; repr. Prospect Heights, Ill.: Waveland Press, 1988), chaps. 2–4. Richard Niemi and John Deegan, "A Theory of Political Districting," *American Political Science Review* 72 (1976): 1304–23.

from voting, nevertheless were to be counted in the population base for districting. (This was not an insignificant change. It allowed Jefferson to beat Adams in 1800.) The Constitution also allowed for regular opportunities to change the geographic areas—redistricting—for the House but prohibited adjustments for population change for the Senate. Incidentally, during the ratification campaign in New York, Federalists initiated the elimination of property qualifications for voting, thus enfranchising mainly the landless laborers in cities, under the apparently correct belief that urban workers favored the Constitution.

By far the most immediate change provided by the framers was, however, in the method of ratification itself. According to the Articles, alterations of that document were to be agreed to in Congress (presumably by nine states) and then confirmed by the legislatures of every state. Although nationalists were twice able to propose alterations, they twice failed to obtain unanimous confirmation. Furthermore, they had every reason to expect that any other centralizing proposal would be similarly rejected, especially any proposal for national taxation. Yet taxation was the core of the problem. Under the Articles, Congress "requisitioned" funds from the states, and state legislatures then chose whether or not to comply. Some did; some did not. The framers were aware, of course, that national taxation threatened state legislators' freedom of choice, and they could reasonably expect their hostility on this matter. So the framers' problem was to find some way around the unanimity rule, that is, to find some other way of counting votes.

They devised two methods. First, they excluded state legislatures from the process. Second, they required only nine, not thirteen, state ratifications. Both of these departures from the Articles' procedure surprised the Antifederalists. A document they had supposed would be easy to defeat had become potentially ratifiable. I believe much of the Federalists' success derives from the Antifederalists' consternation, which impeded their formulation of a coherent response.

The Virginia Plan provided for ratification by popularly elected conventions—as its sponsors would have said, "by the people"—because conventions were the closest that eighteenth-century technology could come to a plebiscite. This provision bypassed state legislatures, just as Madison eliminated them from every other arena of national government.[13]

Although the convention modified the Virginia Plan in some ways, the

13. [[Although these legislatures had just sent a nationalist majority to the convention, the nationalists had reason to fear that their majority might evaporate because legislators were usually elected to one-year terms. Consequently there was the possibility that the tide could quickly turn.]]

plan's method of ratification survived intact. Furthermore, it went through the convention quite easily, preoccupied as the framers were with winning. Most of the delegates seemed to agree with Gouverneur Morris, who urged them to ignore the Articles, saying, "This Convention is unknown to the Confederation."[14] Initially, several delegates did advocate using the method of the Articles.[15] But the plan's provisions were adopted 6–3 with two states divided and confirmed 3–7 by the defeat of Ellsworth's motion to provide for ratification by state legislatures.[16] By the end of the convention, even Sherman and King, who initially favored the Articles' procedure, were enthusiastic proponents of the Virginia procedure.[17]

The reasons given for bypassing state legislatures ranged from the philosophical to the strategic. Madison thought ratification by "the supreme authority of the people" to be "essential" and "indispensable" for the Constitution to prevail over the states. Mason (Va.) also thought it "most important" to refer the Constitution to "the authority of the people," both because they were "the basis of free government" and, more practically, because he wished to forestall the legislatures from subsequently revoking what they had once ratified.[18]

Descending from the high ground of principle, Randolph (Va.), who introduced the Virginia Plan, bluntly defended it on the most practical basis: "Whose opposition will most likely to be excited agst. the System [that is, the Constitution]? That of the local demagogues who will be degraded by it from the importance they now hold. . . . It is of great importance therefore that the consideration of this subject [ratification] should be transferred from the Legislatures where this class of men, have their full influence to a field in which their efforts can be less mischievous."[19]

The most definitive statement, however, was made by Gorham (Mass.), who urged ratification by state conventions rather than legislatures because

> 1. Men chosen by the people for the particular purpose, will discuss the subject more candidly than members of the Legislature who are to lose power which is to be given up to the Genl. Govt.

14. Farrand, *Records of the Federal Convention* 1:92.

15. Ibid.: Sherman (1:122), King (1:123), Ellsworth (2:88), Paterson (2:88), Martin, McHenry, Carroll (2:476–77), and especially Gerry (1:124), who feared popular ratification because the people "have the wildest ideas of government in the world."

16. Ibid., 1:123, 2:93.

17. Ibid., 2:468, 476.

18. Ibid., 1:122, 2:88.

19. Ibid., 2:89.

2. Some of the Legislatures are composed of several branches. It will consequently be more difficult in these cases to get the plan through the Legislatures, than thru' a Convention.

3. In The States many of the ablest men are excluded from the Legislatures, but may be elected into a Convention. Among these may be ranked many of the Clergy who are generally friends to good government, . . .

4. The Legislatures will be interrupted with a variety of little business. [B]y artfully pressing which, designing men will find means to delay from year to year.[20]

One cannot say whether the strategic or the philosophical rationale was more influential in the convention; probably they reinforced each other: Madison's and Mason's appeal to first principles referred to the survival of the proposed Constitution once it was ratified, while Randolph's and Gorham's strategic rationale referred immediately to ratification. Doubtless most delegates thought both kinds of considerations important.

In hindsight, we can see that additional unanticipated strategic considerations were involved in the ratification procedure. An unanticipated disadvantage for the Federalists was that conventions probably took longer than legislatures. Hence Antifederalists had more time to regroup, which they needed most of all. On the other hand, an unanticipated advantage was that short-lived conventions could not haggle with Congress, trading ratification for prior amendments. Antifederalists might have tried just that if the ratification had involved legislatures. As it turned out, the state conventions could not communicate with the disbanded federal convention, with the Congress, or with each other, which made prior amendments difficult and unlikely.

Indeed, one can compare the national agenda for ratification with the agendas for passing bills in the House of Representatives. The Rules Committee of the House may propose either an open rule, which permits amendments on the floor to the bill as proposed by the substantive committee, or a closed rule, which prohibits floor amendments. Obviously, the closed rule gives the substantive committee much more freedom of choice than the open rule. Under an open rule, floor amendments to any committee proposal should result in selection of the median position, whereas under a closed rule the committee can present the chamber with a take-it-or-leave-it choice. This allows the committee to obtain an outcome closer to its ideal than is the chamber median.[21]

20. Ibid., 2:90.
21. This is precisely the situation described in chapter 2 above.

If we interpret the Philadelphia convention as a substantive committee to write a constitution for the states, which are the whole body, then the ratification procedure implied a closed rule because the states were presumably required to vote it up or down. Twice in September, Randolph moved that "amendments to the plan might be offered by the State Conventions, which would be submitted to and finally decided on by another general Convention." But the convention unanimously referred his first proposal to a committee, thus burying it, and unanimously voted down his second proposal.[22] The delegates understood that the closed rule agenda gave them leeway to write a much more centralized Constitution than the median state favored. Similarly, when the Constitution was before Congress, R. H. Lee wanted to amend it, but Madison countered him, saying, "Suppose alters. *made by Congress* are sent to ye State, ye Acts *of some states* requires ye Delegates *to the Constitutional Convention* to report to them — there will be two plans — some will adopt one & some another [.] ys. will create confusion" (CC 95, Melancton Smith's notes). As Madison thus made clear, if the framers had allowed for congressional revision or ratification by state legislatures, the kind of bargaining and confusion envisaged by Randolph and Lee would have been inevitable. And such an open rule would have restricted the delegates' choice.

In the beginning of the campaign, the Federalists insisted on the closed rule. For example, in the Pennsylvania assembly on 28 September 1787, Daniel Clymer insisted that the state convention "must adopt *in toto* or refuse altogether" (RCS Penn., 76). But, as it turned out, the Federalists took a big risk. Suppose they erred about the location of the median; then their proposal could have been voted down. What saved the Federalists from disaster from this error at Philadelphia is that they recouped by changing to something very like a partially open rule in which the successors of the Federalists at Philadelphia were permitted to decide which floor amendments were to be received for consideration.

More important than the method of conventions was the number of state ratifications required to begin the new government. This portion of the framers' agenda for ratification was vital. In view of the absence of Rhode Island from the convention, the framers knew they could not obtain thirteen assents. Gorham stated the matter exactly:

If the last art. of the Confederation is to be pursued the unanimous concurrence of the States will be necessary. But will any one say that all the States are to suffer themselves to be ruined, if Rho. Island should

22. Farrand, *Records of the Federal Convention* 2:561, 631.

persist in her opposition to general measure. . . . The present advantage which N. York seems to be so much attached to, of taxing her neighbours (by the regulation of her trade), makes it very probable, that she will be of the number. It would therefore deserve serious consideration whether provision ought not to be made for giving effect to the System without waiting for the unanimous concurrence of the States.[23]

So the framers were substantially agreed on requiring fewer than thirteen ratifications. The debate concerned exactly how many. Extreme nationalists (for example, Washington, Gouverneur Morris, Wilson, and Madison) favored seven states, a simple majority. On the other hand, some members of groups 2 and 6 from figure 9.1 favored ten or more, even thirteen. I calculate that about ten delegates clearly favored seven states and at least eleven delegates favored ten or more states.[24] Because no more than forty delegates were present on August 31, it seems likely that nine was the Condorcet winner [[(that is, the alternative commanding a majority over *all* other alternatives — see chapter 9)]]. Mason expressed what must have been the definitive argument: "Col: Mason was for preserving ideas familiar to the people. Nine states had been required in all great cases under the Confederation & that number was on that account preferable."[25] So nine it was — and fortunately so for Federalists. Had the number been ten, surely Rhode Island, North Carolina, and New York would have failed to ratify. Just one more loss would have doomed the framers' product.

23. Ibid., 2:90.

24. According to Farrand *(Records of the Federal Convention)*, Wilson (2:468), G. Morris (2:468), Madison (2:469), and Washington (per McHenry, 2:482) favored seven. Virginia voted against requiring either nine or ten (roll calls 423 and 424), though Randolph (2:469) and Mason (2:477) favored nine. I infer therefore that Blair (along with Washington and Madison) favored fewer than nine, South Carolina also voted against both nine and ten, though Butler (2:469) favored nine; so both Pinckneys and Rutledge must have favored fewer than nine. A majority of North Carolina, at least two delegates, favored fewer than nine. Hence at least ten altogether favored seven or eight. Similarly, Sherman (2:475, 478) favored ten or thirteen, and Connecticut voted for ten, so Johnson must also have favored ten. Carroll and Luther Martin favored thirteen (2:475, 469) on the ground that Maryland's constitution required it, and Maryland voted for both ten and nine, so McHenry must have supported them while Jenifer did not (2:477). Georgia (meaning Baldwin and Few), New Jersey (meaning probably Brearley, Dayton, and Livingston), and Connecticut (meaning Sherman and Johnson) voted for ten, and Gerry (Mass.) expressed himself in favor of thirteen (which implies that King and Gorham preferred nine or fewer).

25. Ibid., 2:477.

12

The Nationalist Strategy for Ratification

S O LONG AS THE Constitution was in the friendly hands of the framers, who were significantly nationalist to begin with and increasingly nationalist as the convention progressed, the nationalists controlled the agenda. Once they set the Constitution on its way, however, the members of groups 4, 5, 6, and 7 of figure 9.1 could easily
influence the agenda as well. Here is where the battle over ratification
begins — and it too is a battle for control of the agenda.

UNANIMITY

The nationalists had two clear objectives as they sent forth the Constitution. First, they wanted the appearance of unanimity to overawe the opposition. Second, they wanted the state legislatures to call state ratifying
conventions as promptly as possible. Try as they might, they could not by
themselves force either of these strategic objectives.

Near the end of the convention on 31 August, the nationalist framers
tried to extend their agenda control over Congress. The report of the
Committee of Detail had provided that the Constitution be laid before the
United States in the Congress assembled "for their approbation." On the
motion of Gouverneur Morris (Penn.) and Charles Pinckney (S.C.) approbation was deleted, 8 to 3 (according to Madison), 7 to 4 (according to
the *Journal*).[1] Ten days later Elbridge Gerry (Mass.), who was by then
overtly maneuvering to defeat the Constitution, moved to reconsider the
deletion. He wanted, of course, to require either unanimous consent or at
least consent in Congress, either of which might not be forthcoming. The
convention politely agreed to reconsider (7 to 3 with one divided) but

1. Max Farrand, *The Records of the Federal Convention of 1787*, 4 vols. (New Haven: Yale
University Press, 1964), 2:478, roll call 426.

then rejected reinsertion of approbation 1–10.[2] So a solid majority of seven states opposed giving Congress a voice, and only Connecticut really favored doing so. When Gerry made his motion again, the convention unanimously rejected it.

By so doing, nationalists doubtless hoped to get both congressional unanimity and speed. Of course, when the Constitution did get to Congress, some delegates wanted to approve and others wanted to disapprove and amend. There were three hostile motions — by Dane (Mass.), R. H. Lee (Va.), and Clark (N.J.) — and one favorable one — by Edward Carrington (Va.). The favorable motion could probably have passed by 10 to 1, but this procedure would certainly have revealed disagreement and probably have revealed R. H. Lee's proposed amendments. Consequently, congressional Federalists accepted the least unpleasant of the hostile motions (specifically, Clark's, which simply transmitted the Constitution to the states without comment). This then passed unanimously.[3] Thereby nationalists preserved the appearance of unanimity, just as the framers had arranged. According to Kaminski and Saladino, the general public did not learn of this congressional debate until the end of October (CC 95). So in this instance the nationalist framers may be said to have extended their agenda control to Congress and for a month and a half after the convention, though their stratagem ultimately failed.

But in what perhaps mattered more, the appearance of unanimity in the convention itself, the nationalists failed. On the last day of the convention (17 September), Franklin opened debate with a speech and motion designed to elicit unanimity. After noting that he saw (unspecified) faults in the Constitution, he said that he nevertheless doubted a better one could be written and uttered the hope that "every member of the Convention who may still have objections to it, would with me, on this occasion doubt a little of his own infallibility — and to make manifest our unanimity, put his name to this instrument." He then moved that the signatures be written under the formula "Done in Convention by the Unanimous Consent of the States present . . . IN WITNESS whereof we have hereunto subscribed our Names."[4] Madison noted, "This ambiguous form had been drawn up by Mr. G.M. [Gouverneur Morris, an exceptional heresthetician if ever there was one] in order to gain the dissenting members, and put into the hands of Docr. Franklin that it might have the better chance of success." Hamilton stated frankly the reason for this maneuver: "A few

2. Ibid., 2:561, 563, roll calls 506, 507.

3. Worthington C. Ford et al., eds., *Journals of the Continental Congress*, 34 vols. (Washington: Government Printing Office, 1904–37), 33:549.

4. Farrand, *Records of the Federal Convention* 2:642–43.

characters of consequence, by opposing or even refusing to sign the Constitution, might do infinite mischief by kindling the latent sparks which lurk under an enthusiasm in favor of the Convention which may soon subside."[5] And the formula did gain at least one signature, that of William Blount of North Carolina, who said he could not pledge support but could attest that the states unanimously adopted. Franklin's motion passed 10–0 with South Carolina divided because C. C. Pinckney and Pierce Butler believed the signatures should imply approval. Nevertheless, three of the forty-two delegates present, harbingers of the nine months of disputation to come, refused to sign: Randolph (Va.) of group 5 of figure 9.1 and Mason (Va.) and Gerry (Mass.) of group 6. (Other members of groups 6 and 7 had gone home.) Of course, the three nonsigners refused to be taken in by Morris's subterfuge and interpreted the signature as a show of support, which they refused to grant. Thus, the nationalists could be said to have lost their complete control of the agenda on the last day of the convention. Provincials wrested enough agenda control away from them to guarantee a long, arduous campaign over ratification.

INITIAL FEDERALIST STRATEGIES

Once the convention was over, nationalists — soon to be Federalists — could no longer dominate. Their dominance had derived from previous elections (those that sent nationalists to Congress and the convention), but the effect of those elections dissipated as new ones came due. As always, new campaigns rendered the sides equal in their chance to devise strategies and hence equal in their uncertainty about how these strategies would interact. So it was in October 1787. Each side devised a strategy for the campaign. But neither strategy was a sure winner, so neither side was confident of winning.

The complementary strategies were promptness and caution.[6] The Federalists described caution as unseemly delay, and the soon-to-be Antifederalists — the former provincials — described promptness as unseemly haste and speed. The strategic pattern was so manifest that the contestants often described their own strategies in the somewhat pejorative words of the other side. A widely copied Pittsburgh Federalist resolution proclaimed, "Our prosperity depends on our *speedy* adoption" (CC 270; italics added), and the Antifederalist Federal Farmer (letter V) conceded, "It is

5. Ibid., 2:643, 645.
6. Evelyn C. Fink, "Political Rhetoric and Strategic Choice in the Ratification Conventions on the U.S. Constitution" (Diss., University of Rochester Library, 1987).

true there may be danger in *delay*, but there is danger in adopting" (CC 242; italics added).

The Federalists did not often discuss openly their strategy of speed. Doing so would have suggested that they were bamboozling the electorate. Although they often exhorted people to ratify, only a tiny proportion of their words emphasized promptness (theme #97555), a mere 8,469, only three-tenths of 1 percent. Even adding proposals for later amendments (#97152, 8,587 words) and for ratification after discussion (#97551, 11,179), which together are only six-tenths of 1 percent, the total of all discussions of haste is only 28,235 words, or nine-tenths of 1 percent of the campaign.

By contrast, the Antifederalists frequently discussed strategy. They devoted 49,980 words (#97501) to counseling caution and deliberation and another 26,371 to raising suspicion about Federalists' haste (#97511). These two items were more than 4 percent of their campaign. Furthermore, they devoted even more words to substantive features of delay: 45,207 on prior amendments (#97105), 29,602 on a second convention (#97301), and 15,394 on allegations that the procedure of ratification was unconstitutional (#88013). Together, the procedural and substantive discussions of delay total almost 10 percent of the Antifederalist campaign.

Even though the Federalist 1 percent seems minuscule beside the Antifederalist 10 percent, the Federalists clearly pursued a strategy of haste, however impolitic it was to discuss it openly. We have three kinds of evidence: first, some quite open discussion in the convention, where remarks were protected by the rule of nondisclosure; second, the statistical record of Antifederalists' behavior, which reveals their strategy; and third, the Federalist and Antifederalist behavior in the Pennsylvania campaign, the first state campaign and the beginning of the national campaign.

In the privacy of the convention, two of the Federalists' superherestheticians quite frankly discussed their desire for haste. I have already quoted Alexander Hamilton's fear that "enthusiasm in favor of the Convention . . . may soon subside." Gouverneur Morris was even more specific and prescient. Defending his motion for ratification by state conventions, "which . . . the several Legislatures ought to . . . provide as speedily as circumstances will permit," he argued that his motion would "prevent enemies to the plan, from giving it the go by." Then he prophesied, quite correctly in fact, "When it first appears, with the sanction of this Convention, the people will be favorable to it. By degrees the State officers, & those interested in State Govts will intrigue & turn the popular current against it."[7] Morris's remark must have made a deep impression, at least on one

7. Farrand, *Records of the Federal Convention* 2:478.

future Antifederalist at the convention, because Cincinnatus (possibly Richard Henry Lee or Arthur Lee, according to Kaminski and Saladino, CC 222) cited it almost accurately and hinted broadly that the speaker was Morris: "A member of the late convention . . . , not very honorably distinguished for his moral or political virtue, admonished his associates that, unless they carried the constitution through before there was time for considering it, there would be no probability of its being adopted. When I couple this profligate declaration, with . . . [other evidences of haste] . . . I cannot help apprehending that such advice has not only [been] given, but followed" (CC 307). In a similar citation a month later, Helvidius Priscus remarked, "Let them call for the name of the audacious man, who dared to say . . . in the late convention, that unless they hurried the constitution through before the people had time for consideration, there was no probability it would ever be adopted. And let him be stigmatized with the odium due to the base betrayer of the rights of his country."[8] Helvidius obviously copied Cincinnatus but perhaps believed the speaker was Hamilton.

And if Antifederalists treasured Morris's remark, I think it likely that most Federalist leaders knew about it also.

The passages quoted above are the best evidence from the mouths of Federalists themselves for their strategy of speed, but there is much better statistical evidence from their behavior. Where they had strong support, they almost invariably pressed forward speedily. Where they had weak support, however much they may have sought speed, they usually could not achieve it. Their attempt and failure are evidence not only of their intentions, but also of Antifederalists' contrary intention to delay.

To examine these behaviorally revealed intentions, I have set forth, in the first column of table 12.1, the number of days t (for time) between state legislatures' calls for conventions to the final ratifications in each state. Because all state legislatures acted in the first session held after Congress submitted the Constitution, this column is a measure, adjusted for variations in legislative schedules, of speed: the fewer days, the speedier the ratification. In the second column I have listed the proportion of delegates (or, in Rhode Island, of voters) voting aye, s (for support), in the first decisive vote (either ratification or rejection) in 1787 or 1788. This is a measure of popular support for ratification.

There are some defects in both measures t and s. Consider t first: Maryland, with overwhelming Federalist support, acted slowly, mainly because of delay in the lower house under the influence of Samuel Chase, himself a fine heresthetician. But the Antifederalists' success is less impres-

8. Herbert J. Storing, *The Complete Anti-Federalist*, 6 vols. (Chicago: University of Chicago Press, 1981), 4:154.

Table 12.1   Relation Between Duration of Campaign and Vote Outcome

	t *Days between* *call of convention* *or referendum* *and ratification*	*s* *Proportion* *voting aye* *at first convention* *or referendum*
Delaware	28	1.00
New Jersey	48	1.00
Georgia	66	1.00
Pennsylvania	75	.67
Connecticut	84	.76
Massachusetts	94	.53
South Carolina	127	.67
Maryland	151	.85
New York	156	.53
New Hampshire	190	.55
Virginia	238	.53
North Carolina	715	.31
Rhode Island	820	.08

sive when one realizes that they wished to coordinate their convention with Virginia's, but in fact the timing adopted was such that Maryland ratified before the Virginia convention began.[9] South Carolina was also slower than its support suggests, owing mainly, however, to a local dispute over the location of the state capital.[10] Massachusetts, conversely, acted relatively promptly (though not so promptly as Federalists wished) even though only a small majority of representatives supported the Constitution, mainly, I believe, because the legislature, sitting in overwhelmingly Federalist Boston, did not initially appreciate the large amount of opposition. Indeed, many areas of Antifederal strength did not even send representatives to the General Court (the Massachusetts legislature), which neglect, of course, gave false cues.[11] Finally, in New York Antifederalists generated a long delay, but Federalists did not complain. Federalists in New York believed themselves a minority. So they wanted delay for all the same reasons that Antifederalists generally wanted delay, and further, they hoped that during the delay nine states would ratify before New York, a hope that was realized. Antifederalists by then (1 February 1788) knew that they were

9. Stephen R. Boyd, *The Politics of Opposition: Antifederalists and the Acceptance of the Constitution* (Millwood, N.Y.: KTO Press, 1979), 31.

10. Ibid., 37–39.

11. Ibid., 25.

losing nationally, so they wanted delay in the hope that some other large state would join them in rejection.[12] Note, however, that these New York considerations are not a defect in t because both sides believed themselves weak in the forum that most concerned them. These four cases aside, t is a fair representation of the debates in the legislatures.

There are similar defects in the measure of support, s. Because the document under consideration changed during the Massachusetts convention from that submitted by the framers to some document with unspecified variations, the s values for the ratifications before Massachusetts reflect only groups 1–3 of figure 9.1, while these values for the ratifications in Massachusetts and subsequently reflect groups 1–5. Thus support for the final proposal is underestimated for, at least, Pennsylvania and Connecticut. (It is hard to underestimate for those states that ratified unanimously.) Conversely, support may be overestimated for New York. Although the path by which reluctant delegates became supporters is perhaps irrelevant, some New Yorkers entered group 5 simply because they feared being left out. Finally, some Federalists in Rhode Island, especially in Providence and Newport, boycotted the election. So the 0.08 support is certainly an underestimate.

All this noise notwithstanding, it is apparent even from casual inspection of table 12.1 that speed and support are closely associated, as are delay and opposition.[13] There is no problem here with the direction of causality. For the Federalists high support might have caused speedy ratification (by simplifying the implementation of their strategy). Conversely, speedy ratification might have caused high support (by minimizing the development of opposition). Whether the strategy exploited their advantage or negated the opponents' advantage, clearly the strategy worked. For the Antifederalists low support might have caused delay (by simplifying the implementation of delay) or delay might have caused low support (by maximizing their chance to persuade). Again, whether it exploited the users' advantage or negated the opponents', the strategy worked. Since the two strategies are mirror images of one another, both of them drive the result. Hence the close negative association between time and support is convincing evidence that the two sides were following strategies of speed and delay, respectively.

12. Patrick T. Conley and John P. Kaminski, *The Constitution and the States: The Role of the Original Thirteen in the Framing and Adoption of the Federal Constitution* (Madison: Madison House, 1988), 240.

13. The regression of t on s yields a coefficient of -767 and a constant 715. The r^2 is .70 and the t-value of the coefficient is -5.06, significant at .00018 in a one-tailed test. Omitting the two outliers, North Carolina and Rhode Island, still yields a coefficient of -233 and a constant of 286, with r^2 of .52, significant at .0062.

A third kind of evidence about the two strategies is anecdotal: the calling of the Pennsylvania convention, which was right at the beginning of the campaign and thus allowed each side the chance to implement its strategies. Two temporal considerations set the scene: first, the convention sent the Constitution to Congress, sitting in New York, on 17 September, and the Pennsylvania delegates delivered it to the Pennsylvania assembly on the eighteenth. Congress received it on the nineteenth and on the twentieth read it and placed it on the calendar for the twenty-sixth. Congress debated it on the twenty-sixth and twenty-seventh and reached a compromise on the method of transmission to the states. On the twenty-eighth it actually sent it on to the governors. Second, the Pennsylvania assembly, sitting in September, expected to adjourn on 29 September for elections in October.

These two time constraints put the Pennsylvania Federalists on a tight schedule. They believed it necessary for the sitting assembly to call a convention lest the whole matter be delayed until 1788. As George Clymer (a member not only of the assembly but also of the Constitutional Convention) saw it, "If this House order a convention, it may be deliberated and decided some time in November, and the Constitution may be acted under by December. But if it is left over to the next house, it will inevitably be procrastinated until December 1788" (RCS Penn., 85). Furthermore, Clymer feared that waiting until the next assembly would "have the appearance of our being unfriendly to the new Constitution" (id.). Although they never said so in recorded debate, Federalists may also have worried about the outcome of the assembly elections. Pennsylvania politics in the 1780s were intense, so much so that two named parties had formed: Republicans, who were absorbed into Federalism, and the proto-Antifederalist Constitutionalists (retrospectively a confusing name because prior to 1787 it simply meant support for the Pennsylvania constitution of 1777). Control of the single-house assembly had switched three times in the previous decade: initially the Constitutionalists dominated, but by October 1781, the Republicans had gained control; in October 1784, the Constitutionalists won; and in October 1786, Republicans regained control (RCS Penn., 32–34). It was not unreasonable for Republicans (Federalists) to worry that another switch might occur in 1787. If it did, the future of the Constitution was quite unclear.

Responding to this tight schedule and to their fears of delay, Federalists in the assembly started consideration of a convention on the twenty-eighth, prior to learning of the congressional decision (made on that same day in New York) to transmit the Constitution. George Clymer introduced the appropriate resolutions. Robert Whitehill, a leading Constitutionalist, asked for time "to *consider*" (RCS Penn., 69). Thomas Fitzsimmons, like Clymer a member of the Constitutional Convention, responded, "From the number of petitions on your table, it may be clearly inferred, that it is the wish and expectation of the people, that this House should adopt *speedy* measures for calling a convention" (RCS Penn., 70; italics added). William Findley replied, "Whatever gentlemen say with respect to the importance of this subject is argument to prove, that we should go into it with deliberation" (RCS Penn., 71); and Whitehill detected sinister intent: "The gentlemen that have brought forward this motion must have some design, . . . or why not leave the members at liberty to consult?" (RCS Penn., 72). In general, Antifederalists urged delay until Congress acted: "I should think it unwise to throw out the dirty water . . . before we get the clean" (Findley, RCS Penn., 91). Federalists replied that the Articles were irrelevant and that the confederation had in effect ceased to exist: the Articles "cannot provide for the common defense, nor promote the general welfare" so "if we delay many ill consequences may arise" (Fitzsimmons, RCS Penn., 89–90). Thus, from the very first day of serious debate, the two sides had developed the strategies of speed and delay.

Before lunch on Friday the twenty-eighth the assembly called a convention but delayed decision on details until afternoon. The vote on the call was 43–19. In these numbers the Antifederalists saw their chance to resort to the device of a disappearing quorum, which, with exactly the same numbers, they had used successfully at the end of the September 1784 session (RCS Penn., 110, note 4). By the Pennsylvania constitution, a quorum was forty-six, or ⅔ of the full membership of sixty-nine. The Federalists could not assemble this number. Six members were absent from Philadelphia, which left sixty-three, and of these, nineteen were Antifederalists, as the morning vote revealed. So Antifederalists could, by absenting themselves, limit attendance to forty-four and thus prevent any action before adjournment the next day.

In the afternoon the assembly reconvened with only forty-four present. The Speaker (Thomas Mifflin, also a delegate to the Constitutional Convention) sent the sergeant-at-arms to round up the missing. But the sergeant reported that they would not attend, and the assembly adjourned until the next day.

On the morning of Saturday the twenty-ninth, again only forty-four attended, again the Speaker sent out the sergeant, again he reported that the Antifederalists refused to attend. But the situation was changed now. George Clymer presented the resolution of Congress passed on the twenty-eighth transmitting the Constitution to the states. Although the news was unofficial — it had been sent from New York by a special messenger the day before — it inspired the Federalists to act. A "mob" captured two absentees and brought them to the assembly to make a quorum. James M'Calmont objected strongly, asked to pay a fine for nonattendance (which the Speaker refused to accept because M'Calmont was obviously present), asked for a leave of absence, which the assembly rejected by a large majority, and tried to leave but was physically forced back in by the mob. Having a quorum, the assembly passed the appropriate legislation and adjourned.

The behavior of the so-called mob was not a fortuitous action by an unidentifiable mass. Its main leader was a Capt. John Barry, who left in December for China as master of the ship *Asia,* owned by Robert Morris (RCS Penn., 110–11). One suspects, therefore, that at least some of the mob were Barry's sailors, men effectively in Morris's pay. A secondary leader was Maj. William Jackson, who had been the secretary of the Constitutional Convention. The mob was opportunistically created by well-known Federalists and surely was an application of their strategy of haste. Furthermore, M'Calmont sought redress, but no warrants were ever served, and in February 1788 the case was closed.

A THEORETICAL INTERPRETATION OF THE STRATEGIES OF HASTE AND DELAY

As might be expected, the strategies in general and the event in Pennsylvania in particular inspired considerable discussion not just in Pennsylvania, but nationally. Historians have been fascinated with the Pennsylvania event, mostly because the Federalists' speed seems desperate. By understanding why the two sides adopted strategies of haste and delay we may judge whether or not it is reasonable for historians to condemn the Federalists for haste.

To consider first the motivation, I point out that these strategies are feasible only in circumstances, like those of legislative enactments or this ratification, in which the time of decision is not fixed. For decisions on a fixed schedule, haste and delay are pointless because they cannot alter the time of decision. For unfixed schedules, however, the choice of the date of decision is one method of manipulating the agenda.

Given the uncertainty of the future, if members of a group believe they are now likely to win, it is, of course, advantageous, other things being equal, for them to bring matters to an immediate decision rather than to allow delay. In an inscrutable future, their present advantage might disappear. Conversely, if members of a group believe they are now likely to lose, it is, of course, advantageous, other things being equal, for them to delay decision in the hope that they can persuade, or some unanticipated exter-

Table 12.2   Expected Value of Outcomes in the Hasten-Delay Game

		Prospective losers (L)	
		Delay (D)	Not Delay (~D)
Prospective winners (W)	Hasten (H)	1. $pw - c$, $[(1-p)v]-k$	2. w, $-k$
	Not Hasten (~H)	3. $p'w - c$, $(1 - p')\, v$	4. $w/2$, $v/2$

nal event will itself persuade, others to join them before the decision is finally made.

Setting these considerations up as a two-sided game, as shown in table 12.2, let the prospective winners (W) have alternative strategies Hasten (H) and not Hasten (~H), while the prospective losers (L) have alternative strategies Delay (D) and not Delay (~D). The rationale for the payoffs of table 12.2 is as follows:

1. W gains w if the decision is made and takes the form its members desire. Otherwise it gains zero.

2. L gains v if no decision is made or, if a decision is made, it takes the form its members desire.

3. Cell 1: If W chooses H and L chooses D, then W wins with some probability p, where $0 \leq p \leq 1$. This gives W a gross expected gain of pw. L's choice of D imposes a cost, c, on W, so W's net expected gain is $pw - c$. Because L's chance of gain is the complement of W's chance of gain (and vice versa), L's gross expected gain is $(1-p)v$. W's choice of H imposes a cost, k, on L, so L's net expected gain is $[(1-p)v]-k$.

4. Cell 2: Because W is assumed to have the advantage, its choice of H when L chooses ~D makes W a certain winner. So the expected gain for W is w for certain, while L gains zero and suffers the cost, k, of facing W's haste.

5. Cell 3: If W chooses ~H while L chooses D, then W's chance of winning is p', which is certainly less than W's chance in cell 1, so $p' < p$. Thus W's gross expected gain is $p'w$ and, since L imposes the cost of delay, W's net expected gain is $p'w-c$. Conversely, L's expected gain (gross and net because W goes not impose the cost of haste) is $(1-p')v$.

6. Cell 4: Using the rule of insufficient reason, I assign equal chances to each side, although the story would be the same as long as the gain for W is less than w and $p' < \frac{1}{2}$ so that the expected gain for L in cell 3 is greater than in cell 4.

If we consider the strategies in this game, it is apparent that, for W, the upper row dominates. Because $0 \leq p' < p \leq 1$, then $p'w < pw$; so W's expected value in cell 1 is greater than its expected value in cell 3; and W's expected value in cell 2 is clearly greater than in cell 4. Regardless, thus, of what L does, W gains (in expectation) from the choice of H, that is, H dominates $\sim H$. Other things being equal, therefore, it is anticipated that W would choose H.

L's strategic situation is a bit more complicated. If W chooses H, then it is to L's advantage to choose D because L's expected gain in cell 1 is clearly greater than in cell 2. If, however, W chooses $\sim H$, it is not clear whether or not $(1-p')v > v/2$. It depends on the magnitude of p'. If $p' < \frac{1}{2}$, then L's advantage is to choose D because $(1-p')v > v/2$. But if $p' > \frac{1}{2}$, then L's advantage is to choose $\sim D$ because $v/2 > (1-p')v$. So D does not necessarily dominate $\sim D$. Looking only at its own expected values, L's choice is unclear: D is unequivocally better when W chooses H, but when W chooses $\sim H$, either D or $\sim D$ may be better, depending on external circumstances, that is, on the value of p'. Fortunately, L's information is not limited to its own expected values. L also knows W's expectations, and W's are entirely clear: W invariably benefits from choosing H. So L can infer that W's choice of H is certain, in which case L then knows that its most advantageous choice is D.

By this argument, the best strategies for both sides are H and D, which intersect in cell 1. Because there is thus an excellent theoretical reason for these strategies, they should be expected as a matter of course, unless there is some violation of the *ceteris paribus* condition.

Applying this abstract game to the case of the choices of Pennsylvania Federalists and Antifederalists on 28–29 September, we get the situation of table 12.3. Here the outcomes can be either an early convention or a late convention. The best outcome for Federalists is an early convention and for Antifederalists a late one. For cell 1, there is a toss-up. If Federalists take the extreme action of physically rounding up some Antifederalists, the outcome is an early convention. But any Federalist action less vigorous than a physical intervention means a late convention. Because prior to the event one cannot know just how vigorous Federalists will be, the expected outcome in this cell is some chance, say, one-half, for an early or late convention. In cell 2, where Federalists push for decision and Antifederalists do not attempt delay (that is, do not disappear), the outcome is an early convention for sure. For cells 3 and 4, where Federalists do not push for decision, the outcome is a late convention regardless of whether the Antifederalists use the tactic of a disappearing majority.

For Federalists, cell 1, with some chance of an early convention, is

Table 12.3   Expected Outcomes in the Pennsylvania Legislature,
September 29-30, 1787

		Antifederalists	
		Delay	Not Delay
Federalists	Hasten	½ Early convention ½ Late convention	Early convention
	Not Hasten	Late convention	Late convention

better than cell 3, and cell 2 is absolutely better than cell 4. So Federalists are unequivocally better off to choose the strategy of Haste. Similarly, for Antifederalists, cell 3 is equivalent to cell 4, and cell 1, with some chance of a late convention, is better than cell 2, with no chance for it. So Antifederalists are unequivocally better off to choose the strategy of Delay. Consequently, cell 1 at the intersection of Haste and Delay is the dominant outcome.

These games demonstrate that the strategic choices, both generally and in Pennsylvania, are exactly the ones that rational politicians, acting to maximize their expected utility, would choose. Nonetheless, they have been criticized as foolish choices, especially those by Pennsylvania Federalists. The main charge is that other things are not equal and that Federalist haste raised questions in neutral minds about Federalist motives. Thus Michael Gillespie says, "The manhandling of the minority in Pennsylvania and the newspaper attacks on Massachusetts Antifederalists reawakened the suspicion, first evoked by the Society of the Cincinnati, that a conspiracy was afoot to establish a more aristocratic government."[14] It is certainly true that some people claimed they changed sides because of the Pennsylvania event. One supposedly neutral newspaper editor recited his own history of reawakening:

On reception of the Report of the Convention, I perused, and admired it: — Or rather, like many who still *think* they admire it, I loved Geo. Washington — I venerated Benj. Franklin — and therefore concluded that I must love and venerate all the works of their hands. . . . On the unprecedented Conduct of the Pennsylvania Legislature, I found myself disposed to lend an ear to the arguments of the opposition — not with the expectation of being convinced . . . but because I thought the

14. "Massachusetts: Creating Consensus," in Michael Allen Gillespie and Michael Lienesch, eds., *Ratifying the Constitution* (Lawrence: University Press of Kansas, 1989), 144–45.

minority had been ill used. . . . the address of the Seceders [that is, the Antifederalists whose absence made the quorum disappear] was like the Thunder of Sinai — . . . and I was obliged to acknowledge, not only that the conduct of the majority was highly reprehensible, but that the Constitution itself might possibly be defective. (CC 422; Thomas B. Wait, editor of the Cumberland *Gazette*, Portland, Mass., 8 January 1788)

I am not quite sure how to interpret claims like Wait's. He was answering an accusation that he behaved with a "*violence of passion*" in his opposition to the Constitution, so it may well be that his mental autobiography is simply a fabricated response to a slur. Nevertheless, assuming his autobiography is honest, the appropriate question is, Could the Federalists generally and the Pennsylvania Federalists in particular have behaved differently with less loss?

In order to analyze this question, we need to look at two kinds of costs the Federalists faced. One is the expectation of loss from not choosing Haste, that is, the value of the decline in the probability of winning from choosing not-Haste rather than Haste, or $(p-p')w$. The other is the cost imposed when the Antifederalists choose Delay, c. The latter is externally imposed while the former is self-imposed.

Looking first at the externally imposed costs, we see that Antifederalists' benefits from imposing Delay on Federalists are great, while their costs are small. The benefits of choosing delay are straightforward: Assuming Federalists choose Haste, then Delay brings Antifederalists a net expected benefit of $(1-p)v$. As for their costs, they are usually pretty small. Delay is the losers' strategy, and voters do not usually resent it, whereas they often do resent Haste, the winners' strategy. (In the most famous case of the disappearing quorum — in 1890 — Speaker Thomas B. Reed earned the sobriquet of Czar for stopping it, while Charles Crisp, who organized the disappearance, almost entirely escaped public castigation.) Prospective losers can always rationalize Delay as prudence and caution, so their attempt to manipulate is much less visible than winners' Haste. Because Delay has small costs while seriously hurting the prospective winners, one can expect the prospective losers to initiate delaying tactics whenever they seem likely to be successful.

The internal costs, those that prospective winners impose on themselves when they reject their dominant strategy of Haste, appear quite large, even though they have both positive and negative elements. The positive elements are those implied by Gillespie and Wait, namely, the avoidance of the animosity of the prospective losers. This avoidance probably makes life more pleasant by reducing the amount of ad hominem denunciation, but it is unlikely to prevent the prospective losers from choosing the strategy of Delay. In 1787, Edmund Randolph and Richard Henry Lee had already committed Antifederalists to Delay (that is, requests for a second convention) before the end of the Philadelphia convention and certainly before Congress transmitted the Constitution to the states. In Pennsylvania the Constitutionalists (Antifederalists) had already decided on Delay by the time the Republicans (Federalists) chose Haste. For example, as early as 24 September, David Redick, a Constitutionalist who was appalled by the popular enthusiasm for the Constitution in Philadelphia, wrote to William Irvine, a Pennsylvania delegate to Congress, "I hope Congress will be very deliberate and digest it thoroughly before they send it recommended to the states" (RCS Penn., 135; Redick ultimately supported the Constitution in 1788). In the assembly on 28 September, it seems probable that the Federalists expected Delay when they chose Haste. They may not have anticipated the disappearing quorum until the afternoon, but they certainly understood that Delay was imminent.

Given the Antifederalists' choice of Delay, the amount $(p-p')w$ is probably very small. As Hamilton and Morris forecast, support for the Constitution would surely erode; active efforts to delay would guarantee substantial erosion, enough perhaps to defeat it. So comparing the very modest benefits of forbearance with its substantial costs suggests that $p-p'$ might even be as large as ½.

Reverting now to the main question, Could the Federalists have behaved differently with less loss? I think the answer is no. Because the Antifederalists could cheaply and advantageously choose Delay, they could be expected to do so. Hence, Federalists would have borne the cost c regardless of what they themselves did. Furthermore, Haste dominates Not Haste. And $(p-p')$ is probably very large, large enough to guarantee the failure of the Constitution. Consequently, it would have been both foolish and improper for the Federalists to choose Not Haste: Foolish because the choice of a dominated strategy is enough to turn a prospective winner into a loser; and improper, at least by democratic standards, because it is immoral of representatives to fail to act as best they can to serve the values and interests of those who elected them, especially when their electors were, as in Pennsylvania and all other states in which Federalists were able to impose their choice of Haste, clearly a majority of the voters. Historians who have criticized the Federalists' strategy have not, I think, thought through the strategic and moral situation. The Federalists chose as they did, first, because it was reasonable to do so, and, second, because it was democratic.

Doubtless those who condemn the Pennsylvania Federalists' strategy will continue to do so, but they should remember that nothing the Federalists could do, short of losing, would moderate the party spirit on both sides. Given this state of affairs, the Federalists surely chose the best strategy politically. They did attempt, once they obtained a quick election with a two-to-one Federalist result, to mollify their opponents with a long convention in which opponents had ample time to state their case. Of course, this did not mollify them because they knew from the beginning that they had lost, and they continued to blame it on what they thought of as Federalist perfidy in refusing to acquiesce in the tactic of the disappearing quorum. Subsequent historians have too easily been taken in by the Antifederalist complaint that their undemocratic maneuver failed to work.

APPLICATIONS OF THE STRATEGY OF HASTE AFTER THE PENNSYLVANIA CONVENTION CALL

After the example of Pennsylvania, Federalists usually pushed for quick decisions in the other states where they expected to win. Various local considerations doubtless influenced their degree of success. In one special case, Georgia, the desire to have a national government for military assistance was compelling. Georgia was at war with Indians in what is now south central Alabama, a war encouraged and partly financed by Spain. Not surprisingly, Georgia ratified quickly and unanimously.

A more general consideration influenced the small coastal middle Atlantic states and Connecticut. Cut off as they were from westward expansion by New York, Pennsylvania, and Virginia, they had resented the barrier ever since they began to fill up. They had been an important force for Robert Morris's program of transferring western lands to the central government because, after that transfer, they could at least share in the potential revenue. Connecticut had actually sold lands in its western claim in the Wyoming valley in northeastern Pennsylvania, and, although it ultimately lost on these, it did manage to secure its claim to distribute land in the so-called Western Reserve of Ohio, even after Virginia gave up most of its claim to the old Northwest Territory. But New Jersey, Delaware, and Maryland had no western claims comparable to Connecticut's. So, given the assurance of equal treatment in the Senate, they were as Federalist as any states in the Union.

Finally, Connecticut and New Jersey had another special concern: their imports mostly passed through the port of New York, where a New York tariff took in almost enough money to pay the cost of New York's government. Landholder asserted that Massachusetts, Connecticut, and New Jersey lost fifty thousand pounds per year to New York in this way (CC 371), but A Plebeian (a New York Antifederal pamphleteer) denied this, saying that the New York impost produced no more than fifty thousand pounds a year in its entirety.[15] Landholder's figure seems high, and he had a strong motive to exaggerate. Yet it is also true that New York had very low land taxes. Consequently, the voters in western Connecticut, northern New Jersey, and even western Massachusetts had good reason to prefer national taxes from which they could expect to benefit themselves. Because the bulk of the population in Connecticut was in the Connecticut River Valley and the bulk of the population in New Jersey was in the north, these states were strongly Federalist. New Jersey ratified unanimously and more quickly than any state except Delaware. Connecticut ratified about as quickly as Pennsylvania and by a three-to-one ratio.

Two other middle Atlantic states, Delaware and Maryland, lived in the shadow of giants. They feared neighborly domination and so were extremely nationalistic, once they had assured themselves of a national voice. Delaware was the first and fastest state to ratify — in less than a month — and did so unanimously.

Maryland, however, was a different case, even though its basic situation was similar to Delaware's. There, Federalist efforts at speed simply did not work. Maryland had a strongly nationalistic history in Congress: four nationalist delegations and one tied in the previous five years. But in 1786–87 its internal politics were closely divided, and the issue of paper money dominated and divided the legislature sharply. Consequently, it split its delegation to the Philadelphia convention, and the split was even more complicated when half the delegates initially chosen rejected the job. So Maryland's delegation was split three nationalist to two provincialist, next to New York the least nationalistic delegation at Philadelphia, but highly unrepresentative, as it turned out, of Maryland's enthusiastic ratification by a ratio of five-to-one.

Maryland Federalists wished to ratify quickly and in the fall elections put forward their best candidates for the House of Delegates and recaptured it.[16] But their control was marginal. The house proposed an April election with a convention on 21 April 1788, a good six months away. Samuel Chase, the leading Antifederalist, probably influenced this decision. Because he then represented the extremely Federalist town of Baltimore, he did not come out directly against the Constitution; but, according to Daniel Carroll, he wrote a letter under the name Caution in which he repeated the usual Antifederalist advice for careful consideration and

15. Storing, *Complete Anti-Federalist* 6:128–47, 139.

16. Daniel Carroll to Madison, in Robert Rutland, *The Papers of James Madison* (Chicago: University of Chicago Press, 1977), 10:226–27; Norman K. Risjord, *Chesapeake Politics 1781–1800* (New York: Columbia University Press, 1978), 281.

debate, exactly what the six-month campaign provided.[17] The senate, with a strong Federalist majority, proposed instead a March convention, then conceded when the house stuck to its proposal by a one-vote, but apparently firm, margin.

Thus, in Maryland the Federalist strategy of speed did not work. Federalists had the will and indeed the popular support of, but not the necessary votes in, the lower house. The result was an intense campaign that, in the end, revealed a huge popular majority for the Constitution — so large, in fact, that the Maryland convention, like no other in 1788 after Massachusetts, adamantly refused to recommend amendments and a bill of rights.

The only other state in which Federalists, with a large elected majority, might have used the strategy of speed was South Carolina, which, like Pennsylvania, ultimately ratified with a two-to-one majority. We have less information about the reason for the delay in South Carolina, but it seems to have had something of the same motivations as in Maryland, and the Antifederalists were stronger.

The political disputes in South Carolina in the 1780s centered on the conflict of interests between the coastal regions, which depended on the export trade, and the backcountry regions, which practiced subsistence agriculture. Complicating this division was the heavy in-migration and extremely swift population growth upcountry. Hence, the mostly nationalist low country was heavily overrepresented: it had more than 60 percent of the seats in the House of Representatives, but it represented only about 20 percent of the white population in 1790, or less than 40 percent of the weighted population calculated as all of the whites and three-fifths of the black population.[18] Although there had been several disputes about reapportionment — which, according to the state constitution, should have occurred in 1785 — the typical conclusion was a compromise: low country members conceded on a substantive issue, and upcountry members conceded apportionment.[19] Although the legislature added six seats for the upcountry in the convention, presumably to equalize apportionment, the upcountry gain was spurious because the seats went to areas of the 96th district that elected Federalists.[20] So the convention was as badly districted as the legislature.

17. Rutland, *Papers of Madison*. "Caution" is reprinted in Paul Leicester Ford, *Essays on the Constitution of the United States* (repr. New York: Burt Franklin, 1970), 327–28.

18. Fink, "Political Rhetoric," 187.

19. Ibid., 190.

20. Michael E. Stevens and Christine M. Allen, eds., *Journals of the House of Representatives 1787–88. The State Records of South Carolina* (Columbia: University of South Carolina Press, 1981), 402–04. Jonathan Elliott, ed., *The Debates in the Several State Conventions on the Adoption*

When the legislature held a three-day debate on the Constitution in January 1788, the resolution to hold a convention passed unanimously. But when it came to deciding when and where, the outcome was very close. The Senate proposed an election on 21–22 February for a convention in Charleston. The House disagreed with both features. The vote on Charleston (as against Columbia) was 76 to 75 for Charleston. Charleston may have lost on the voice vote because a Charleston representative called for the yeas and nays.[21] Further, the House adopted 11–12 April, nearly two months later than the Senate.[22] We do not know the vote on this, but I infer that, because no one called for the yeas and nays, the margin in favor of the later date must have been substantial. Both of these outcomes suggest that Antifederal strength in the legislature was substantial, enough to restrain Federalist enthusiasm for haste.

It is a bit difficult to reconcile unanimity for holding a convention with great Antifederal strength in favor of delay, which I think is clear in the change from February to April. Main believes that the vote on Charleston also shows Antifederal strength, although this is less evident.[23] Evelyn Fink has attempted to explain the apparent inconsistency by suggesting that Antifederalists were quite skillfully hiding their strength to lull the Federalists into accepting a long campaign. She notes that five of the ten main Antifederal leaders of the convention sat in the house, were completely silent during the three-day debate, and voted unanimously for holding the convention.[24]

Whether forced or lulled into a three-month campaign, the Federalists probably suffered from the delay. They apparently expected easy victory and did not campaign ardently. Antifederalists, however, were very active.[25] Fink has provided good statistical evidence of their intensity. The upcountry Antifederalists rejected a large proportion of their legislators for the convention, presumably because they were insufficiently Antifederal, while low country Federalists rejected few.[26] Only a strong, self-conscious Antifederal campaign could have produced that result. Although the Federalists were in no danger of losing — they had apportionment on

of the Federal Constitution as Recommended by the General Convention at Philadelphia in 1787, 2d ed. rev., 5 vols. (Philadelphia: J. B. Lippincott, 1836), 4:333.

21. Stevens and Allen, *Journals,* 330–32.

22. Ibid.

23. *The Antifederalists: Critics of the Constitution* (1961; repr. New York: W. W. Norton, 1974), 216–18.

24. "Political Rhetoric," 207–13.

25. Boyd, *Politics of Opposition,* 115; Fink, "Political Rhetoric," 214–28.

26. "Political Rhetoric," 217–21.

their side — they faced tougher opposition in the convention than they had in the legislature. Ultimately they achieved a two-to-one victory (149–73), and they were strong enough to accept only quite limited recommendatory amendments as well as to reject a proposal for a bill of rights. But they did generate more opposition than they intended or expected — and for that I believe they can thank the legislature for imposing the delay of a three-month campaign. Strong as the Federalists were, the Antifederalists were able to grab a bit of agenda control. This outcome emphasizes the wisdom of the Federalist strategy of haste in the five states in which they could carry it through.

13

Massachusetts:
The Federalist Coalition Expands

I N MASSACHUSETTS, the ultimate Federalist victory made the difference between ratification and rejection for the entire country. Initially Federalists thought they had an advantage and thus sought
speed; but it turned out that they were short of votes and could only
partially control the agenda, so they changed to a strategy of delay and
heresthetical manipulation of the situation: the Federalists reorganized
their coalition by expanding from groups 1–3 of figure 9.1 (p. 135) to
include groups 4 and 5. Groups 1–3 had been enough to carry the nationalists through the Philadelphia convention, but they were not enough
to carry them through the Massachusetts convention. The result was that
in several subsequent conventions (New Hampshire, Virginia, and New
York) the new Massachusetts-like coalition was necessary for Federalist
victory, and that fact led to some change in the Constitution itself.

The problem for nationalists (group 1 or 1–3 Federalists) was perfectly
straightforward. As I have already noted, the Philadelphia convention had
sent the Constitution out as if it were under a closed rule. There was to be
no new national convention or national legislature to which disputatious
ratifying conventions could return the Constitution for amendments, forcing voters to vote the Constitution up or down. This strategy reduced the
groups to two sides, 1–3 against 4–7. Such bifurcation was successful as
long as group 1 (as revised in Philadelphia to include groups 2 and 3) was
an absolute majority of the people and of the convention—or at least of
the convention, as in the middle Atlantic states, Connecticut, South Carolina, and Georgia. But in Massachusetts the revised group 1 was probably
not a majority of either. Groups 4–7 were quite large, and potentially
groups 4 and 5 were pivotal between the two extremes.

In this situation the nationalists of group 1—for there were probably
no members of 2 and 3 in Massachusetts—had these alternatives: they
could stick with the closed rule and almost certainly lose or they could

devise a way around it and thus try to win. Of course, if the Constitution lost, there might be a second federal convention. But such a convention, if it formed at all, would likely write a much less nationalistic constitution than the one written at Philadelphia. And that would be a hard blow to group 1 Federalists, who already had five of the necessary nine state ratifications when Massachusetts met and would ultimately get seven entirely on their own. What, then, should they do to extricate themselves from this procedural restriction? How could they circumvent the closed rule?

They approached the problem in two ways in Massachusetts. First, they tried to proselytize from groups 4 through 7. But, as I shall show, they were only partially successful. So, second, they invented or adopted an amendment device that divided supporters of amendments into groups 4, 5, and 6 and turned members of groups 4 and 5 into supporters of the Constitution as it stood. Thereby they turned their own, presumably unalterable closed rule into what amounted to an open one, over which, however, they had more than the usual control. This is one of the most interesting and successful heresthetical maneuvers in the entire political history of the United States.

The Federalists' maneuver opened the closed rule in the following way: Imagine, by way of analogy, a bill under a closed rule in a contemporary legislature. Initially, the bill's managers obtain a closed rule because they believe they can thereby force a majority, some of whom may be reluctant, to support the unamended bill, which is far from the median. But as they solicit votes, they run into trouble because they have only about half the number they need. Of course, if they cannot round up any more votes, they may simply allow the bill to die and start over next session. But, if they fear they will never get a comparable bill out of the committee, they can say to marginal opponents, "We know the closed rule won't permit amendments. But if you think the basic idea is good, then vote for the bill as it stands and we promise we will, after the next election, amend the bill to your liking." It is difficult to believe that such a device could work, either now or then. After all, the bill's managers would have no control over the next legislature, just as the group 1 Federalists of 1788 had no control over the actions of the group 1 Federalists of 1789 and later. Nevertheless, this is the promise that group 1 Federalists made to opponents who advocated a bill of rights, thereby creating group 4 and group 5 Federalists. And the members of groups 4 and 5 accepted it, even though they recognized there was considerable doubt that amendments would in fact be proposed or adopted.

By means of this remarkable heresthetical maneuver, the group 1 Federalists expanded their coalition to take in groups 4 and 5. They obtained thereby the sixth ratification, pointed the way for ratification in the New Hampshire convention, and (probably) importantly influenced the Virginia elections. With Maryland and South Carolina ratifications subsequently obtained by the old group 1, ten states had ratified, and the Constitution could begin operating. Very shortly New York came in under duress, and within two years the recalcitrants in North Carolina and Rhode Island realized they could no longer stay out of the Union.

There has been considerable misunderstanding of the authorship of this maneuver. In the nineteenth century, and even today, those in the provincial tradition credit the members of groups 4 and 5 such as John Hancock and Samuel Adams, while those in the nationalist tradition credit members of group 1 such as Rufus King and Theophilus Parsons. But, of course, it is impossible to distinguish the contribution of the groups. Both contributed and both were Federalists in that sense, though not necessarily in the sense of membership in the subsequent Federalist party of Washington and Hamilton. It is not possible even to say which groups were pivotal. Members of 4 and 5 may appear pivotal because they joined later than group 1. But the members of 4 and 5 really wanted the Constitution, and the members of group 1 appear pivotal in the sense that they agreed on recommendatory amendments.

The difficulty in understanding the maneuver arises because interpreters view the situation as being static, as if there were the same Federalists and Antifederalists from beginning to end. Actually, however, groups 4 and 5 did not exist in the beginning. Initially, groups 1–3 and 6–7 alike interpreted amendments as rejection. Gerry's letter, which opened the Antifederal campaign in Massachusetts and thus defined the terms of the debate, specifically urged amendment prior to ratification: "Cannot *this object* [amendment] be better attained before a ratification, than after it?" (CC 227A). This made sense especially in Massachusetts, where a proposed state constitution was rejected in 1778 and a revised proposal adopted in 1780. Only after recommended amendments were invented in late January 1788 were groups 4 and 5 created. So in the beginning amendments meant rejection, but by the end they meant ratification. Hence a person like Samuel Adams, who favored amendments, was necessarily an opponent together with members of group 6 during the campaign, but emerged as a member of group 5 after recommendatory amendments were proposed.

GROUP 1 FEDERALISTS IN THE MASSACHUSETTS LEGISLATURE

The first indication that nationalists would lose control in Massachusetts came when the legislature considered the call of a convention, 18–25

October 1787. The 1787–88 legislature had been elected in April 1787 and was considerably less nationalist than the 1786–87 legislature, which had in March 1787 elected mostly nationalist delegates to the Philadelphia convention. What made the difference between the two legislatures was Shays' Rebellion in the latter half of 1786 and early 1787. In the winter of 1786–87, Gov. James Bowdoin had put down the uprising with military force, which was heartily approved by the legislature, especially in the Senate under the leadership of Sam Adams. But the bulk of the voters in central and western Massachusetts, though probably disapproving of armed insurrection, sympathized with the rebels, victims of agricultural distress and tax foreclosures. Consequently, in April, voters in these areas turned out Bowdoin and his legislative supporters and called back John Hancock, who had been governor from 1780, when the office was instituted, until his resignation in 1785. As governor again, Hancock acted with moderation, pardoned the Shaysites, and restored peace and confidence in the west. Meanwhile, to loosen credit, the lower house voted for paper money as legal tender.

The legislature that considered the Constitution in October was not, therefore, automatically nationalist. After Hancock delivered the Constitution to the legislature — the General Court — on 18 October, the senate immediately (and apparently unanimously) passed a call for a ratifying convention to meet on 12 December. A two-month campaign was part of the Federalist strategy of speed. But when the resolution went to the assembly, some of its leaders expressed the usual Antifederal warnings for caution and careful consideration, and the assembly increased the campaign to three months with a convention to meet on 9 January 1788.

On the whole, however, this was not a bad outcome for Federalists. One Antifederal leader had argued urgently against consideration at all, and another, William Widgery, one of the three or four main Antifederalists in the convention, proposed to submit the Constitution to town meetings rather than to a state convention on the ground that towns could not afford to send delegates to Boston. This procedure would almost certainly have defeated the Constitution, just as it had defeated the Massachusetts constitution of 1778, because each town would, more or less independently, have found something to revise before ratification. Thus there would have been many disparate negatives with no agreement even about how to perfect the document. Fortunately for the Federalists, they were able to counter Widgery's argument with an agreement for the state to pay the delegates' expenses and wages. (Who knows what would have happened had Widgery put his proposal on the less easily countered ground that ratification by towns was more republican?)

The one-month extension of the campaign was in itself no disaster —

indeed, this was a better result for the Federalists than they would achieve in any remaining state. It was, however, a harbinger of what might be expected in the campaign and in town elections, which resulted in an unmistakable majority against unconditional ratification and perhaps against ratification at all.

GROUP 1 FEDERALISTS LOSE THE ELECTION

It is difficult to specify the initial composition of the convention. We know that Antifederalists carried most of the inland towns, from western Middlesex county on west to the New York border, as well as the inland parts of Maine. There were pockets of Federal strength: the Connecticut River valley and some of Berkshire, which perhaps reflected the hostility to New York that made western Connecticut so Federalist. On the other hand, Federalists carried the seacoast from Maine to New Bedford. But we have no reliable count of the house in the beginning. We do not know the number of group 1 Federalists as against those who started in group 6 or 7 and were persuaded to join group 1 or were attracted to groups 4 and 5 after recommended amendments were invented.

Our ignorance is not accidental. Federalist leaders, aware of their weakness, avoided confrontation until they were sure of victory. Rufus King, who was the Federalist floor leader (for example, he spoke more frequently than anyone else on either side), wrote Madison on 27 January 1788, just a week before debate ended, "We have avoided every Question which would have shown the division of the House, of consequence we are not positive of the numbers on each side."[1]

Difficult as a precise estimate of the strength of the several groups may be, we have some assurances that opponents of ratification as it stood (that is, groups 4 to 7) outnumbered the nationalists of group 1. We have information about three informal counts of the house. The Antifederalist leader Samuel Nasson wrote to George Thatcher (a Federalist member of Congress) that the Antifederalist advantage was 144–192, and Matt Cobb quoted Widgery as saying that their advantage was 138–228. On the other hand, Gen. Henry Jackson, an ardent Federalist in regular attendance in the gallery, wrote to U.S. Secretary of War Henry Knox that the Federalists had the advantage 194–166.[2]

1. Robert A. Rutland, ed., *The Papers of James Madison* (Chicago: University of Chicago Press, 1977), 10:437. The same day King wrote to Secretary of War Henry Knox, "From motives of policy, we have not taken any question which has divided the House, or shown the strength of sides" (Knox papers, roll 21, item 121).

2. "The Thatcher Papers," *The Historical Magazine*, 2d series, 6:266, 268, 22 January and 24 January 1788. Knox papers, roll 21, item 113, 20 January 1788.

It is difficult to reconcile these supposed counts. Jackson's is the closest to the final outcome, but he must have included all of the members of what later became groups 4 and 5 in his count of Federalists. (From internal evidence in his count, he included at least Governor Hancock as a Yea, though other Federalists were unsure about him until ten days later.) I am skeptical of Widgery's count also because right up to the end, when Nathaniel Gorham was sure his side would win, the Antifederal leadership (mainly Widgery) claimed a majority of ten.[3] Nasson's count of 144–192 is possible, but it is about thirty members short. Among contemporary analysts, Evelyn Fink, who has made the most careful study of this question, believes that the initial division was an Antifederalist advantage of 158–203, including the later members of groups 4 and 5 in the Antifederal column.

Turning from the evidence of counts of the house, we have indirect evidence, which seems to me more compelling than the counts. First, the Federalist leaders, unsure of their situation, adopted a strategy of delay. Thus, on the motion of Caleb Strong, a framer and a Federalist, the convention adopted the procedure of discussion by paragraphs without votes until after a general discussion at the end, when the main question was to be put. I have already quoted King's explanation of this maneuver as "policy," and it seems a strategy of delay, adopted in the hope of persuading some members of group 6 to convert. The group 1 Federalists stuck by this strategy resolutely, rejecting (with the compelling assistance of Samuel Adams) an Antifederalist motion to take up the whole Constitution rather than reading by paragraphs.

Second, beyond the new Federalist strategy of delay, which clearly indicates their own belief in their weakness, we have their decision to adopt the device of recommendatory amendments. This adoption signals that the Federalist leaders (all of whom were members of group 1) believed that they could not win by themselves and had to have the members of the soon to be formed groups 4 and 5 as well.

Third, throughout the convention there are hints of conversions to support of the Constitution. Considering the closeness of the outcome, this suggests that the members of group 1 were not initially numerous enough to ratify the Constitution. Evidence of the conversion is, however, both anecdotal and indirect. For example, one can follow Rufus King's increasing confidence in his letters to Madison and Knox: in table 13.1 I have listed and described these nine letters.[4] The point of this lengthy

3. Knox papers, roll 21, item 129, 3 February 1788.
4. Charles R. King, *Life and Correspondence of Rufus King* (New York: G. P. Putnam's Sons, 1894), 1:313–17; Rutland, *Papers of Madison*, 10:376, 400, 411, 436, 465, 475; Knox papers, roll 21, items 121, 127.

Table 13.1   Rufus King's Degrees of Confidence, 16 January to
6 February 1788

---

16 January (to Madison): Federalists acquiesced in Antifederalists' request to send Elbridge Gerry (who has not been elected to delegate) to "answer questions," thereby avoiding a trial of strength because of their "doubt of issue."

20 January (to Madison): ". . .the opponents affirm to each other that they have an unalterable majority on their side. The friends [i.e., of the Constitution] doubt the strength of their adversaries, but are not entirely confident of their own."

23 January (to Madison): "Our prospects are gloomy, but hope is not entirely extinguished" (because of the idea of recommendatory amendments).

27 January (to Madison): " . . . by the last calculation we made on our side, we were doubtful whether we exceeded them, or they us."

27 January (to Knox): "Our hopes do not diminish, although our confidence is not complete. The opposition are less positive of their strength and those few among them who are honest and capable of reflection appear uneasy concerning the Fate of the Question—yesterday's Centinel contains a proposal for a conditional ratification, said to have come from Sullivan, the opposition gives it some countenance—I mention the circumstance rather to show that our opponents are not so confident of their numbers, since hitherto they have reprobated the Suggestion of Amendments and inserted among their party on a Total Rejection of the Constitution. . ."

30 January (to Madison): " . . . our hopes are increasing. . ."

3 February (to Madison): After John Hancock had introduced and Samuel Adams supported the recommendatory amendments, "We flatter ourselves that the weight of these two characters will ensure our success, but the event is not absolutely certain."

3 February (to Knox): "Hancock has committed himself in our favor, and will not desert the cause. . . the Federalists are united in that system and as Adams has joined on this, we are encouraged to then how success is probable."

6 February (to Madison): The Constitution has been ratified by 186-168, which majority "although small is extremely respectable."

Sources: see ch. 13, note 4.

recital is to show the increasing confidence of one main Federalist leader as the convention progressed. This increase of confidence can mean only that the nationalists thought that they were gaining converts as the convention progressed and that they were initially a minority.

We have similar evidence from the Antifederal side. I have already mentioned the Antifederalist motion to cease reading by paragraphs in order to discuss the whole Constitution. This was undoubtedly a motion to speed up discussion, the kind of motion made by people who think they are winners at the moment but fear they may not be in the future. Additional evidence of this sort, external to the convention, was the publication on 21 January 1788 in the *Boston Gazette and Country Journal* of the following squib: "BRIBERY AND CORRUPTION!!! The most diabolical plan is on foot to corrupt the members of the Convention who oppose the adoption of the new Constitution. Large sums of money have been brought from a neighboring State for that purpose, contributed by the wealthy. If so, is it not probable there may be collections for the same accursed purpose nearer home? Centinel."[5] The squib implies that by 20 January some members of group 6 had begun, at least, to waver. Why else publish this accusation unless to scare off both the waverers and their persuaders? The convention demanded detail from the publisher and nothing more was heard of it. Nevertheless, this squib (21 January) and the motion to shorten discussion (23–24 January) suggest that the Antifederalist leaders believed time was against them because of conversions to support the Constitution. Poor as the counts of the house may be, we can be fairly certain that the group 1 nationalists lost the elections for delegates to the Massachusetts ratifying convention.

PERSONNEL ADVANTAGES OF GROUP 1 FEDERALISTS

Of course, losing an election usually means losing control of the agenda. First of all, it reverses the strategic situation. The nationalist-Federalists, who had carried five states easily with their strategy of speed, now were no longer the winners, and speed was no longer an advantage for them. Without any hesitation they reversed strategy. I have already mentioned their successful support for the motion to read by paragraphs. This delaying tactic gave them a chance to persuade and convert, and to some degree it kept the agenda in their hands. Their leaders, King, Gorham, Theophilus Parsons, and others, were skilled and experienced parliament men, and in spite of losing the election they retained enough control of the agenda so that, with some compromise, they could carry the day. Their partial control allowed them to structure the form of the compromise, and this structure carried them to success.

How are we to explain this partial success, given that members of group 1 lacked the initial majority? One part of the answer is, conventionally, the overwhelming proportion of outstanding men in group 1 compared to

5. *Debates and Proceedings in the Convention of the Commonwealth of Massachusetts Held in the Year 1788* (Boston: William White, 1856), 150.

those in the initial groups 6 and 7. There is reason to be a bit skeptical about this tradition, however. It is certainly misleading to the degree that it is based on a reading of the *Debates,* preserved in Elliot (1836), and as recorded by reporters for the two extreme Federalist papers, the *Massachusetts Centinel* and the *Independent Chronicle.* These *Debates* report Federalist speeches at great length (an average of 34 lines) and Antifederalist speeches briefly (an average of 16.6 lines). They record 140 Federalist speeches out of 242, or about 58 percent. By contrast, Parsons, although an ardent Federalist, gave equal attention in the *Minutes* he kept to speakers on both sides and recorded 129 Federalist speeches out of 249, or about 52 percent.[6] After the convention, the Antifederalist Nasson wrote bitterly about the press, "You may Depend upon it, you do not Get the Truth by the papers. All the argumental parts are left out on one side — this from the Printer. I cannot stand to the judgment they frame of me."[7]

To test the possibility of a false picture of Federalist glory derived from the *Debates,* I have counted the delegates whom twentieth-century historians have seen fit to memorialize in the *Dictionary of American Biography.*[8] In table 13.2, I have assigned them to groups 1, 4, 5, 6, and 7. As the table shows, the Federalist dominance was overwhelming. Of twenty-two listed (about 6 percent of the convention), nineteen are definitely in group 1; John Hancock, who was silent until the end, may have been group 1 or, when possible, 4; Samuel Adams, who sounded like a group 6 opponent in December, appeared to be a crypto-group 1 Federalist through most of the convention, until he ended up in group 4 or 5; Samuel Holten, who became ill early in the convention, belonged to 6 or 7 — or perhaps 5. The significance of this disparity is revealed in table 13.3, which identifies the floor leaders of each side by the number of their speeches and their listings in the *Dictionary.* The striking feature of this table is that all of the Federalist floor leaders in Parsons's *Minutes* and all but one in the *Debates* were later selected for the *Dictionary.* None of the Antifederalist floor leaders were. So the tradition that Federalists had better leaders is probably correct. The reason is that most of the Antifederalists who might have been leaders, such as Gerry and James Warren, lived in coastal cities, where Federalists dominated at the polls. Hence experienced Antifederalists were not elected.

The disparity between Federalists and Antifederalists in experience and achievement makes a great difference in at least two ways. First, the

6. *Debates and Proceedings.* Parsons's *Minutes* are printed with the debates. Note that Parsons's *Minutes* cover only 15–28 January 1788.

7. "Thatcher Papers," 347.

8. *Dictionary of American Biography* (New York: 1928–).

Table 13.2 Delegates to the Massachusetts Convention with Memoirs in the *Dictionary of American Biography* (1928)

| Group | Name | Notable achievements | | Remarks | Vote on constitution |
		Prior to 1787	Subsequent to 1787		
6 or 7	Samuel Holten	Continental Congress		Became ill during convention	— —
1, 4 or 5	Samuel Adams	Patriot leader, Boston Continental Congress, Massachusetts Senate	Massachusetts Legislature, Governor	See text	Yea
1 or 4	John Hancock	Patriot Leader, Boston President, Continental Congress, Governor	Governor	See text	Yea
1	Fisher Ames		Congressman		Yea
1	Isaac Backus	Baptist divine			Yea
1	James Bowdoin	Boston merchant			Yea
1	James Bowdoin, Jr.	Dorchester merchant	Diplomat	Later Jeffersonian	Yea
1	John Brooks	Revolutionary General			Yea
1	Francis Dana	Continental Congress, Judge, Revolutionary Diplomat			Yea
1	John Glover	Marblehead merchant, Revolutionary General			Yea
1	Nathanial Gorham	Charlestown merchant, Philadelphia Convention			Yea
1	William Gray	Salem merchant, Lt. Governor			Yea
1	Rufus King	Continental Congress, Philadelphia Convention	Diplomat, Senator, Presidential candidate		Yea
1	Benjamin Lincoln	Revolutionary General, Lt. Governor, Suppressed Shays			Yea
1	Theophilus Parsons	Legislator	Chief Justice (Massachusetts)		Yea
1	Theodore Sedgewick	Continental Congress, Suppressed Shays			Yea
1	Caleb Strong	Philadelphia Convention, Governor			Yea
1	Increase Sumner	Judge			Yea
1	Israel Thorndike	Beverly merchant			Yea
1	Cotton Tufts	Physician, Legislator			Yea
1	Joseph Varnum	Revolutionary General		Later Jeffersonian	Yea
1	Samuel West	Congregational divine			Yea

Table 13.3   Floor Leaders in the Massachusetts Convention, with *Dictionary of American Biography* Biographees in Italics

| Speakers in Parson's Minutes *with Six or More Speeches* | | | | Speakers in Debates *with Six or More Speeches* | | | |
| Federalist | | Antifederalist | | Federalist | | Antifederalist | |
Name	Number	Name	Number	Name	Number	Name	Number
King	20	Thompson	17	*King*	15	Taylor	15
Parsons	12	Taylor	13	*Parsons*	9	Thompson	12
Gorham	11	Widgery	13	*Dana*	9	Widgery	12
Sedgewick	9	Dench	10	*Gorham*	7	Nasson	9
Dana	8	Cooley	9	*Adams	7		
Brooks	7	Randall	7	*Ames*	6		
Strong	6	White	6	*Strong*	6		
				Dawes	6		

*Member of Group 4 or Group 5

Federalist leaders were all experienced parliamentarians who understood rhetoric and legislative strategy, and this helped them to keep some control of the agenda. Although some Antifederalists had legislative experience (for example, Thompson had served several terms and Nasson, Taylor, and Widgery one term each), none had been leaders. But more of this advantage later. Second, the Federalist leaders had some rhetorical advantage. It is true that some Antifederalists tried to counteract this by making anti-intellectual appeals. For example, Amos Singletary referred to "these lawyers, and men of learning, and moneyed men, that talk so finely and gloss over matters so smoothly to make us poor illiterate people swallow down the pill."[9] Some present-day writers have interpreted such talk as an Antifederalist advantage.[10] But this very speech of Singletary's was responded to by Jonathan Swift of Lanesborough (Berkshire), who called himself a plough-jogger and who asked if it would not be better to have these "lawyers, moneyed men, and men of learning on the farmers' side" when all must sink and swim together. So it seems more likely that the anti-intellectualism simply reveals the Antifederalist sense of disadvantage, as ruefully expressed, for example, by Benjamin Randall, who also made an

9. *Debates and Proceedings,* 203.
10. Michael Allen Gillespie, "Massachusetts: Creating Consensus," in Michael Allen Gillespie and Michael Lienesch, eds., *Ratifying the Constitution* (Lawrence: University Press of Kansas, 1989), 148, 165.

anti-intellectual appeal: "Mr Randall talks a great deal, and says, as he sits down, that he has done better than he expected."[11]

This rhetorical advantage made a difference because conversions did occur partly at least owing to rhetorical superiority. Charles Turner of Scituate was initially sensitive on this score, resenting King's supposed ridicule of his inept metaphor — King instantly apologized. But in the end Turner converted, using all the usual Federalist arguments about crisis, as did others.[12]

THE POTENTIAL FOR COMPROMISE

Some important figures in Massachusetts politics were initially determined not to take sides publicly. The chief of these was John Hancock, the governor and without question the most popular politician in the state. He had a long history of avoiding commitment until the lineup was clear, and he followed that policy in this case. When the General Court met on 17 October 1787, Hancock presented the Constitution. Although he avoided personally endorsing the document, he spoke of it in quite laudatory terms:

> The general convention . . . having reported to Congress, "a constitution for the United States of America," I have received the same from that honorable body, and have directed the secretary to lay it, together

11. *Debates and Proceedings,* 138; *Minutes,* 303.

12. *Debates and Proceedings,* 273–76, 289. Two others, like Turner, announced their conversion in the convention. One was William Symmes, a student of Theophilus Parsons (Samuel B. Harding, *The Contest over Ratification of the Federal Constitution in the State of Massachusetts* [Cambridge: Harvard University Press, 1896], 42), and the other was Nathaniel Barrell, who described his "folly . . . till powerful reason . . . bore down . . . deep root of prejudice" ("Thatcher Papers," 339, 271, 341). The "Thatcher Papers" suggest three more: Judge Thomas Rice and David Sylvester (Pownalsborough) and Capt. Samuel Grant (Vassalborough). Sylvester, Turner, and Barrell were elected as opponents to the committee to consider Hancock's amendments, but later they voted for the Constitution. Jackson Turner Main (*The Antifederalists: Critics of the Constitution* [1961; repr. New York: W. W. Norton, 1974], 206) lists John Sprague (Lancaster) and Isaac Snow (Harpswell), but I doubt this attribution because they both gave Federalist speeches early in the convention, and Sprague served on the amendments committee as a supporter of the Constitution. Main also lists J. Williams (Taunton), but I doubt this as well because, after his election, two other clearly Antifederal delegates were "illegally" elected — obviously to counter Williams. After the convention Jeremy Belknap, pastor of the church in which the convention was held, wrote to Ebenezer Hazard (the notorious postmaster general) that the conversions included about the same number of people in other counties as were in the three Maine counties ("The Belknap Papers," *Collections of the Massachusetts Historical Society,* 5th ser., 3 [1877]: 18). We know of four from Maine (via the Thatcher papers) so this suggests at least about ten more — or if Maine be counted as one county, then about thirty-five more. Belknap himself guesses about one hundred were converted, but that is clearly too high.

with the letter accompanying it, before the legislature, that measures may be adopted for calling a convention in this commonwealth, to take the same into consideration. It not being within the duties of my office to decide upon this momentous affair, I shall only say, that the characters of the gentlemen who have compiled this system, are so truly respectable, and the object of their deliberations so vastly important, that I conceive every mark of attention will be paid to the report. Their unanimity in deciding those questions wherein the general prosperity of the nation is so deeply involved, and the complicated rights of each separate state are so intimately concerned, is very remarkable; and I persuade myself that the delegates of this state when assembled in convention, will be able to discern that, which will tend to the future happiness and security of all the people in this extensive country. (CC 177)

On the basis of this indirect praise, most people at the time assumed that Hancock favored the Constitution.[13] And it is certainly true that his entourage encouraged this belief. The letters of Cassius (probably James Sullivan, Hancock's closest advisor) combine an ardent defense of the governor's administration with an equally ardent support of the Constitution.[14] John Avery, another close associate of Hancock and the secretary of state, was a convinced and ardent supporter of the Constitution, though it is not clear that he said so publicly.[15] In any event, most group 1 Federalists probably assumed that, if they could show they were close to victory, Hancock would announce his support for the Constitution.

Sam Adams, in the sixties the radical leader of the Sons of Liberty but now the fervently anti-Shays leader of the state senate, was also in an equivocal position. Privately, as we know from his letter to Richard Henry Lee, he wanted conditional amendments, which, at the beginning of the campaign, put him squarely in the Antifederal camp. (He wrote to Lee on 3 December 1787, "As I enter the Building I stumble at the Threshold. I meet with a National Government, instead of a federal Union of Sovereign States" — CC 315.) But he said nothing publicly, though some Federalists suspected him sufficiently to leave his name off several Federalist tickets. He won a seat easily, however. Most Federalists accepted him, perhaps because, like Christopher Gore, they hoped election would "damp his opposition" (CC 388). Adams exposed his hand on 3 January 1788 at a

13. Van Beck Hall, *Politics without Parties: Massachusetts, 1780–1791* (Pittsburgh: University of Pittsburgh Press, 1972), 256; CC:388, 448; CC:4:562–64.

14. Paul Leicester Ford, ed., *Essays on the Constitution of the United States* (1892; rept. New York: Burt Franklin, 1970), 1–48.

15. "Thatcher Papers," 337.

dinner given by ex-Governor Bowdoin for the ten Boston delegates; as Gore wrote to King, Adams on this occasion was "open & decided agt it," saying it "ought not be adopted, but on condition of such amendments as would totally destroy it" (CC:424A). Adams's opinion is confirmed by Gorham, who wrote to Knox that "one of the company" reported that Adams "opened fully and positively in opposition." Furthermore, Gorham reported that "Clark, Rhodes, and Truman three of the greatest Leaders at the North End . . . intended . . . to have the most numerous Caucas ever held in Boston to consider what was to be done in consiquence of Mr. Adams declaration" (CC:424B).

The Boston caucus held on 7 January 1788, which was indeed large — overflowing the Green Dragon Masonic Hall with possibly 380 — must have been chastening for Adams. Its final resolution, prepared by a three-man committee consisting of the chairman, John Lucas, Paul Revere, and Benjamin Russell, widely known as the intensely Federalist publisher of the *Massachusetts Centinel*, proclaimed that the voters chose as delegates "such men, and such only" as would "promote the adoption" of the Constitution "without any conditions" (CC 424C). Most writers have argued that this sharp rebuke from his political base deflected Adams's opposition. Indeed, his surprising "silence," "contrary to his own Sentiments,"[16] is good evidence that the Green Dragon caucus restrained him. Gillespie, however, attributes his silence to the death of his son.[17] Of course, such an event was devastating, even though it had long been expected. Still, Adams was regularly present during the convention, and at every point that he intervened, both before and after his son's death, he took the side of group 1 Federalists. He behaved, as is fairly evident from table 13.4, exactly like a crypto-Federalist. The Green Dragon resolutions induced Adams to abandon his initial preference for conditional amendments, but when recommendations became the Federalist position, he welcomed Hancock's amendments. He went too far, accidentally I believe, in offering his own; so he withdrew them, just as a crypto-Federalist should.

With Hancock and Adams thus prepared to ratify the Constitution, the group 1 Federalists could hope to win with some kind of compromise.

CONTROL OF THE AGENDA

A fascinating feature of the Massachusetts convention is that members of groups 6 and 7 initially had the numerical advantage, yet they failed to

16. King to Madison, in Rutland, *Papers of Madison* 10:465.
17. "Massachusetts: Creating Consensus," 150.

Table 13.4   Samuel Adams in the Ratifying Convention

a. January 9, moved for morning prayers by clergy of all denominations (Debates pp. 48, 98). Since this accommodates the mostly Antifederalist Baptists, it is a pro-federalist move. Were Adams to lead Antifederalists, it would be unnecessary, even hurtful. But if he planned to play a Federalist part, it was a useful move.

b. January 11-12, served on a committee that seated a challenged Federalist (pp. 48, 53).

c. January 15, asked why the Constitution provided biennial rather than annual elections and declared himself satisfied with the answer (pp. 103, 108).

d. January 16, criticized General Thompson, the most frequent Antifederal speaker, as out of order (p. 293).

e. January 18, invited delegates to his son's funeral on the 19th (p. 62).

f. January 24, spoke against an Antifederal motion to speed up consideration by ceasing to read by paragraphs. Here, as elsewhere, he expressed a desire for full explanation, which was, of course, the federalist rationale for delay (p. 196).

g. January 25, rebuked an Antifederalist who called to order the Federalist "plough jogger" (p. 203).

h. January 26, rejoiced that the Constitution permitted annihilation of the slave trade at a certain data. The context was that Antifederalists criticized the Constitution for not abolishing the slave trade (p. 209). (The Debates have no entries for January 29, 30, though the Journal indicates that the convention met.)

i. January 31, moved and praised Hancock's proposed recommendatory amendments as removing his doubts about the Constitution. Note that Hancock's proposal was the new position of the group 1 Federalists. Adams accepted the proposal even though he explicitly recognized that the proposed amendments might never pass (p. 227).

j. February 1, spoke at length in support of Hancock's amendments (pp. 232-35).

k. February 6, introduced a bill of rights to go with Hancock's amendments, then withdrew them as they "did not meet with the approbation of those gentlemen whose minds they were intended to ease" (p. 266). This explanation is mysterious. It might mean that Antifederalists, bent on outright rejection, resented them; but an Antifederalist reintroduced them and Adams then voted against this motion. (See Ralph V. Harlow, *Samuel Adams, Promoter of the American Revolution: A Study in Psychology and Politics* (New York: Henry Holt and Co., 1923), p. 334; see also Gillespie, *op. cit.*, p. 157.) Alternatively, it might mean that group 1 Federalists thought the motion broke the agreement, so Adams conceded. Finally, then, Adams voted that day for ratification.

Source: *Debates*, 1856.

obtain control of the agenda. To begin with, the convention chose the Federalist George Minot as secretary.[18] Then, although it elected the ambiguous Hancock as president, it also elected the group 1 Federalist William Cushing as vice president. Because Hancock was absent during January 9–29, Cushing usually presided. This put committee appointments, some potentially important, in his hands. Group 1 Federalists dominated the committees (see table 13.5). The only significant committee dominated by Antifederalists was one of four committees investigating disputed elections. It upheld two challenged Antifederalists, but the other three committees upheld three challenged Federalists.

The worst Antifederal failure was the committee elected to consider Hancock's amendments. An Antifederalist, Josiah Whitney, whom King referred to as a "doubtful character," proposed this committee with the understanding that it would consist of two members from each county, one announced for, the other against, to be chosen by the county delegations. Because Dukes county (Martha's Vineyard) had only two delegates, both of whom were group 1 Federalists, no opponent could be chosen. Automatically Federalists had a 13–12 majority (and King immediately crowed to Madison and Knox that Federalists dominated).[19] But it was even better than that for the Federalists, because two of the elected opponents actually announced their conversion, and a third also voted for the Constitution. In the end, the committee reported favorably, 15–7, with one absent and one not voting.

This committee was crucially important because it dealt with the agenda on Hancock's amendments. Opponents wanted to vote up or down before voting on amendments.[20] Federalists, of course, wanted a simultaneous vote: to ratify and recommend. This is what the committee reported.

It is difficult to understand how Antifederalists could have permitted this to happen. Only inexperience can explain such ineptitude.

Just as Antifederalists failed on committees, so they failed on procedure. When the convention began discussion on 14 January, it adopted two important procedural motions: to discuss by paragraphs, with no vote until this was completed, and to seat Gerry for the purpose of answering questions. Discussion by paragraphs amounted to delay and was the essence of group 1 Federalist strategy. As King told Madison, it also precluded amendments, which, if made conditional for ratification, were the Federalists' main fear. At the same time Federalists supported the motion

18. Main, *The Antifederalists*, 202.
19. King, *Life and Correspondence* 1:318–19.
20. *Debates and Proceedings*, 404–05, Benjamin Lincoln to George Washington.

Table 13.5   Committee Membership

Date	Subject	Appointed (A) Elected (E)	Group 1 Federalist	Antifederalist	Uncertain
9 January	On Returns	?	4	1	1[a]
10 January	revised	?	4	1	1
10 January	revised	E	4	1	1
9 January	Tellers for Secretary	A	3	1	
9 January	Monitors (Tellers)	E	3	2	
10 January	revised	E	3	3	
9 January	On Rules	A	5	2	
9 January	To Notify Hancock	A	3	2[a]	
9 January	To View Brattle Church	A	5	2	2[a]
10 January	To Accept Brattle Church	E	1	1	1[a]
11 January	Disputed election - Sheffield	A	4	2[a]	S. Adams
11 January	Disputed election - Great Barrington	A	4	2	1
11 January	Disputed election - Williamstown	A	6	1	
11 January	Disputed election - Taunton	A	2	3	
11 January	To Seek a New Hall	A	4	3	
14 January	To Notify Gerry of Invitation	A	-	3	
15 January	To See a New Hall	A	3	3	1[a]
17 January	On Payroll	?	2	3	
21 January	On Newspaper Libel	?	5	2	
2 February	On Hancock's Amendments	E	13	12[b]	

[a] including one who voted for ratification
[b] including three who voted for ratification: Barrell, Sylvester, Turner

to seat Gerry—in order, King said, to moderate emotion and to avoid a trial of strength that they might lose.[21] To me, the two motions look like a deal, especially since the convention had rejected an invitation to Gerry two days earlier.[22] If so, Federalists got the better of it. The procedure of discussion by paragraphs survived through the whole convention, but Gerry dropped out. On 19 January he intervened, unasked, to defend his action in the Philadelphia convention as a member of the committee on the Connecticut compromise, which Strong had described in a way that made Gerry appear to have sold out the interest of Massachusetts. Francis Dana objected sharply to Gerry's speaking unasked.[23] So Gerry retired, saying by letter that he would not return until allowed to defend himself. The letter went unanswered, and Gerry never reappeared. So Antifederalists entirely lost on the bargain.

A second Antifederal failure on procedure was Nasson's motion, made on 24 January, to cease discussion by paragraphs, a hurrying motion as Antifederal strength subsided. With forceful help from Adams, group 1 Federalists quashed this motion on a voice vote. Clearly neither Nasson nor anyone else had bothered to plan for this motion. By contrast Federalists worked in caucus "as hard as in convention."[24] No wonder Antifederalists lost.

The worst failure of the Antifederalists was, however, in the coordination of their strategy. Although some, like Gerry and Adams in his pre-Green Dragon mode, had from the beginning been willing to ratify on condition of amendments (group 6), the floor leaders and the most aggressive Antifederal newspaper writers, such as Agrippa, Helvidius Priscus, and Republican Federalist, were for flat-out rejection (group 7). Toward the end of the convention, however, Antifederalists outside seemed better at counting votes than did those inside because outsiders, like Hampden, began urging conditional amendments.[25] But the inside leaders were

21. Rutland, *Papers of Madison* 10:376.
22. "Belknap Papers," 5.
23. *Debates and Proceedings*, 65–75; Rutland, *Papers of Madison* 10:400–01.
24. Eben F. Stone, "A Sketch of Tristrom Dalton," *Historical Collections of the Essex Institute* 25:1–20.
25. Evelyn Fink, "Political Rhetoric and Strategic Choice in the Ratification Conventions on the U.S. Constitution" (Diss., University of Rochester Library, 1987), 167–70. "Hampden," 26 January, proposed ratification on condition that Congress, in its first substantive action, submit state recommended amendments, to be included in the Constitution when seven states ratified: Herbert J. Storing, *The Complete Anti-Federalist*, 6 vols. (Chicago: University of Chicago Press, 1981), 4:199. King properly called this conditional ratification and interpreted it as a revelation of Antifederal weakness: Eben F. Stone, "Parsons and the Constitution Conventions of 1788," *Historical Collections of the Essex Institute* 35:81–96 at 93. Gillespie ("Massachusetts: Creating Consensus," 164) calls Hampden's amendments recom-

frozen into an agenda for an up or down vote. A Republican Federalist had the good sense on January 30 to urge adjournment, for he recognized that the Federalists were by then winning the debate.[26] John Taylor, one of the main floor leaders, immediately picked this up, but he was too late because Hancock had already made his proposal.[27] No other Antifederalist pursued this idea until February 5 — after the Hancock amendments were reported out — when Dench moved to adjourn to take them back to constituents.[28] This was debated and then defeated 115–214, again demonstrating poor preparation.

But the problem was deeper than poor preparation. The floor leaders were irrevocably wedded to outright rejection and could not see that they were losing. An appropriate Antifederal strategy might have been to respond to Hancock and Adams with, "Yes, your amendments are a good idea, but they aren't safe; so let's make our ratification conditional on their adoption." This is what Hampden and Agrippa suggested, and Republican Federalist was moving in the same direction. Except for Taylor (in part) and Dench, the Antifederal leaders stuck doggedly to the strategy of voting up or down, emphasizing that recommended amendments were illegal or unlikely to be adopted.[29] So they lost all the votes that Hancock won.

---

mendatory, but this is clearly not what Hampden thought because he used the words "upon the following conditions" and said that he expected seven states to agree before the Constitution went into effect (Storing, *Complete Anti-Federalist* 4:201). A propos of Hampden's letter, General Lincoln reassured Washington that the convention would never adopt with conditions (*Debates and Proceedings*, 402–03). On 5 February, Agrippa, while preferring amendments of the Articles and entirely rejecting recommended amendments, did propose amendments as a condition for ratification (Storing, *Complete Anti-Federalist* 4:111–12). This was a great change for Agrippa because before and during the convention he wanted outright rejection and then amendment of the Articles (Storing, *Complete Anti-Federalist* 4:88–90, 98–99). But his conversion came too late because it was published the day before the convention voted on ratification with recommended amendments. Nevertheless, crabbed and late as Agrippa was, he showed more resilience than the Antifederal leaders in the convention.

26. Storing, *Complete Anti-Federalist* 4:181–82.

27. *Debates and Proceedings*, 227.

28. Ibid., 265–66.

29. Following are the responses of the Antifederal floor leaders with citations to the *Debates and Proceedings* (1956) (the names of those in table 13.2 are italicized):

(a) *Taylor*: "He did not see any constitutional door open for them [i.e., amendments]. We are . . . treading on unsafe ground" (227). "He concluded by objecting to the amendments because no assurance was given that they would become a part of the system" (265).

(b) *Widgery*: "He did not see the probability that these amendments would be made, if we had the authority to propose them" (240).

(c) Pierce: "It appears to me very uncertain whether they are ever a part of the Constitution" (242).

(d) *Thompson*: "We have no right to make amendments; it was not the business we were

Antifederal leaders plainly were inept. In this recital of their defects I have several times emphasized that they apparently made no count of the house, thus leaving the fate of their motions up to chance and to their fixed, inflexible strategy. By contrast, Gorham wrote to Knox on February 3, three days before the final vote and indeed the day before the committee on amendments reported, "I think the numbers will be about 185 for to 160 or more against it — though the Antis say they shall have a majority of 10 — I confess that I shall be more mortified if they are right in their confidence than I have ever been in my life" (Knox papers 21:129). The actual outcome, 187–169, shows Gorham's count to be almost dead-on for ratification and just a few off on the against. The reason, of course, that he would have been mortified by an error is that he had what he thought was an excellent count, and he would have been professionally shamed if it had turned out to be wrong. On the other hand, to believe, as Gorham says his opponents did, that the outcome would be about 173–183 means that they were about fourteen off on each side. Clearly the Federalists had the better caucus.

The superior quality of their count was a major reason the Federalists won. They knew where they were at all times and so could invent recommendatory amendments when necessary. The Antifederalists, however, did not know where they were and so were precluded from offering, say, conditional amendments.

And the Federalists' success and Antifederalists' failure on the count is just one example of a more general feature of the convention: the Federalists, despite beginning as a minority, kept substantial control of the agenda throughout.

COMPROMISE WITH RECOMMENDED AMENDMENTS

However much group 1 Federalists and moderate opponents like Hancock and Adams wanted an accommodation, none appeared so long as both sides interpreted amendments as rejection. The crucial event is, therefore, the development of the idea of recommended amendments, which group 1 could accept and which allowed groups 4 and 5 to become Federalists themselves.

---

sent for . . . but they might be voted for by someone — he did not say Judases" (243).

(e) Lusk: "He did not see any reason to suppose they [i.e., amendments] ever would be adopted" (250–55).

(f) *Nasson, Taylor, Thomas* "did not think it was probable they would be inserted" (243).

Thus all the main floor leaders and several lesser ones simply refused to consider amendments.

According to Samuel Harding, the earliest known proposal of this sort is a letter of 12 January written by a Republican Federalist (possibly James Warren); but that letter merely proposed to amend the Articles through their unanimity procedure. Simultaneously, the author observed that the ⅔ procedure in the Constitution would not work.[30]

This is just the Gerryesque argument for rejection by amendment. Harding's second source for recommended amendments is a private letter of 19 January from Avery to Thatcher. This letter has the germ of the idea and is important because Avery was close to Hancock. Avery wanted the supporters to "discover a conciliatory disposition," in order, perhaps, to ratify unanimously: "My Wishes are that they may adopt it and propose Amendments which, when agreed upon, to transmit to the several States for their Concurrence." Possibly this puts ratification first and amendments second, as the convention ultimately provided. But just as easily it may mean amendments first and ratification second. Avery is thinking of a procedure, sometimes used under the Articles, of communication between state legislatures, not the amendment procedure of the Constitution. Unclear as it is, however, it does indicate that something like what came to be recommendatory amendments was in the air.[31]

The earliest unambiguous statement that I can find of recommendatory amendments is in King to Madison, on Wednesday, 23 January, on what was apparently a caucus decision earlier in the week: "We are now thinking of amendments to be submitted not as a condition of our assent and Ratification; but as the opinion of the convention subjoined to their Ratification." Jeremy Belknap, outside the inner circle, repeated this on 25 January: "to annex some amendments *recommended* to be adopted by the first Congress."[32]

From this point to 31 January, the history of the idea is obscure because the Federalist caucus treated it as a secret. In a letter of 30 January by Tristram Dalton we read, "I will tell you as a confidential communication, that Mr. S. Adams will come out in favor of the Constitution. [He did so the next day.] This and the Governor on the same side will settle the matter favorably — All this is scarcely known out of our caucus," to which Theophilus Parsons added a postscript: "Our friend D.'s communication will give you all the information we are at liberty to put on paper. We have stolen a moment in caucus to write this."[33]

30. Harding, *The Contest over Ratification*, 84; Storing, *Complete Anti-Federalist* 4:174, 176.
31. "Thatcher Letters," 265–66.
32. Rutland, *Papers of Madison* 10:411; Massachusetts Historical Society, *Collections of the Massachusetts Historical Society*, vol. 3, 5th ser, "Belknap Papers" (Boston: Massachusetts Historical Society, 1877), 11.
33. Stone, "Sketch of Tristrom Dalton," 20.

What was secret, of course, was the wooing of Hancock and the construction of amendments. Hancock was waiting on the sidelines, husbanding his physical strength and waiting for such assurances of victory as a favorable count of the house. But group 1 Federalists were not sure of him until he actually gave his speech on January 31: Thus in King to Knox, Sunday, 27 January, we read, "Hancock is still completely confined, he appears to me to wish well to the Constitution, but don't care to risque anything in its favor."[34] The same day Gorham wrote Madison a broadstroked description of the convention, mainly showing that the Antifederalists had insignificant leaders, while his side was star-studded. He included two governors (Hancock and Bowdoin), three supreme court judges, fifteen senators, and so on but said they still could not win without recommendatory amendments.[35] This letter displays an assurance of Hancock's support, but it does not suggest that Hancock was willing to risk anything. Even as late as Wednesday, 30 January, Gorham, writing in caucus to Knox, did not include Hancock in his calculations: "We cannot gain the question without some recommendatory amendments — With them I presume we shall have a small majority — They are preparing and will be ready for tomorrow — we shall then present them — if a proper pause offers." On the same day in the same caucus, however, Dalton seemed sure of Hancock.[36] At least he said that Adams and the governor on the same side would settle the matter favorably. Evidently the members of the caucus had Hancock's promise of support, but not even Gorham — at the center of the caucus — could count on Hancock to present amendments. Indeed, it seems to me that the caucus had already picked a backup, Gen. William Heath, a respected elder who had also been out sick for ten days. Heath proposed recommendatory amendments on Thursday morning, 31 January, with an appeal very much like that Hancock used in the afternoon. That is, Heath deplored conflict and urged unanimous ratification with recommended amendments. It seems that Heath had been primed and then, in fairness, could not be displaced once Hancock agreed. So Heath broached the idea in the morning, Hancock presented amendments in the afternoon, and Adams then seconded them enthusiastically.

On Sunday, 3 February, King explained to Knox just what had gone on: "You will be astonished when you see the list of names [of those voting for ratification] that such a union of men has taken place on this Question.

---

34. Knox papers 21:121. Note, however, that by 30 January, the day before Hancock's speech in favor of the Constitution, Dalton and Parsons seemed totally confident of both Hancock and Adams. Stone, "Sketch of Tristrom Dalton."

35. Rutland, *Papers of Madison* 10:436.

36. Knox papers 21:121, but see n. 34 above.

Hancock will hereafter receive the universal support of Bowdoin's friends, and we tell him that if Virginia does not unite, which is problematical, that he is considered as the only candidate for President."[37] So Hancock was pulled off the fence by the idea of recommended amendments and the promise of future support.

Adams was, I think, less of a problem for the group 1 Federalists. He was regularly acting as a crypto-Federalist and, now that amendments were proposed, he could openly support them as if they were what he had wanted in November and December. Of course they were not. There is a vast difference between amendments required before ratification and ones recommended for adoption after ratification. The latter method guarantees ratification, the former neither guarantees nor indeed holds out much hope for ratification. But by glossing over this difference Adams could appear to gain his point and thus publicly endorse Hancock's amendments.

One might well ask why some apparently Antifederalist delegates accepted the recommended amendments. There is no problem about Hancock and Adams. Both were Boston men, living in an environment in which a huge proportion of the population favored the Constitution and in which economic advantage dictated quick ratification. In fact, in my opinion, Hancock was all along in favor of ratification without any kind of amendments. His interest in offering amendments was simply to aid the cause. At least, there is no evidence to the contrary, and his warm quasi-endorsement in October 1787 suggests that he began as a group 1 Federalist. Adams, on the other hand, clearly began in group 6 but was persuaded by his constituents to move, so he became a crypto–group 1 Federalist. But once the idea of recommended amendments surfaced, he was glad, for the sake of apparent consistency in favoring amendments, to join what appeared to be group 4 or 5.

The puzzle is, instead, about those apparently convinced Antifederalists who followed Hancock and Adams. At least two Federalists told them that the recommended amendments might never be ratified.[38] And Antifederal leaders were unanimous in doubting adoption (see note 29 above). Yet Gorham and King thought recommended amendments carried them over the top. And we have the direct testimony of Nathaniel Barrell, Charles Turner, and William Symmes that the proposal of recommended amendments converted them.[39] They convinced themselves that

37. Knox papers 21:127.
38. *Debates and Proceedings*: Adams (225), and Ames (261).
39. Ibid., 264, 274, 278.

there was a "moral certainty" or "no reasonable doubt" the amendments would be adopted. And then they repeated the usual Federalist arguments that crisis demanded the immediate ratification of the Constitution. This indicates that these men were waverers, people who sympathized with the Federalist arguments. All they needed was an excuse to convert, and they grasped at the amendments, however uncertain their fate.

In any case, the recommended amendments transformed the ratification process not only in Massachusetts, but later in several other states. These recommendations appeared to open up the closed rule, but the opening was more apparent than real because it left control of the agenda and the amendments in the hands of group 1 Federalists, provided they won the national elections in 1788. Because they did win, they could pick and choose among amendments to comply with the implied promise in Massachusetts and elsewhere. They chose only those that they found palatable (that is, the bill of rights) and ignored the proposals for structural change in the institutions provided for in the Constitution. So the Antifederalists who prophesied the amendments' failure had a better prediction than the Federalists who were confident of adoption. Nevertheless, the Federalists could claim that they kept their promise and subsequent generations have on the whole chosen to believe them.

Besides transforming the process of ratification, the Massachusetts ratification boosted the chances of ratification immensely. Six states, including two of the three largest, had ratified, and, though the Federalists lost Rhode Island in April, they easily gained Maryland and, in May, South Carolina. So the tough struggle in Massachusetts gave them eight of the nine they needed. Surely the probability of a ninth success, to come from New Hampshire, Virginia, New York, or North Carolina, was very high.

ALTERNATIVE INTERPRETATIONS

Michael Gillespie has interpreted the Massachusetts ratification in a quite different way from me. His purpose is to refute the proposition made by Stanley Elkins and Erik McKitrick that the young, vigorous, commercially oriented Federalists were the founders of American political life, and he seeks to prove that the more idealistic old revolutionaries, who regarded the Constitution as the completion of the Revolution, were crucial to ratification.[40] For this reason he endeavors to show that Hancock and Adams stepped in to save the ratification with conciliatory propositions when the

40. "Massachusetts: Creating Consensus"; Stanley Elkins and Eric McKitrick, "The Founding Fathers: Young Men of the Revolution," in Jack P. Greed, ed., *The Reinterpretation of the American Revolution 1763–1789* (New York: Harper and Row, 1968), 378–95.

group 1 Federalists had nearly blown their chances. Although the dispute between Gillespie and Elkins and McKitrick seems unresolvable because of the imprecision of terms — given the continuity of life, sharp distinctions of generations are difficult to dispute — I think that Gillespie's interpretation of events in support of his view is highly dubious. To make it work he must show that two old enemies, Hancock and Adams, came together to impose what had been Adams's position all along. Neither feature of this interpretation holds up.

Gillespie's basic evidence for a conscious alliance between Hancock and Adams is a paragraph in William Wells's *Life of Samuel Adams* of 1865 that recounts a story that Joseph Vinal "related early in this century."[41] Vinal visited Hancock, found Adams with him, and then observed to come in, "several gentlemen . . . who appeared to be a committee. They desired to know specifically the objections of Hancock and Adams to the Constitution and to endeavor to remove them by some means that would conciliate their favor and support." Then Adams listed objections, so Vinal continued, and Hancock agreed and offered to present amendments. This story sounds apocryphal to me. It provides that all the interesting detail of the convention be determined while the narrator is conveniently present to observe it. If there is any truth to the story, however, it only supports a portion of Gillespie's contention, that portion in fact on which we are agreed. True, Adams and Hancock are together as two crypto-Federalists might well be. But the initiative — the request for objections — is in the hands not of Adams, but of the committee, presumably a delegation from the Federalist caucus. And if it is such a committee, then the amendments must be the recommendatory ones, not the conditional ones that Adams initially desired.

Gillespie's argument also depends on Adams's having the same position all along, and this requires blurring the distinction between ratifying only on condition of amendments and ratifying with recommendations for amendments. This blurring is probably what led to his misreading of Hampden's proposal (see note 25 above), which Gillespie says amounted to recommendatory amendments, but which King, Lincoln, and Hampden himself, as well as modern editors like Storing, say were conditions on ratification. Only by treating the two kinds of amendments as equivalent can Adams's position remain unchanged throughout the campaign and convention. But, as I have pointed out, there is a great difference between ratification now with recommended amendments and ratification at some

41. William V. Wells, *The Life and Public Service of Samuel Adams* (Boston: Little, Brown, 1865), 3:259–60.

later time when conditions are satisfied. Agrippa thought that the Articles could be amended in about two years, and I suppose optimistic Antifederalists would agree. So at very minimum there is a two-year difference in the time of ratification for the two kinds of amendments, and, of course, the experience with the impost suggested that a conditional ratification would mean no ratification at all.

Adams clearly favored conditional ratification in December and January. He abandoned this position when he became a crypto-Federalist after the Green Dragon resolutions. When he sponsored recommended amendments he was taking a position much closer to the original group 1 Federalists than to the position he had himself held in December. Indeed, by voting against his own amendments when they were again offered by an Antifederalist, he identified himself entirely with the Federalist position and rejected his own earlier position. In short, the group 1 Federalists, by favoring recommended amendments, converted Adams publicly and effectively co-opted him to their cause.

Finally, Gillespie's argument depends on Hancock's acting exclusively on principle, for which there is no evidence. Hence Gillespie denies that Hancock might have been influenced by the promise of support from Bowdoin's friends. Instead, Hancock presumably sponsored amendments because he agreed with them. This attributes more knowledge of Hancock than we have. We know nothing of his opinions between the time he praised the Constitution to the General Court and the time he offered amendments. On the basis of his remarks to the General Court he appeared to be a group 1 Federalist, an appropriate stance for a Boston merchant. When he introduced recommendations he was still acting as a group 1 Federalist, for that group had changed positions. We have no reason, one way or another, to attribute a desire for amendments themselves. Instead, he appears to be, as King remarked, a cautious politician who did not wish to risk anything until he was sure of the outcome. So, given the offer of Bowdoin's support, it is difficult to see such a man regarding it with indifference. By the very act of supporting the Constitution, Hancock was offending the very people — the westerners — who had elected him in 1787. As the elections of 1788 approached, therefore, most politicians would be concerned about rebuilding support. He must have thought that Bowdoin's friends looked pretty attractive. But, of course, this is speculation both on my part and on Gillespie's.

14

The Federalists Regain Momentum

T HE MASSACHUSETTS ratification substantially changed both the Constitution and the process of ratification. The remaining states really had a choice of two documents to ratify, either the one drafted at Philadelphia or the as-yet quite fuzzy one allowing possible revisions after ratification. Two states, Maryland and Rhode Island, acted on the original document; three states, Virginia, New York, and North Carolina, acted on the post-Massachusetts document; and it is not clear what New Hampshire and South Carolina acted on.

The main consequence of the Massachusetts ratification was that group 1 Federalists retained control of the agenda and their momentum. This fact was well recognized in 1788: Edward Carrington, a strongly Federalist Virginia delegate to Congress, wrote to Henry Knox (CC 508), "The decision of Massachusetts is perhaps the most important event that ever took place in America, as upon her in all probability depended the fate of the Constitution." And Washington wrote to Madison (CC 583), "The decision of Massachusetts, notwithstanding its concomitants, is a severe stroke to the opponents of the proposed Constitution in this State; and with the favorable determinations of the States . . . before, and . . . after, will have a powerful operation on the Minds of men." Contemporary historians share this judgment: Kaminski and Saladino, quoting Carrington's letter (CC 508), remark that without the recommendatory amendments "it is unlikely that the Massachusetts Convention would have ratified . . . or the required nine states."

Naturally, the Federalists were jubilant. Although Boston's celebration went unreported nationally, it contained at least 1,625 marchers.[1] And a

1. Cited from the *Massachusetts Centinal,* 9, 13 February 1788, in *Debates and Proceedings in the Convention of the Commonwealth of Massachusetts Held in the Year 1788* (Boston: William White, 1856), 323–29.

poem about the event was printed twenty-two times, for 11,264 words (CC 552) in my sample. Elsewhere celebrations were given 9,889 words (New Haven, CC 4:516, 1,820 words; New York, CC 4:517–18, 7,304 words; Philadelphia, CC 4:522, 765 words). The significance of the event garnered 14,990 words, and praise of the Massachusetts Antifederalists for their ready acquiescence amounted to 16,567 words, about two-thirds of which came from Washington ("the candid and conciliating behavior of the [Massachusetts] minority," CC 638B). Altogether, the Federalist commentary on the Massachusetts ratification was 52,710 words. Of course, the Antifederalists spat out some sour grapes, mostly about "only a majority of nineteen" (CC 4:528) or allegations of unfairness (CC 570). But the total Antifederal attention to the Massachusetts ratification was only 6,990 words. So the ratio of Federalist to Antifederalist words was about 7.5 to 1, which is approximately four times the expected ratio and thus amounts to persuasive evidence of the Federalist recognition of their momentum and continued agenda control.

The rest of the campaign is characterized by a fairly successful Federalist effort to keep their momentum going in the new circumstances of an open rule.

THE FEDERALIST SETBACK IN NEW HAMPSHIRE

The Federalist campaign in the next state after Massachusetts, New Hampshire, resulted in a setback, from which, however, the party recovered handsomely. Initially, New Hampshire Federalists lacked confidence about ratification. But they did have control of the agenda. President John Sullivan delayed calling the legislature until 1 November. Then he called a special session for 5 December. In its delay portion, this composite tactic gave Federalists time to persuade voters and provided for a convention after Massachusetts, which, the president hoped, would serve as a model for New Hampshire's ratification. In its special session portion, this tactic guaranteed a safely Federalist legislature as against an unknown legislature to be elected for a late January session. In this special session, the Senate was overwhelmingly Federalist, and, although the full membership of the House was probably Antifederalist by a big margin, only a Federalist majority actually attended. This Federalist legislature then performed as expected. It called a convention for 13 February, well after Massachusetts. It set the convention in Federalist territory at Exeter, near Portsmouth. It provided that the towns send the same number of delegates as representatives, as against an Antifederal plan to double representation in order to minimize the impact of the more experienced rhetors and herestheticians on the Federal side. It allowed unrepresented towns to send delegates. And it allowed the mostly Federalist state officeholders, such as judges, to serve as delegates.[2]

This was a pretty good beginning, and it was based entirely on agenda control. Although both sides then conducted intensive campaigns, the Federalists believed that they were quite persuasive, and they were certainly buoyed up by the Massachusetts ratification. John Langdon thought that "if Massachusetts adopted . . . , N. Hampshire would not be one week in Session" (CC 4:61). Madison, in close touch with New Hampshire Federalists, wrote to Jefferson after the Massachusetts ratification that in New Hampshire "adoption is a matter of certainty" (CC 541).

But, as it turned out, the New Hampshire Federalists' initial doubts were justified. The Federalists elected all the delegates from seacoast towns and a big majority of delegates in the Connecticut River valley, but they elected very few in the central part of the state, which was an extension northward of the geological and ideological pattern of Worcester and Hampshire counties—Shays country—in Massachusetts. Even though Federalist campaigners persuaded several previously unrepresented towns to elect delegates, the election went against them. Furthermore, Antifederalist campaigners persuaded between twenty-five and forty towns (out of about one hundred) to instruct their delegates against the Constitution.[3]

As with the election in Massachusetts, this was a major Federalist setback. But the Federalists still controlled the agenda. This authority, coupled with effective persuasion, ultimately permitted them to triumph. First, consider agenda control: By arriving promptly and organizing the convention exactly on time, while Antifederalists dawdled or were kept in legislative session by President Sullivan, the Federalists selected a Federalist chairman and a Federalist committee on credentials that was also to determine (not simply recommend) the rules. They seated two Federalists in disputed election cases. Further, their rules provided, quite unconventionally, that only the vote on adoption be recorded (so delegates instructed against the Constitution could safely vote for adjournment), that a motion to adjourn take precedence over any others (so, if Antifederalists threatened a negative vote on the Constitution, the convention could avoid it by adjournment), and that a motion to reconsider require as many

2. Jere R. Daniell, *Experiment in Republicanism: New Hampshire Politics and the American Revolution, 1741–1794* (Cambridge: Harvard University Press, 1970), 212; Jere R. Daniell, "Frontier and Constitution: Why Grafton County Delegates Voted 10–1 for Ratification," *Historical New Hampshire* 43 (1988): 207–29, 218.

3. Daniell, *Experiment,* 213–14.

voters as the original motion (so, if Federalists once passed a motion to adjourn, they could prevent reconsideration of it by simply not voting). It would be hard to imagine a set of rules better devised for Federalist floor managers to stop the momentum that the Antifederalists had acquired from their electoral success. And these procedural devices worked. The Federalists did not have a majority, but they prevented a vote on the Constitution.

Two observers constructed a count of the house soon after adjournment.[4] One, relying on a Federalist floor leader, wrote that there were forty-five certain Federalist votes out of one hundred and five present, or eight short of a majority. The other observer, more optimistic, probably less well informed, and clearly wrong about three votes, wrote that there were fifty certain Federalists. Still not enough. However, there were eleven cross-pressured delegates who, while instructed against, wished to vote for the Constitution. When the Federalists moved to adjourn in the hope that the instructions could be rescinded, these eleven voted for adjournment without directly violating their instructions on a recorded vote. (In table 14.1, the eleven are those on lines 2, 7, 8, 10, one on line 6, and one discussed in note b in the table.) They provided the margin with the forty-five certain Federalists to adjourn from February 21 until June 18 at Concord.

In the interim both sides scrambled for votes, although the Federalists scrambled harder. By an amazing stroke of luck the Federalist count of the house at Concord has survived as well as the two observers' estimates of the February vote on adjournment. Jere Daniell has carefully and brilliantly analyzed these counts, and I have used his estimates to construct table 14.1, which summarizes just what happened between sessions. One result of the intensive campaigning was a wash: three towns on each side unrepresented at Exeter sent delegates to Concord. Otherwise, the Federalists did better. True, the Antifederalists' instructions disciplined four delegates against the Constitution (line 10) who otherwise would have voted for it. But the Federalists were better at persuading. One town rescinded instructions (note b). Another replaced an Antifederalist delegate (line 7) with a Federalist (line 3). A possibly cross-pressured delegate who had not voted at Exeter voted for the Constitution at Concord (line 2). Four more, who voted with the Antifederalists against adjournment, voted for the Constitution (line 11). Then nine more simply did not vote in the second session. They either stayed away, walked out, or voted present (lines 5–9).

4. Jere R. Daniell, "Counting Noses: Delegate Sentiment in New Hampshire's Ratifying Convention," *Historical New Hampshire* 43 (1988): 136–55.

Table 14.1   Reconciliation of the Vote on Adjournment in the First Session of the New Hampshire Convention at Exeter and the Vote on the Constitution in the Second Session at Concord[a]

Line Number		Yea	Nay	Not Voting
1[b]	Adjournment	56	49	
2[c]	Additions: Not recorded on Adjournment; Yea on Constitution	+1		
3[d] 4[d]	Not present at Exeter: Yea on Constitution Nay on Constitution	+4	+3	
5[c]	Subtractions: Nay on Adjournment; not recorded on Constitution		−1	
6[e,f] 7[c,d,e]	Absent from Concord: Yea on Adjournment Nay on Adjournment	−2	−3	
8[f] 9[c]	Not Voting on Constitution: Yea on Adjournment Nay on Adjournment	−2	−2	2 2
10[f] 11[c]	Additions and Subtractions: Yea on Adjournment; Nay on Constitution Nay on Adjournment; Yea on Constitution	−4 +4	+4 −4	
12[b]	Constitution	57	46	4

[a] based on Daniell, see note 4.

[b] lines 1, 12. While the usual allocation of votes is 56-51 on adjournment and 57-47 on the Constitution, Daniell's sources give respectively 51-49 and 57-46 with 4 not voting. One delegate instructed against voted for adjournment, persuaded his town to withdraw instructions, and voted for the Constitution. So he appears only on lines 1 and 12.

[c] lines 2, 5, 7 (2 delegates), 9, 11: I think Federalists persuaded eight or more (perhaps eleven) of these to vote for or not to vote against the Constitution. All came from towns bordering Federalist concentrations near Portsmouth or in the Connecticut River valley.

[d] lines 3, 4, 7 (one delegate): Campaigners stirred up three new votes on each side and a town meeting replaced an Antifederalist on line 7 with a Federalist on line 3.

[e] lines 6 (one delegate), 7 (two delegates): These three may have skipped for personal reasons or they may have been cross-pressured and persuaded.

[f] lines 6 (one delegate), 8, 10: These seven delegates, while instructed against, voted for adjournment without violating instructions.

Some of these did not vote for personal reasons, but some were persuaded not to by political arguments. The net result of all this movement was a Federalist gain of one and an Antifederalist loss of three. So the Constitution passed 57 to 46 with four not voting.

Nevertheless, when the convention reassembled in June, the outcome was far from certain, at least from the viewpoint of the Federalist manager of the count, Pierce Long. Describing the situation to Paine Wingate, a New Hampshire delegate to Congress, Long characterized the debate as "dry arguments gone over again until both sides were quite tried [*sic*] out." So Federalists "determined to take the question — when we saw a probability of obtaining it — if by a majority of one only. . . . Accordingly though we could count but upon that number [that is, 54 out of 107] we took it, and to our surprise had a majority of eleven, three of the opposition were excused from voting and one left the house — and three or four whom we did not expect voted in favor."[5] (Daniell believes that three of the surprise votes were on line 11 of table 14.1. If so, they must not have been entirely a surprise because all three were from river towns in the Connecticut River valley and must have felt cross-pressured from Federalist domination in the area.)

In any event, in New Hampshire, as in Massachusetts, Federalists won after a setback by reason of superior rhetorical and heresthetical performance. As in Massachusetts, Federalists had the bulk of the experienced parliament men, and they were careful to keep control of the agenda, even when they did not necessarily have the votes. We know they did not win the election (because they had to adjourn), but we also know that they got a majority of votes in the convention. How did this happen? Their agenda control allowed them to keep the momentum and to clear the path for persuasion. And they were, as it turned out, successful persuaders.

What did they say to persuade? I cannot answer definitively because my sample ends on March 31. (We must await further volumes of commentaries on the Constitution.) But we know that the strongly Federalist *Hartford Courant* circulated widely in the state.[6] Furthermore, my sample does contain *Landholder X* and *XI*, which were addressed particularly to New Hampshire. Only two of the previous nine letters were reprinted at all in the state, but editors copied X and XI four and three times, respectively, out of five papers in the state. Only the writings of Washington, Franklin, and Wilson were copied as often. So New Hampshire editors must have thought these two Landholder essays relevant. In the tenth essay he warned the state against invasion from Canada, and in the eleventh he

5. Ibid., 139.
6. Robert Allen Rutland, *The Ordeal of the Constitution* (Norman: University of Oklahoma Press, 1966), 123.

promised the state greater benefits from forestry, fisheries, and national imposts. The potential for British invasion must have greatly concerned farmers in the northwest, which was almost unanimous for the Constitution, just as frontiersmen in Pennsylvania, Virginia, and Georgia were more Federal than frontiersmen in other backcountry areas. Similarly, the promise of fisheries and forestry must have appealed to the coastal area, which wanted such trade.

More important than these arguments, however, were the objective changes in the political situation between February and June, changes that fit into Federalist arguments and cut the ground from under Antifederalists. First, two additional states, Maryland and South Carolina, ratified in the interim. Thus New Hampshire, if it ratified, would be the definitive ninth. Furthermore, three states had yet to vote, so the Constitution looked like a winner. These facts were influential in Virginia, whose convention also met in June, and must have been influential in New Hampshire as well.

Second, the constitutional document had changed by June. After Massachusetts proposed recommendatory amendments, South Carolina did too. So the pattern of treating the process of ratification as a quasi open rule was then well established, even though Maryland ratified and refused to recommend amendments. So New Hampshire Federalists could win a few votes by recommending as well. The leading Antifederalist, Joshua Atherton, refused to consider recommendatory amendments. Clearly he belonged to group 6 or 7. But there were also some moderate opponents who would become Federalists in group 4 or 5 if they were given just a bit of encouragement. So the group 1 Federalists, the forty-five sure votes, offered the compromise. First, they modified the Massachusetts amendments in minor verbal ways. For example, the first Massachusetts amendment reads: "All Powers not expressly Delegated . . . are reserved to the several States"; New Hampshire's version says "expressly and particularly." Then, they added three more amendments to prohibit standing armies unless provided for by three-fourths of both houses, quartering of soldiers in private houses, laws about religion, and disarming of citizens. I can easily visualize the process by which these ad hoc, unrationalized words and sentences were added: The Federalist floor managers say to a wavering group 6 delegate, "What do you think we should add?" The waverer says, "Well, I'm not sure that 'expressly' is strong enough in the first one." So a manager replies, "Will you be satisfied if we add 'particularly'?" So "particularly" is added. My point is that the additions are not well thought out, but they make perfect sense as a set of ad hoc adjustments to win a few votes.

Though in the end the Federalist managers created a majority coalition, the four-month delay probably hurt the Federalist momentum. Federalist leaders tried hard to put the best possible face on adjournment: Langdon wrote to Rufus King (CC 554A),

> I am sorry to inform you that our Convention adjourned yesterday (to meet again in June next), without compleating the important business. ... [C]ontrary to the expectation of almost ev'ry man of reflection ... a majority appeared against the plan a great part of whom had positive Instructions to Vote against it. However, after spending ten days ... a number of opponents came to me, and said, they were convinced and should be very unhappy to Vote against the Constitution, which they (however absurd) must do, in case the question was called for. I therefore moved adjournment which was carried though much opposed by the other side. This question determined a majority in favor of the Constitution had it not been for their Instructions.

When the substance of this letter appeared in the Massachusetts *Centinel* (CC 554B) the editor explained that the adjournment allowed time to get instructions changed. Wherever this rationale was explained, Federalists seemed pretty confident of ultimate success.[7] But when they thought simply of delay without knowing about the justification, Federalists were depressed.[8] In the public press, however, Federalist confidence suppressed depression: confident accounts used 7,195 words, depressed accounts only 5,861 words. Because Antifederalists were not particularly jubilant, I am inclined to believe that the general public impression was one of confidence. Antifederalists devoted only 2,842 words to the subject, and those words were, mostly, more bitter than triumphant. I think the Federalists probably got their message across so that delay did not seriously slow down their momentum.

RHODE ISLAND: FEDERALIST SETBACK OR NONEVENT?

In the abstract, one might expect that Rhode Island's overwhelming defeat of the Constitution would have set the Federalists back, yet it probably had little effect on their momentum. The reason is fairly clear. As we have learned from the observation of presidential primary campaigns in our

7. See Knox to Washington, CC 610, in which Knox reports President Sullivan's assurance that the next session "will adopt ... by a majority of three to one"; Congressman John Brown (Va.) to James Breckenridge, CC 621; Rufus King to Tench Coxe, CC 623; Congressman Paine Wingate (N.H.) to Timothy Pickering, CC 653.

8. Madison to Randolph, CC 587; Cyrus Griffin to Thomas Fitzsimmons, RCS Va., 1: 453; Madison to Washington, RCS Va., 1:454, though Madison fully explained Langdon's rationale; Nicholas Gilman to John Sullivan, CC 637; Cyrus Griffin to Madison, CC 640. Kaminski and Saladino cite a number of similarly depressed Federalist letters, CC 4:183.

era, events that turn out about as expected do not change popular percep-
tions of the ultimate outcome.[9] On the whole, Federalists expected little
from Rhode Island. Early in October, William Ellery, a Rhode Island signer
of the Declaration of Independence, warned Postmaster Ebenezer Hazard
— and hence the New York and congressional center of Federalist communications — that Rhode Island would "stand out as long as it can; but if nine
States agree to it they will be compelled to come in" (CC 163). This view
spread quickly among Federalists. Between 14 October and 8 November
Madison wrote seven letters to Virginians appraising the chances for the
Constitution. In all of them he predicted that Rhode Island would resist
ratification.[10] Doubtless other congressmen and national leaders did the
same.

Newspaper squibs in my sample kept the public well informed. Denunciations of Rhode Island (#96251), all of which referred to the ratification
decision, accounted for 32,164 words (about 1 percent of the Federalist
campaign and all prior to the Rhode Island decision), and defenses of
Rhode Island by Antifederalists accounted for 2,959 words (only about
one-sixth of 1 percent of the Antifederalist campaign). All 35,123 words,
however, gave the public a clear expectation about Rhode Island's prospective decision.

The process went as follows: On November 3 the legislature rejected a
convention. Because this was prior to any other state convention, the rejection can be interpreted as an effort to defeat the proposed Constitution by
ignoring it. On March 1, however, after six ratifications and one adjournment, more positive action seemed necessary. So the legislature provided
for decision in the town meetings. Of course, this procedure violated the
provisions of the Constitution and the instructions of Congress, but passed
by 42 to 15, a harbinger of the probable outcome. The town meetings on
24 March rejected the Constitution 239 to 2,711. The actual preferences
were not quite so lopsided as this vote suggests because Federalists in
Providence and Newport, where they were probably the great majority,
boycotted the meeting — there were only 12 Federalist votes in both cities.
By contrast, 89 Federalist votes came from Bristol and Little Compton, the
two ratifying towns whose Federalists had not, apparently, heard about the
boycott. Of course, Federalists got a scattering elsewhere in the state. Nevertheless, the boycott was effective for it reduced the total vote by about
1,200 from the previous assembly election.[11] But, as in New Hampshire

9. Larry M. Bartels, *Presidential Primaries and the Dynamics of Public Choice* (Princeton:
Princeton University Press, 1988).

10. Robert Allen Rutland, *The Papers of James Madison* (Chicago: University of Chicago
Press, 1971), 10:194, 200, 216, 221, 224, 232, 244, 532.

11. Rutland, *Ordeal*, 126.

and Massachusetts, the urban seaports were Federalist while the rest of the state was, like central New Hampshire, a continuation, both geologically and ideologically, of Worcester county (Shays country) in Massachusetts.

After the election was over, Federalist Carrington wrote from New York to Madison in Virginia about the elections, "The business of the Constitution as referred to the Town meetings of Rhode Island, is over without producing any effect."[12] That, I believe, must be the interpretation today: Rhode Island's decision did not seriously harm the Federalists' momentum because everyone expected Rhode Island to be hostile.

FEDERALISM BACK ON TRACK:
MARYLAND AND SOUTH CAROLINA

From the point of view of campaign developments, very little happened in the Maryland and South Carolina conventions that had not previously been determined by the tastes of the voters whether from the campaign and ideological conviction or from local political interests. Of course, ratifications in these two states brought Federalists close to victory. But it was not the conventions that did it, so in this survey of heresthetical manipulation we can pass over them lightly.

In Maryland the candidates were all publicly committed during the campaign.[13] Except for the agriculturally poor counties at the upper bay, the Chesapeake country, both eastern and western shore, was pretty solidly Federalist. The people of Baltimore City, unlike those in the county but like those in all other urban places, were enthusiastically for the Constitution. The westerners, who shared agriculture, ideology, and fears of Indians with western Virginia, were also solidly Federalist. So it is not surprising that the Federalists elected 64 of the 76 delegates and ratified the Constitution 63–11 after a five-day convention. Antifederalists tried to recommend amendments; but they were too aggressive and so, by a vote of 47 to 26, Federalists adjourned without acting on them.

If New Hampshire and Rhode Island set Federalists back somewhat, Maryland more than made up for those delays. It was especially significant because Maryland's position was not well understood nationally. Luther Martin's writings and behavior at the Philadelphia convention gave the impression that Maryland was deeply divided. Thus when Maryland came through with about a six to one ratification it gave the Constitution a boost.

That boost can easily be seen in South Carolina. As I have already

12. Robert Allen Rutland, *The Papers of James Madison* (Charlottesville: University Press of Virginia, 1977), 11:30.

13. Norman A. Risjord, *Chesapeake Politics, 1781–1800* (New York: Columbia University Press, 1978), 288.

shown, its ratification was pretty much a sure thing because Federalists in the tidewater were overrepresented and the back country Antifederalists underrepresented. Group 1 and group 3 Federalists easily controlled the convention, ultimately ratifying by two to one. Big as the Federalist majority was, however, it clearly benefited from the new momentum generated in Maryland.

The debate began on 12 May. Federalists adopted a conciliatory stance. They allowed for detailed debate, and by Monday, 19 May, they had finished Article I. On that day came the news that Maryland had ratified on 26 April. The moderate Antifederalist floor leader, Peter Fayssoux, resigned his opposition (though he still voted nay). On Tuesday, 20 May, the convention debated Articles II through VII. On Wednesday, 21 May, Gen. Thomas Sumter, an Antifederal diehard, moved adjournment until October — typically a loser's desperate attempt to delay. It failed 89 to 135, perhaps a better indicator of sentiment than the final vote. On Thursday, 22 May, in a remarkable strategic move, the Federalist leader Edward Rutledge moved for recommendations of amendments. A committee of six Federalists and three Antifederalists met immediately, reported amendments — obviously already prepared — and the convention adopted them as recommendations to the new Congress. Three amendments moved by Antifederalists were rejected. On Friday, 23 May, the convention ratified 149–73.[14]

The most interesting feature of the South Carolina convention was its recommended amendments. All along amendments had been the Antifederalist device. In Massachusetts, when group 1 Federalists wanted compromise, they adopted a watered-down version of the Antifederalist proposal — ex post amendments rather than ex ante ones. Thus, in Massachusetts, amendments, even if only recommendatory, were understood to be of Antifederal origin. But in South Carolina the amendments were strictly Federal. Although they may have increased the Federal majority by fourteen votes, this was surely not the purpose. Almost all the Federalists were members of groups 1 or 3. Unlike Massachusetts Federalists, they did not need to attract groups 4 and 5. Instead, the South Carolina Federalists treated the amendments as a grand conciliatory gesture. They actually proposed significant constitutional changes: returning to the method of requisitions and providing state control of national elections. Nevertheless, as I will show later, South Carolina trivialized the notion of amendments, transforming them from a genuine compromise to a sop to losers.

14. For the clearest and most detailed account of this convention, see Evelyn Fink, "Political Rhetoric and Strategic Choice on the Ratification Conventions on the U.S. Constitution" (Diss., University of Rochester Library, 1987), 173–239.

15

Virginia and the Failure of Antifederalism

THE LEADING Antifederalists in Virginia, Richard Henry Lee, Patrick Henry, and George Mason, thought they could stop the Constitution there. But Federalists had the momentum and they controlled the national agenda. And in Virginia, they had the votes. There was nothing Antifederalists could do about that. Antifederalists might have had some chance to stop the Constitution if they had controlled the agenda. But to wrest control of the agenda from the Federalists they would have had to win the elections in 1787 and the spring of 1788, and that they could not do. The best that Antifederalists could hope for, therefore, was to break the Federalists' momentum. But Federalists could use their momentum to keep things moving and, of course, that is exactly what they did.

The Federalists' control of the national agenda consisted mainly of the dispatch of the Constitution from the convention, through Congress, to the states. States under Federalist control of course acted quickly to start the ratification process. Consequently, no matter when or where Antifederalists intervened, they would be late — usually, as it turned out, far too late. There is no better example of ill-timed delay than the process in Virginia, which, along with New York, was the Antifederalists' best hope for twisting the agenda in their favor.

Virginia, like most other states, considered the convention call in October 1787. As usual, Federalists pushed for an early convention.[1] This turned out to be impossible. The main issue on 25 October was whether to authorize the convention to propose amendments. The compromise was to call the convention for "full and free" discussion, which, without men-

---

1. Kaminski and Saladino print instructions from four places for a convention "immediately": Alexandria, Fredericksburg, Frederick County, and Petersburg (RCS Va., 1:23, 85, 91–92, 96–97).

tioning amendments, was understood to authorize them (RCS Va., 1:111–20). Finding the legislature closely divided, Federalists apparently hesitated to dispute other issues and so accepted a convention on 2 June. James Monroe, by then an open Antifederalist, explained the rationale to Madison: "The object in the postponement of . . . our Convention to so late a day was to furnish an evidence of the disposition of the other States. . . . If they or many of them were agnst. it our State might mediate between contending parties & lead the way to an union more palatable to all" (RCS Va., 1:354–55). Delay coupled with the ultimate hope of revision is a good strategy only if many states were in fact against it. Simple delay without other plans was not enough, though I doubt that Antifederalists could have carried any more hostile provisions through the legislature in October. As it was, Federalists simply conceded the point, accepting 2 June in spite of contrary instructions because, according to a Federalist member, they were "willing to delay it 'to see what other states would do' " (RCS Va., 1:123).

Of course, a late convention implies, by Monroe's rationale, that Antifederalists would organize immediately to bring other states into their coalition and to act in concert. This they did not do. But by December, Antifederalists apparently felt stronger. Seizing the occasion of a bill to pay delegates, they moved appropriations for, among other things, deputies to confer with other states and a second federal convention to consider amendments. Naturally Federalists resisted, and the bill as finally passed (12 December) appropriated simply for Virginia delegates to communicate with other conventions "which may be then met." This was, of course, a clear invitation for others to use Virginia's timetable, and on 27 December the legislature instructed the governor to forward the act to other state executives. This he apparently did on the same day (RCS Va., 1:189–93). So, by the end of December, Antifederalists had acted to generate national cooperation on their side. But Federalists had a three-month head start.

The Virginia Antifederalists' gambit was too late for five states that ratified by 9 January and for four more states whose conventions had already been set. The gambit could, in fact, influence only South Carolina and New York. But South Carolina called its convention on 19 January, and it would have been indifferent to Virginia's proposal anyway. This meant that Virginia could influence only New York, which was already half Antifederalist. All other state executives received their letters from Randolph by 22 January, but Gov. George Clinton in New York did not receive his until 7 March. New York had set its convention for 1 February. So Patrick Henry's initiative really had no effect (RCS Va., 2:788–93).

Why did Clinton receive his letter so late? Clinton complained to Randolph on 8 May, and Randolph unsuccessfully attempted from August to October to prove that he had dispatched the letter on 27 December. It is reasonable to believe Randolph's protestation because in December he was still in favor of amendments. The alternative is that the post office mishandled the letter, an explanation that would appeal to Antifederalists, even if the mishandling were not malicious. The reason for the delay remains a mystery, but the consequences are clear: It delayed cooperation between Antifederalists in Virginia and New York by another four months, by which time seven states had ratified and another was soon to do so.

However blameless Randolph may have been — from an Antifederal point of view — in sending out the act of 12 December, he worked against Antifederalists in his next contact with New Yorkers. Clinton wrote to Randolph on 8 May to stress the need for communication. Acting now clearly in the Federal interest, Randolph sat on that letter, not revealing it until it was too late to affect the Virginia ratification on 25 June. Earlier, Randolph had written to Madison that he would wait at least until Maryland decided before deciding himself whether to press for prior amendments or immediate ratification (RCS Va., 2:741). Maryland ratified on 27 April, and Randolph would certainly have known about that before Clinton wrote his letter. (Randolph announced for immediate ratification on 4 June; RCS Va., 2:936.) When he received Clinton's letter, he consulted his council, which advised him that it was a public, not private, letter. So he could justify saving it for the next meeting of the legislature, which met in special session on 23 June. He submitted it then, and it was read on 26 June, the day after the convention, sitting in the same town, had ratified. Naturally, when Antifederalists discovered this deliberate delay, they were furious. Two days later George Mason drafted resolutions to provide for an *elected* committee of the legislature to interrogate Randolph about the reasons for concealing the letter (RCS Va., 2:788–93). But ten states had ratified — nine that Mason knew about. So nothing came of his draft, probably because it would have served no public purpose other than to exact revenge.

This incident is perhaps trivial — even having received Clinton's letter Virginia would probably have ratified. But it does reveal the large Federalist advantage in controlling the agenda. Not only were eight — nearly nine — ratifications in hand before Antifederalists attempted to wrest control of the agenda, but an Antifederalist public official with crucial authority to trip them up had, by reason of this very fact, turned up in group 4 as a Federalist.

New York Antifederalists tried one last time to reach Virginia Antifederalists before ratification. The Federal Republican Committee, led by John Lamb, the state collector of customs, had been active all year in distributing Antifederal literature. In mid-May Lamb wrote letters to prominent Antifederalists in several states between the Virginia, New Hampshire, and New York conventions to seek their cooperation in forcing amendments. Because Antifederalists distrusted the post office, Lamb sent his letters to Mason, Henry, and William Grayson by Eleazar Oswald, the editor of the *Philadelphia Independent Gazetteer* (which published Centinel and Philadelphiensis). Oswald arrived in Richmond on 7 June and was back in New York by 16 June with the proposal that New York take the lead in appointing a delegation to meet with Virginia. But, of course, Virginia had ratified before Clinton could inform Virginians of New York's proposed amendments. Another instance of concrete Antifederalist action coming far too late.

What made Virginia Antifederalists reluctant to agree to immediate and decisive action was that they did not control the Virginia convention. The elections probably produced a small Federalist majority, though it was not large enough to instill Federalist confidence or Antifederalist despair. Madison believed that the convention debates did not alter the election results. On 20 June he wrote to his father, "It is not probable that many proselytes will be made on either side," and on 22 June, when debates were nearly over, he wrote to Rufus King, "The attack has apparently been less formidable than I apprehended. Independently of some particular interests, the objections against it have not been calculated in my opinion to make any deep impressions."[2] Of course, part of the reason was Madison's own activity. Although he made fewer long, flourishing speeches than Patrick Henry, Madison was constantly engaged in damage control and was on his feet sixty times as against Henry's thirty-eight. Nonetheless, to this reader of the Virginia debates, Madison's judgment rings true. Each side had fine debaters (for the Federalists: Madison, George Nicholas, Randolph, Edmund Pendleton, Henry Lee, John Marshall; for the Antifederalists: Henry, Mason, William Grayson, James Monroe). In a sense, therefore, they canceled each other out. No argument went unanswered, so no argument could indisputably persuade.

If Madison's judgment is correct, the outcome in Virginia was decided at the polls in March, not at the convention in June. In this respect, then, the Virginia campaign and convention differ from those in Massachusetts and New Hampshire and instead parallel those in Delaware, Pennsylvania, New Jersey, Georgia, Connecticut, Maryland, and South Carolina, where the elections, not the conventions, were decisive.

There are several calculations of how the elections turned out. The

2. Robert Allen Rutland, *The Papers of James Madison* (Chicago: University of Chicago Press, 1971), 11:158, 167.

Table 15.1   Reconciliation of Henley List Predictions with Vote on Ratification in the Virginia Convention

	Federalist	Antifederalist	Doubtful	Unfilled
Henley List Predictions	85	66	3	16
Absent (paired?)	−1	–	–	−1
Doubtful	+1	+2	−3	
Unfilled Seats on Henley List				
Kentucky	+2	+7		−9
Northwest	+4	+0		−4
Southwest	+0	+2		−2
Errors				
Wrong Winners Listed	−2	+2		
Wrong Predictions				
Listed F, voted AF	−3	+3		
Listed AF, voted F	+3	−3		
Vote on Ratification	89	79	0	0

Source: F. Claiborne Johnston, Jr., ed., "Federalist, Doubtful, and Antifederalist: A Note on the Virginia Convention of 1788," *The Virginia Magazine of History and Biography,* Vol. 96 (1988), pp. 333–44.

most impressive is in a letter by David Henley, a New York lawyer who was a frequent visitor to Virginia as a commissioner to settle some of its claims against the United States. Henley received a list predicting how the convention delegates would vote on the Constitution from a Virginia source, copied it, and forwarded it to his father in Boston, where it was preserved. The source of the list is unknown, though F. Claiborne Johnston speculates that it may have been compiled by George Nicholas, a Federalist delegate from the Shenandoah Valley whom Madison described to Washington as "among the best judges" of election returns.[3]

Wherever the Henley list came from, it is surprisingly accurate. In table 15.1 I have reconciled the list with the actual outcome. There are 8 actual errors out of 151 predictions, which is about 5 percent — as good as most survey research today. This high degree of accuracy means that the positions of the candidates were well known, not just in their home counties, but to good political managers throughout the state. Consequently, the decision on the Constitution must have been made by the voters in the election choosing delegates with well-known intentions, and not by the delegates themselves in the convention.

3. F. Claiborne Johnston, Jr., ed., "Federalist, Doubtful, and Antifederalist: A Note on the Virginia Convention of 1788," *Virginia Magazine of History and Biography* 96 (1988): 333–44. Rutland, *Papers of Madison,* 11:20.

In spite of the accuracy of knowledge about the election, during most of the convention the managers on both sides were uncertain about the outcome. In table 15.2 I have compiled all of Madison's known estimates of the outcome. Note that from 4 June, two days after the convention opened, to 11 June Madison was pretty confident. This reflects, I suppose, his reading of a list like that in Henley's letter. But Henley had not predicted Kentucky and western counties, where the vote was late to come in. When the vote did come in, most of Kentucky (except for the Louisville area) went Antifederalist, and this bloc must have worried Madison very much. By 18 June, however, he was more confident. He did not mention Kentucky, and he spoke of a "3, 4, or 5 or 6" Federal majority. On 19 June, Archibald Stuart, an active Federalist delegate from the Shenandoah Valley, estimated "82 members unmovably fixed for it, 12 doubtful and the balance against as unmovable." Stuart went on to list six of the doubtfuls — all of whom voted Federalist — and said, "Any three [of these six] will give us a majority."[4] Three of those on his doubtful list were Kentuckians, and the previous day William Grayson, an Antifederalist manager, had conceded them. Grayson wrote, "We have got 80 . . . inflexible, and eight persons . . . fluctuating" and included "ten out of thirteen Kentucky members, but we wanted the whole."[5] Having the Stuart list and perhaps knowledge about Kentucky, Madison was certainly justified in regaining confidence. On 23 June, however, he was absolutely confident. On the twenty-second he was pushing his majority to five or six in a letter to Rufus King, but on the twenty-third he had the evidence of seeing and hearing Mason's despair, which told him, of course, that their count agreed with his. So it seems clear that the head count, almost finished before the convention began, was absolutely certain two days before the final vote.

On this analysis, it seems that the main purpose served by the convention was not to examine or persuade but to count the votes as determined by the local elections. Of course, it is possible that some were persuaded by events in the local campaigns; but even this is not likely. Kaminski and Saladino collected some detail on local elections in thirty-four counties (sixty-eight delegates), and of these there is some evidence about the party attachment of sixty, about 88 percent. In short, in these sixty cases, and perhaps the remainder, the voters knew exactly what they were doing. It was they, not the delegates, who made the choice.

The issue of whether voters or delegates made the decision is interesting because it touches on the subject of how many delegates were in

4. Johnston, "Federalist, Doubtful, and Antifederalist," 334.
5. Ibid.

Table 15.2   Madison's Reports of Federalist Votes, 4 June to 25 June

4 June (to Rufus King): "The Govr. has declared the day of previous amendments past, and thrown himself fully into our scale. . . .[t]he federal party are apparently in the best of spirits. There is reason to believe nevertheless that the majority will be but small, & may possibly be yet defeated" (XI, 76).

4 June (to Washington): "The federalists are a good deal elated. . . .I dare not speak with certainty as to the decision. Kentucke has been extremely tainted" (XI,77).

9 June (to Hamilton): ". . .The chance at present seems to be in our favor. . ." (XI, 101).

9 June (to King): "I think we have a majority as yet, but the other party are ingenious. . ." (XI, 102).

11 June (to Tench Coxe): "The parties are pretty nicely balanced and pretend each to be sanguine of victory. I think the majority has been as yet in favor. . . ." (XI, 102).

13 June (to King): "The issue. . .is more doubtful than. . .when I last wrote. . . [T]he vote of Kentucky will turn the scale. . . .the majority on either side will be small and at present the event is as ticklish as can be conceived" (XI, 133).

13 June (to Washington): "Appearances at present are less favorable. . . .British debts, the Indiana claim, and the Mississippi. are the principal topics of private discussion and intrigue. . . .[T]he event may depend on Kentucky members; who seem to lean more against. . ." (XI, 134).

16 June (to Hamilton): "The parties continue to be nicely balanced. If we have a majority at all it does not exceed three or four. . . . If we lose it Kentucke will be the cause. . . ." (XI, 144).

18 June (to Tench Coxe): "Each hopes for victory. There will not probably be half a dozen for a majority on either side. I hope and think that if no accident happens the Constitution will carry. . . (XI, 151).

18 June (to King): "There is not a majority of more than three or four on either side. Both sides claim it. I think however it rather lies as yet in favor. . ." (XI, 152).

18 June (to Washington): ". . .The majority on either side will not exceed more than 3,4, or 5 or 6. I indulge a belief that. . .the Constitution [has] the advantage. . ." (XI, 151-52).

20 June (to Hamilton): "At present It is calculated that we still retain a majority of 3 or 4. . ." (XI, 157).

20 June (to James Madison, Sr.): "The calculations on different sides do not accord. . . .[T]he friends of the Constitution are most confident. . .3 or 4 or possibly more" (XI, 157).

22 June (to Hamilton): ". . . success by 3 or 4, or possibly 5 or 6. . ." (XI, 166).

Table 15.2   Continued

---

22 June (to King): ". . .a majority of 3 or 4, possibly of 5 or 6. . ." (XI, 167).

23 June (to Washington): "Tomorrow some proposition for closing the business will be made. . . .The opposition will urge previous amendments. Their conversation today seemed to betray despair. Col. Mason in particular talked in a style which no other sentiment could have produced. He held out the idea of civil commotions. . . .We calculate on a majority, but a bare one" (XL, 168).

24 June (to Ambrose Madison, his younger brother): "I do not know that either party despairs absolutely. The friends of the Government seem to be in the best spirits. . ." (XI, 170).

25 June (to Hamilton?): ". . .ratified by 89 ays agst 79 noes. . ." (XI, 177).

25 June (to King): ". . .89 ays to 79 noes. . ." (XI, 178).

25 June (to Washington): "On the question today for *previous* amendments the votes stood 80 ays - 88 noes - on the final question the ratification passed 89 ays - 79 noes. . ." (XI, 178).

Source: Rutland, *Madison,* vol. 11.

groups 4 and 5. Most delegates who voted for the Constitution were clearly in group 1 or 3, committed Federalists — but some were not. Randolph, for example, whose fence sitting was tolerated by his electors, was in group 6 until persuaded before the convention (presumably by the Maryland outcome) to become a group 4 Federalist — much like Hancock. How many others were like him? One way of looking at this question is through the votes on proposed amendments.

The test vote on the Constitution was a motion for referring amendments to other states before ratification, a motion that failed 80 to 88. On the motion to ratify one delegate changed sides, bringing the vote to 79 to 89. This delegate, David Patteson, seems to me to belong to group 5.

After the Constitution was ratified, a committee reported a number of amendments to be recommended, namely, a bill of rights with twenty paragraphs and twenty substantive amendments. The Federalists made a stand against one amendment that permitted states to collect excises if they wished. On the motion to delete that article, the vote was Yea 65 to Nay 80, so it was not struck out. The delegates who changed sides between the votes on ratification and on the proposed deletion are likely candidates, I believe, for identification with groups 4 or 5. In table 15.3 I have reconciled these votes, showing that thirteen persons changed sides. (I suspect that many of the absentees were paired, though one or two may have been trying to avoid revealing their positions.) Of these thirteen,

Table 15.3   Reconciliation of Votes on Ratification and on the Motion to
Delete Article 3 of the Recommended Amendments

	Yea	Nay
On Constitution	89	79
Absent on Motion to Delete	−11	−12
Shifted Yea to Nay	−13	+13
On Motion to Delete	65	80

Patteson is listed as doubtful in Henley's letter, and he also shifted from
favoring prior amendments to favoring ratification. Two more are on
Stuart's list of doubtfuls: Paul Carrington, the state chief justice, and William Fleming (Boutetourt County). According to Hugh Blair Grigsby, the
voters instructed Fleming to vote for the Constitution, but he apparently
voted his own tastes on the amendment (RCS Va., 2:573–74).[6] Finally, William McKee (Rockbridge County), whom Henley (and presumably Stuart)
counted as Federalist, was, again according to Grigsby, instructed against
the Constitution and then, presumably, broke ranks on the amendment.[7]

The remaining delegates who switched were all strong Federalists from
the tidewater areas, and their actions thus appear to be more a matter of
conciliation than conviction. Still, with Randolph, the four nontidewater
switchers would have been enough to cause a tie in the convention, 84 to
84, in which case the Constitution would have failed. So I think group 4
was large enough in Virginia to be essential to the victory of the Constitution. Virginians probably also contributed to the trivialization of the idea
of amendments because they proposed twenty items for a bill of rights and
twenty substantive amendments.

6. *The History of the Federal Convention of 1788* (repr. New York: Da Capo Press, 1969),
2:13–14. Originally published in *Collections of the Virginia Historical Society,* 1891.

7. Grigsby, *History of the Federal Convention* 1:340, 347. Grigsby cites no source for this
assertion, and Kaminski and Saladino say nothing of it in their comments on the Rockbridge
election (RCS Va., 2:609). But Grigsby asserts in detail that the other delegate, Andrew
Moore, consciously disobeyed instructions, returned and explained, and triumphantly won
reelection to the legislature against the same Antifederalist he had opposed in the election
for the convention. This suggests that the less well-known delegate, McKee, sought a compromise with the electors: after disobeying instructions (perhaps), he voted according to their
tastes for the proposed amendment.

16

New York: Federalists Outflank Antifederalists

NEW YORK WAS THE ELEVENTH PILLAR, the last state to ratify in 1788. New York's ratification was, however, extremely difficult, and it seems likely that, in the absence of recommendatory amendments, New York would have held out for a second convention. Whether it could have obtained one is, of course, unknowable. If a second convention had been held, we also do not know what states, if any, would have attended. And if the second convention had not been held and if New York had not ratified, we cannot even guess what the transactions between New York and the Union would have been. Still, without knowing the answer to these conditionals, we can be certain that without New York, the path of the Constitution would have been rockier. So the fact that the Federalists were able to agree to recommendatory amendments is important for the Constitution, even though more than the required number of states had ratified before New York.

Like the Federalists in Virginia, those in New York were able to force unconditional ratification by reason of their control of the agenda, and the significant features of that control again were the requirement of nine rather than thirteen ratifications to begin operations, the speed with which Federalists carried through the first six ratifications, and the change from a closed to an open rule. Almost up to the end of the convention Antifederal leaders apparently believed that, even if they ratified only conditionally, they would still be allowed to participate in the new government. On 17 July, Governor Clinton, speaking in favor of ratification conditional on the new government starting a process of amendment, rather plaintively asserted, "Congress may without a violation of the Constitution, receive the states in terms of the ratification proposed into the union."[1] Even at that late date, only nine days before ratification, the Antifederal leader

1. Herbert J. Storing, *The Complete Anti-Federalist* (Chicago: University of Chicago Press, 1981), 6:187–88.

did not seem to comprehend the significance of the Federalists' control of the agenda — that they could operate a government without Rhode Island and New York. But in fact, the Federalists, through good planning, needed only nine states, and, through efficient operation, they obtained seven ratifications easily and three more by changing the rule. So it was indeed true that the Federalists could exclude New York, and when Antifederalists finally understood that fact they ratified promptly. Had they not continued to control the agenda, Federalists would have failed, I think, to obtain this and several other ratifications.

What makes the Federalist achievement in New York so impressive is that they did not have electoral control either in the state government or in the convention. Their victory was achieved by means of heresthetical maneuver.

Of the twelve states that called conventions, New York was the last to call and the next to last to meet. Unlike the governors of other states without fall legislative sessions, Governor Clinton did not call a special session to plan a convention. Undoubtedly his delay was motivated by partisanship. When the legislature did finally assemble on 17 January, it delayed action until 1 February and set the convention for 17 June, later than any other state except North Carolina. Because four and a half months is perhaps not excessive for a campaign in a large state, most of the credit for the delay can be attributed to Clinton's action.

In the legislature, both sides were apparently willing to delay. Both houses were closely divided, so both parties believed they needed time for persuasion. In addition, the Federalists probably believed their position would be stronger with each subsequent ratification, and the Antifederalists probably believed that they might, as on the impost of 1783, find another large state to join them in rejection. But the Federalists did have a slight majority in both houses — on key votes the assembly divided 27–25 and the senate 10–9. Consequently the Federalists were able to wrest three advantages in the call: there was never a question, as in Rhode Island, of no convention at all; the Antifederalists failed to attach either specific permission for the convention to amend or a statement that the Philadelphia convention exceeded its authority; and the Federalists attached a provision for adult male suffrage, the first democratic rule on the continent. Because the city favored the Constitution and because most men without freeholds were urban mechanics, this provision aided the cause of the Constitution. According to John Kaminski, Antifederalists were uneasy, but found themselves sandbagged.[2]

2. "New York: The Reluctant Pillar," in Stephen L. Schecter, ed., *The Reluctant Pillar: New York and the Adoption of the Federal Constitution* (Troy, N.Y.: Russell Sage College, 1985), 75.

The delegate election campaign in New York lasted three months and, according to Kaminski, was the most furious of any state.[3] The outcome was a huge victory for Antifederalists, who obtained 70 percent of the seats and probably about 55 percent of the citizens' votes. The Federalists carried only New York, Kings (Brooklyn), Richmond (Staten Island), and Westchester counties, roughly a circle around the city. Antifederalists carried all of upstate and most of Long Island. So when the convention met on 17 June, the Antifederalists could reasonably expect victory for whatever they wanted. Furthermore, unlike the Massachusetts Antifederalists, who also won their election, the New Yorkers had plenty of experienced leaders: Clinton, Lansing, Melancton Smith. Of course, the Federalists did too: Hamilton, Jay, Chancellor R. R. Livingston. But this matching of abilities precluded a Federalist rhetorical success comparable to the one enjoyed in Massachusetts.

Nevertheless, the Federalists won: they obtained unconditional ratification. Of course, they conceded recommendatory amendments, as they had elsewhere. Even more, they conceded a "circular letter" inviting other states to a second convention; but because ten states had either Federalist majorities or blocking strength, this concession turned out to be trivial. So the interesting question about New York is how the Federalist minority was able to win. Victory came about through a combination of Federalist agenda control and ineffective Antifederalist strategy.

The fatal defect of Antifederalists' strategy in New York was to delay to the end of the process. Their gamble was as follows: If Virginia rejected or required conditions, then New York could do the same, and these two states would separate the ratifiers into geographic thirds, a development that would doubtless be enough to force considerable revision. If Virginia ratified, on the other hand, New York would have to go it alone. A priori, this might appear at least a fifty-fifty chance. But coordination with Virginia could perhaps improve the chance to, say, 75 to 25. And, of course, the same proposition holds for Virginia. But neither cluster of Antifederalists sought to improve its chances. Moreover, the New York Antifederalists did not recognize until too late that, as the last major convention, they held a different place on the agenda from Virginia. In the end, New York Antifederalists really had less than an even chance with their strategy, and they took only a toddler's steps to improve it.

By contrast, Federalists had had a clear strategy ever since September.

3. Ibid., 77; John P. Kaminski, "New York: Adjusting to Circumstances: New York's Relationship with the Federal Government, 1776–1788" in Patrick T. Conley and John P. Kaminski, *The Constitution and the States: The Role of the Original Thirteen in the Framing and Adoption of the Federal Constitution* (Madison: Madison House, 1988), 241.

They hurried ratifications so that by the time the Virginia and New York conventions came around, they were nearly home. Publicly they made much of their victories. As pointed out earlier, about 20 percent of the Federalist campaign consisted of celebration of victory. Privately, the Federalist leaders coordinated and kept in close touch with each other. One great Federalist advantage was that Congress, sitting in New York, was predominantly Federalist, and congressmen like King, Madison, Hamilton, and Carrington as well as national officials like Jay and Knox served as a communications center. Antifederalists had Nathan Dane as well as the state impost collector, John Lamb; but they were not good correspondents. Outside New York, Gerry and Mason communicated some with other Antifederalists, but together they did not compare with Washington, who was himself another Federalist communications center in Virginia. Of course each campaign and convention were locally run, but Federalists explained their strategies to each other and thus enabled other states to consider similar ones. (Steven Boyd argues that the Antifederalists also had a network. This is true, but theirs was pretty skimpy compared with the Federalist one.)[4]

At the beginning of the convention, the Federalists again had better detailed strategies. As a first stage, they intended to spin out the convention until New Hampshire and Virginia acted. They hoped, of course, that both would soon do so, and, by reason of their good communications, they were pretty sure of New Hampshire. Hamilton and King arranged for a swift courier to bring the New Hampshire results.[5] As their second stage, they intended to use the nine or perhaps ten ratifications they had in hand as leverage to split the Antifederal party. The weak point of the Federalist plan was Virginia's ratification, but, again because of good communications, they had reason to be confident about that.

As for the detailed Antifederal strategies, most delegates probably wanted to temporize. This was how they had defeated the impost of 1783. Most agreed that the Articles should be strengthened, so the best delaying device was to attach conditional amendments. However, they had not thought out what to do if New Hampshire and Virginia both ratified and New York did not. Most apparently assumed that they would continue to sit in Congress, just as, for example, Maryland had sat in the Continental Congress during the time it refused to ratify the Articles. But they had no plan for the contingency that the Federalists, but not they, knew to be

4. *The Politics of Opposition: Antifederalists and the Acceptance of the Constitution* (Millwood: KTO Press, 1979).

5. Harold C. Syrett, ed., *The Papers of Alexander Hamilton*, vol. 5 (New York: Columbia University Press, 1962), 5:2, 5.

Table 16.1   Hamilton's Judgment of Federalist Chances, 8 June to 24 July 1788, in Letters to Madison

8 June ". . .the more I can penetrate the view of the Antifederal party in this state, the more I dread the non-adoption of the Constitution by any of the other states, the more I fear an eventual disunion and civil war"

19 June "It is not easy to conjecture what will be the result. Our adversaries greatly outnumber us. . .So far the thing is not to be despaired of. A happy issue with you must have considerable influence with us"

27 June ". . .slight symptoms of relaxation in some of the [i.e. Antifederal] leaders. . .Our arguments confound but do not convince"

2 July "Some of the leaders appear to me to be convinced *by circumstances*. . ."

8 July "We have good reason to believe our opponents are not agreed, and this affords some ground of hope"

19 July ". . .the footing [i.e., ratification conditional, not on amendments, but on an amending process] is the best on which it can be placed; but everything possible will yet be attempted to [obtain] . . .an unqualified ratification. Let me know your idea of the possibility of our being *received* [i.e., into the union] on that plan.

22 July ". . .there is so great a diversity in the views of our opponents it is impossible to predict anything. Upon the whole however our fears diminish"

Source: Harold C. Syrett, ed., *The Papers of Alexander Hamilton* (New York: Columbia University Press, vol. 5, 1962), 3, 10, 91, 141, 147, 177, 187.

highly likely. When this contingency occurred, Antifederalists were forced to concede.

That the Federalist strategy was effective throughout can be seen easily in table 16.1. Note that before the convention began on 17 June, Hamilton was very gloomy. But things looked a bit better to him as soon as the convention began. Ten days later (after New Hampshire) he seemed to see some gains, and his confidence increased on 2 and 8 July (after Virginia). On 19 July he was ready to compromise, which is, actually, an improvement because earlier no such possibility was apparent. And by 22 July, he sensed real victory. So on the whole I think the Federalist strategy worked well throughout the convention.

To implement the first phase of the Federalist strategy Chancellor Livingston began by moving, as had his counterparts in Massachusetts and Virginia, for reading by clauses with no votes until the end of the reading. The Antifederalists agreed, thereby guaranteeing several weeks of debate, by which time news from New Hampshire and Virginia had arrived. Although Antifederalists had the votes to act immediately on ratification and amendments (as had Federalists in Maryland), they supported Livingston's motion. Antifederalists outside were worried by this decision; Yates explained it to George Mason in response to the Lamb-Oswald letter: "We yielded . . . provided that . . . we should suggest amendments . . . we deemed necessary . . . — Fully relying on the Steadiness of our Friends."[6] Of course, Yates's friends were not as steady as he supposed.

With these parameters established, the debates were politically insignificant, however rhetorically grand they might have been. Both sides had good debaters and good floor managers to keep their troops in line. Hamilton reported (2 July), "Our arguments confound but do not convince."[7] However, the debate did allow time, as was probably intended, for Antifederalists to assemble amendments and for Federalists to await decisions from elsewhere.

When the news from New Hampshire arrived on 24 June, Federalists rejoiced, but to their surprise Antifederalists seemed indifferent. Chancellor Livingston explained on 25 June, "The circumstances . . . were greatly altered, and the ground of . . . debate changed. The Confederation was now dissolved."[8] But Melancton Smith replied that the change "had not altered his feelings. . . . He had long been convinced nine states would receive the Constitution," and Lansing rather cavalierly proclaimed, "Since nine states have acceded to it, let them make the experiment."[9] Indeed, it was official Antifederalist policy: in the letter from Yates to Mason, Yates, the elected Antifederalist floor leader, asserted, "You may rely on our fixed Determination that we shall not adopt the present constitution without previous Amendments."[10] So the debate continued.

When the news came from Virginia on 2 July, Antifederalists again appeared unperturbed — though Hamilton sensed some worries (see table 16.1). Antifederalists continued to offer and debate amendments. But Federalists suddenly fell silent. Nathaniel Lawrence, an Antifederalist who finally voted for the Constitution, was puzzled: "The information from Virginia seems to have no effect on *us,* tho' it has on the other party. . . . [T]hey have disputed every inch . . . but to day they have quietly suffered us to propose our amendments without a word in opposition to them. What

6. Robert A. Rutland, *The Papers of George Mason*, 3 vols. (Chapel Hill: University of North Carolina Press, 1970), 3:1111–12.

7. Syrett, *Papers of Hamilton* 5:141.

8. Jonathan Elliot, *The Debates in the Several Conventions on the Adoption of the Federal Constitution as Recommended by the General Convention at Philadelphia in 1787*, 5 vols. (Philadelphia: J. B. Lippincott, 1836), 2:222.

9. Ibid., 2:324–25.

10. Rutland, *Papers of Mason*, 3:1111–12.

their object is I know not."[11] In spite of Lawrence's confusion and his apparent incomprehension of the effect of Virginia, it seems clear that Federalists now had simply to let the significance of Virginia sink in, as ultimately it did, even to Lawrence.

The second phase of Federalist strategy was to use the other ratifications to split the Antifederalists. To moderate Antifederalists they urged that any conditions were unacceptable, while themselves offering modest concessions. Moderates wavered, offered several formulas of their own, all of which Federalists rejected, though they seriously considered one. In the end the moderates voted to ratify, just as moderates elsewhere had. This is an instance of a fundamental heresthetical maneuver of changing the grounds of decision by introducing a new dimension of discussion.[12] Most of the real action in the New York convention centers on this heresthetic, the success of which reveals the real genius of Hamilton and Jay as politicians.

The play of motion and countermotion from 10 to 26 July began with the Antifederalists' initial plan, produced after two days of caucusing and introduced by Lansing on 10 July. It provided three kinds of amendments to be adopted prior to ratification: explanatory (for example, a bill of rights), conditional, and recommendatory (that is, amendments to be considered after ratification).[13] The conditional amendments provided that until a general convention considered New York proposals, Congress could not (1) call New York militia out of state for more than six weeks without its legislature's consent, (2) regulate federal elections in New York, or (3) collect taxes in New York without first requisitioning so that the legislature could provide, if it chose, for state taxes to pay the requisition.[14] The Antifederalists regarded this plan as a magnanimous concession that Federalists, as a minority, should be happy to accept. Of course, Antifederalists had totally failed to understand the actual position they were in. They thought that because they had won the state election they were entitled to pass whatever motions they wanted. They seemed totally unaware that they also had to deal with another body: the new government of the ten ratifying states.

Federalists responded the next day with their alternative: uncondi-

---

11. Cited in Linda Grant De Pauw, *The Eleventh Pillar: New York State and the Federal Constitution* (Ithaca: Cornell University Press, 1966), 216.

12. William H. Riker, *The Art of Political Manipulation* (New Haven: Yale University Press, 1986).

13. Elliot, *Debates,* 2:410.

14. Kaminski, "New York: Reluctant Pillar," 108.

tional ratification, with all amendments recommendatory.[15] Jay pointed out that, unless New York joined (that is, ratified unconditionally), it could have no part in the new government: "These are not threats. This is prudence."[16] This Federalist response began to frighten moderate Antifederalists, those who would ultimately end up in group 5. They had, it seems, not realized up to this point that they might be excluded. The formal break appeared on 15 July—though Linda Grant De Pauw cites evidence that Samuel Jones (Queens) was wavering on 14 July.[17] On the fifteenth, however, Hamilton and Jay moved to add specific recommended amendments to Jay's original Federalist motion. This was an attempt at accommodation in the sense that Federalists agreed to specify defects in the Constitution. Jay explained, "We honestly think Congress must reject such [a conditional] Adoption."[18] Instead Melancton Smith responded by moving Lansing's earlier proposals of 10 July, not, however, as amendments that had to be made *prior* to New York's entry, but rather as amendments to be made *subsequent* to New York's entry by a constitutional convention to be called as soon as the new government started. Smith pointed out that these conditions affected only New York and were not, as Jay and Hamilton alleged, an attempt to dictate to other states. Although Clinton probably despised this change from conditions prior to conditions subsequent, he supported Smith vigorously and argued (as already quoted) that Congress could admit New York, and only political expediency would keep it from doing so. Would not, he asked, the other states rather have New York on this basis than have New York reject the Constitution?[19]

Evelyn Fink points out that this motion was the first irrevocable Antifederalist step down the path to unconditional ratification.[20] Smith accepted Jay's and Hamilton's argument that New York must think in terms of being accepted by the new government. But that is, of course, hindsight. At the time, it looked as if Smith's concession might pass, especially since Clinton accepted it. After all, Antifederalists abandoned prior amendments for amendments subsequent. So Federalists tried to adjourn (à la New Hampshire) but got only three Antifederalist votes.

As Federalists waited for defeat, they won a reprieve from Smith himself, who proposed (on 17 July) a new form of ratification: New York would

15. Elliot, *Debates*, 2:140.
16. Cited in De Pauw, *Eleventh Pillar*, 222.
17. Ibid., 241.
18. Ibid., 223.
19. Storing, *Complete Anti-Federalist*, 6:189.
20. "Political Rhetoric and Strategic Choice in the Ratification Conventions on the U.S. Constitution" (Diss., University of Rochester Library, 1987), 257 ff.

ratify unconditionally but would reserve the right to secede if their amendments were not considered under Article V within a specified number of years. Antifederalists, who had first abandoned prior amendments for an agreement on subsequent amendments, were now abandoning specific subsequent amendments for a subsequent process. Reluctantly and slowly they were approaching unconditional ratification.

Federalists seem to have seriously considered a deal on Smith's new basis. Hamilton wrote on 19 July to Madison (see table 16.1) asking if New York could be "*received* on that plan. . . . The only qualification will be the reservation of a right to secede in case our amendments have not been decided upon" under Article V, "within . . . 5 or 7" years.

But if Federalists were willing to consider Smith's new plan, Antifederalists were not. So on 19 July Lansing moved to take up his original proposal of 10 July. But now there was a big difference because Smith and his dozen or so followers were truly and publicly worried about being left out of the Union. The matter came to a head on 23 July, when Lansing's motion came up for a vote. This motion had two parts:

> 1. Relevant to New York's proposed bill of rights and amendments: " . . . on the express condition that the rights afore said will not and shall not be lost, abridged or violated, and that the said Constitution shall in all cases above particularized receive the construction hereinbefore expressed, . . . and that imperfections . . . will . . . be submitted to . . . a general convention." Although this does not require a prior convention and prior amendments, it does require that the new government interpret the Constitution as New York desired and that a subsequent convention be called. Clearly this is a conditional form of ratification.
>
> 2. Relevant to ratification: "We . . . ratify . . . upon Condition nevertheless that until Amendments shall have been submitted to and determined upon by a general Convention to be called in the mode prescribed in the . . . Constitution." This is a condition that federal powers be curtailed in New York until after a convention and amendments.[21]

With the Antifederalists now sharply divided, Smith moved to replace part 1 with a passage that read "in confidence that the rights and explanations . . . are consistent with the Constitution, and . . . that the amendments will receive an early and mature consideration." Smith's amendment avoided imposing New York's interpretations and simply expected, but did not require, a subsequent convention. Because this was getting back to

21. Syrett, *Papers of Hamilton*, 5:193–94.

something pretty close to Smith's first concession of 15 July, which Clinton had supported in the interest of party harmony, he now supported this version. It passed thirty-nine to nineteen, with nineteen Federalists and twenty Antifederalists voting aye. But of course it did not harmonize the Antifederalist party because nineteen Antifederalists continued to vote nay.

With Lansing's first clause of 23 July now emasculated, Samuel Jones moved to delete "upon condition" in part 2 and replace it with "in full confidence that." This removed the restriction on federal powers in New York and so turned all the amendments into recommendations, not conditions. Jones's motion passed thirty-one to twenty-nine, and the majority consisted of nineteen Federalists and twelve Antifederalists. So the Federalists now had what they had most wanted in the beginning: ratification with recommendatory amendments.

But this is not quite the end. The next day (24 July) the intransigent Lansing tried again to unite the Antifederalists on a new motion to ratify with the right to secede, about the same content as the motion Jones had the previous day defeated. In response Hamilton read the answer he had received from Madison on just this point. (See Hamilton's request of 19 July in table 16.1.) Madison's answer was tough — unconditional ratification or nothing:

> My opinion is that a reservation of a right to withdraw if amendments be not decided on under the form of the Constitution within a certain time, is a *conditional* ratification, that does not make N. York a member of the New Union, and consequently that she could not be received on that plan. Compacts must be reciprocal, this principle would not in such case be preserved. The Constitution requires an adoption *in toto,* and *for ever.* It has been so adopted by the other States. An adoption for a limited time would be as defective as an adoption of some of the articles only. In short any *condition* whatever must vitiate the ratification. . . . P.S. This idea of reserving right to withdraw was started at Richmond & considered as a conditional ratification which was itself considered worse than a rejection.[22]

Madison thus indicated that the motion was unacceptable in four different, emphatic ways.

After that opinion from an influential and dominant congressman who had a majority of Congress behind him, there was little hope for Anti-

22. Robert Rutland, *The Papers of James Madison* (Chicago: University of Chicago Press, 1977), 11:189.

federalists. The Federalists made one peace offering to them: a circular letter to óther states asking that two-thirds join New York in a call for a second convention. Then the convention ratified the Constitution 30–25 in the committee of the whole and finally on 26 July the engrossed copy, 30–27.

It is easy to understand why the Antifederalists split. The thirty persons in the majority for ratification consisted of eighteen Federalists (one had gone home) and twelve Antifederalists. The Federalists were from the counties in and around New York City: eight (earlier nine) from New York (Manhattan), two from Kings (Brooklyn), two from Richmond (Staten Island), and six from Westchester (now Bronx and Westchester). This was the area that would lose international trade if New York separated. It would also lose the national capital, which was thought to bring in about one hundred thousand pounds per year in hard money. And, most of all, it was the area of potential civil war. The twelve Antifederalists were from counties in a wider circle around New York City: four out of four from Queens (mostly now the borough of Queens), three out of four from Suffolk (the rest of Long Island outside Kings and Queens), four out of six from Dutchess (the county just north of Westchester), and one from Orange (across the river from what is now the Bronx). In the very first speech of the convention Chancellor Livingston emphasized the inability of New York State to defend Long Island and Staten Island from the potentially unfriendly powers, Connecticut and New Jersey. He also pointed out that the surrounding states had no interest in allying themselves with New York, which was a broad hint that the southern counties would have considerable interest in secession and alliance with the neighboring states. So throughout the convention these Antifederalists from the south had to face the question of their future in an isolated New York State, a future that might include secession and civil war, realistic concerns considering that New York had, only a few years earlier, lost Vermont.

As long as these Antifederalists could believe, with Clinton, that there was a place for a conditionally ratifying New York within the Union, they could ally with the Clintonian party. But Jay and Hamilton and Livingston reiterated again and again that such a nice accommodation was not to be, and Madison confirmed that the new Union would not tolerate any kind of condition. Thus these Federalist leaders impressed a new dimension of judgment on Antifederalists from the south of the state. Samuel Jones was from Queens, a county geographically separated from upstate by the counties of New York and Westchester. Melancton Smith had started his political career in Dutchess county, but he lived and practiced law in New York City. (He ran for a seat in the convention in both counties but won only in Dutchess.) He too could hardly have been insensitive to the implied threats of division.

So if Federalist rhetoric did not persuade, Federalist heresthetic did. As Hamilton recognized, "Our arguments confound, but do not convince"; but, as he also pointed out, "Some of the leaders . . . appear to me to be convinced *by circumstances.*"[23] However, circumstances do not convince unless they are recognized, and the Federalist achievement in the New York convention was to make certain that the vulnerable Antifederalists clearly recognized the circumstances that would convince them. By enforcing such recognition, the Federalists, who started off as a minority with about 29 percent, ended up as a majority of about 53 percent.

Thus Federalists won by remarkable heresthetic: their long-term national strategy of a speedy campaign with only nine ratifications required and their short-term New York strategy of forcing the true political circumstances into Antifederal consciousness.

23. Syrett, *Papers of Hamilton,* 5:140.

17

Forging the Final Constitution

EVENTS SUBSEQUENT to the ratification by New York in July 1788 had a significant effect on the final Constitution. These events were a clear combination of rhetoric and heresthetic. New York was the last to ratify, but North Carolina was the last to hold a convention. Still, North Carolina's rejection in the summer of 1788 had no effect on the ratification and implementation, nor did Rhode Island's rejection in the spring. Actually, the absence of Rhode Island from the last Confederation Congress and the absence of both states from the first session of the first Congress under the new Constitution probably smoothed the way for implementation.

It is true that Madison continued to worry through 1788 and 1789. But as we know from his letters about the expectation of ratification in Virginia, he worried excessively. He need not have been so concerned because the Federalists had almost as large a majority in the Confederation Congress in 1788 as they had had in 1787. Hence, the implementation of the new Constitution went through easily.[1] The only thing the congressmen disputed about the new government was the location of the capital, and that had been a constant issue throughout the later history of the confederation.[2] When the new government was formed, Federalists again had a majority in both houses and, of course, won the presidency. So there was no difficulty about implementing the Constitution. Many Federalists from the states that ratified without recommendatory amendments were

---

1. Robert A. Rutland, *The Papers of James Madison* (Charlottesville: University Press of Virginia, 1977), 11:222.
2. Calvin Jillson and Rick K. Wilson, *Congressional Dynamics: Structure, Coordination, and Choice in the First American Congress, 1774–1789* (Stanford: Stanford University Press, 1994), 281–85.

opposed to the promised amendments, although most Federalists who debated the question were from Massachusetts, New York, and Virginia.[3] But the few Antifederalists in Congress as well as Federalist leaders like Madison were determined to adopt amendments, and they succeeded fairly easily.

Madison had been challenged in the 1788 elections to Congress by James Monroe, in a district gerrymandered for Monroe to win, but Madison won (by 2 to 1, as it turned out), probably because he promised to obtain amendments, and he felt strongly obligated to do so. The amendments went through Congress in 1790 and were ratified by 1792. Thus, the Constitution, begun in 1787, was completed finally in five years, although for all practical purposes it had been finished in fourteen months.

MAKING THE PROPOSED AMENDMENTS STICK

One place where rhetoric and heresthetic converge is in the construction of the bill of rights amendments. The crux of the Federalist strategy in the later ratifying conventions — those in, at least, Massachusetts, New Hampshire, Virginia, and New York — was the promise to consider proposed amendments. They might have ignored this promise, but then they would probably have had much less time to implement the new Constitution. Moreover, reneging would have given Antifederalists a perfect campaign issue. So instead the Federalists adopted amendments, as promised, but not at all the kind of amendments that hard-core Antifederalists (that is, groups 6 and 7) wanted.

The reason this odd strategy worked for the Federalists is, I believe, a combination of the Antifederalists' rhetoric and their ambiguous strategic position. Federalists used the particular themes of Antifederalist rhetoric to fashion amendments that, to all public appearance, seemed to satisfy Antifederalist criticism of the Constitution while pleasing Federalists and annoying Antifederalists in groups 6 and 7. Thus, Federalists heresthetically exploited Antifederalist rhetoric to accomplish Federalist ends.

Federalists were able to carry out this maneuver because many of those who ended up in, especially, group 6 believed that some kind of reform was necessary. I have already cited James Monroe and Nathan Dane to that effect, and I could cite many more. George Mason and Elbridge Gerry proved by their enthusiastic participation in the Philadelphia convention

---

3. Goodhue, Mass.: "There appeared to be a large majority against amendments, when the subject was first introduced, and he had no doubt that the majority still existed," 21 August 1789. *Documentary History of the First Federal Congress*, 11:1992.

that they shared this belief, as did also those who, like Samuel Adams and Edmund Randolph, started out as Antifederalists and ended up as group 4 or 5 Federalists. Since twelve state legislatures had, in the spring of 1787, sent delegates to propose reform, the spirit of reform was general, and it was difficult to oppose. The only feasible arguments left to Antifederalists were that the reform was in some way wrong: illiberal, too consolidated, and so on. And, of course, to the argument that the principle of reform was acceptable but the practice unacceptable, the Federalists' perfect answer was, "Then let us plan reform together." It was difficult for group 6 Antifederalists to reject that argument, and so many of them became, perhaps reluctantly, group 4 and 5 Federalists. This is the most obvious way in which the heresthetic, that is, the quasi-open rule, and the rhetoric, that is, the allegations of consolidation and illiberality, work together—to the Federalists' advantage.

But there is an even deeper way in which the Federalists' heresthetic set a trap for the Antifederalists' rhetoric. The Antifederalists' own argument paved the way for Federalists to satisfy the demand for amendments with amendments about which group 6 and group 7 Antifederalists did not care very much.

To understand the tightness of the trap, it is necessary to review the amendments proposed in the ratification conventions. Kenneth Bowling, the leading student of the adoption of the Bill of Rights, distinguishes between two kinds of proposed amendments: "alterations" refers to "fundamental changes in the balance of power between state and federal governments and in the structure of the federal government, or both," while "bill of rights" refers to changes in the guarantees of personal liberties.[4] As Bowling points out, the word *amendment* in the first part of the campaign referred both to alterations and bills of rights. By the time of the Virginia and New York ratifications the distinction was well understood, and in both states the convention proposed a bill of rights and, separately "amendments" of the sort Bowling called alterations. But the distinctions drawn in June and July of 1788 were far too late to affect opinions formed in the earlier state campaigns. This failure to distinguish turned out to be a rhetorical trap for Antifederalists, even in Virginia and New York.

Altogether, there were 124 recommendations for amendments (some of them duplicates) in the five states (Massachusetts, South Carolina, New Hampshire, Virginia, and New York) that recommended them.[5] Of these,

4. " 'A Tub to the Whale:' The Founding Fathers and Adoption of the Federal Bill of Rights," *Journal of the Early Republic* 8 (1988): 223–51.

5. Sometimes writers on this subject include the North Carolina proposals as well as

58 were bill of rights items and 66 were alterations.[6] In table 17.1 I have listed the overlaps to indicate in some rough way what the recommending conventions, taken together, thought were most important. The most interesting fact about table 17.1 is that five states agreed on two alterations and on one ambiguous amendment that was not clearly in one class or the other. Four states agreed on one alteration and one bill of rights item. Only when one considers the three-state agreements do bill of rights items predominate, and there Congress rejected the one ambiguous item. The policy of Congress in accepting or rejecting recommendations was to accept some bill of rights items and reject all alterations (see tables 17.2 and 17.3). Only one ambiguous item (now the Tenth Amendment: powers not delegated reserved to states) got through Congress, perhaps because it was regarded by Madison as a bill of rights item. Otherwise, only bill of rights items passed. All but two of those came from the state proposals: Congress itself added the Ninth Amendment (the enumeration of rights does not preclude others not enumerated) and a passage in the Fifth Amendment, "nor shall private property be taken for public use without just compensation." In Congress there were twelve amendments, the first two of which were alterations: an amendment concerning the number of citizens represented by a congressman (thirty thousand) and a restriction that pay raises apply only to the next Congress; but these two amendments were not ratified by the states (until the latter one became the Twenty-seventh Amendment). Of the first ten amendments, then, nine were clearly bill of rights items, and the tenth was interpreted either as an alteration or as a right.

This was too consistent to be accidental. And indeed it was not. Madison stated the rationale when he introduced the amendments on 8 June 1789:

---

those by the minorities in Pennsylvania and Maryland. But North Carolina's proposals were made at a time when it did not join the Union and it was unrepresented in the first session of the first Congress that proposed amendments to the states. The proposals from the minorities in Maryland and Pennsylvania were specifically rejected by their conventions. So I regard the proposals from these three states as unofficial and not, therefore, properly before Congress when it proposed amendments.

6. There are two ambiguities. The Virginia list actually contained 20 alterations, but the motion to pass it mentions 21. I have used the number 20. One state (New York) proposed an ancestor of the Tenth Amendment as a bill of rights item, another (Virginia) as an alteration. The other three states did not distinguish, but in the Massachusetts convention Samuel Adams said that its version of the Tenth Amendment "appears to my mind to be a summary of a bill of rights." *Debates and Proceeding in the Convention of the Commonwealth of Massachusetts Held in the Year 1788* (Boston: William White, 1856), 223. Because New Hampshire followed Massachusetts almost word for word, I have included these ancestors to the Tenth Amendment as bill of rights items in all states but Virginia.

Table 17.1   Recommended Amendments from Five, Four, or Three States

Alteration (Alt) or Bills of Rights (BR)	Subject	States Recommended	Adopted by Congress and States
I. Five States			
Alt.	Prohibition of Congressional Regulation of Federal Elections Unless States Fail to Regulate	MA, SC, NH, VA, NY	No
Alt.	Prohibition of Direct Taxes with "Improved" Procedure for Requisitions	MA, SC, NH, VA, NY	No
BR? Alt?	Powers not Delegated to the United States Reserved to States	MA, SC, NH, VA, NY	Yes
II. Four States			
Alt.	One Representative for Every 30000, until Congress Reaches 200 (100)	MA, NH, VA, NY	No
BR	Trial by Jury in Civil Cases	MA, NH, VA, NY	Yes
III. Three States			
Alt.	Prohibition on Granting Monopolies	MA, NH, NY	No
Alt.	No Congressional Consent for a Foreign Title for a U.S. Officer	MA, NH, NY	No
BR? Alt?	No Standing Army in Peacetime Without Consent of Congress	NH, VA, NY	No
BR	Free Exercise of Religion and No Establishment of Religion	NH, VA, NY	Partial
BR	Indictment by Grand Jury	MA, NH, NY	Yes
BR	Right to Keep and Bear Arms	NH, VA, NY	Yes
BR	No Peacetime Quartering of Soldiers in Private Houses	NH, VA, NY	Yes

Table 17.2   Action on Items Proposed by Three, Four, or Five States

	Alteration	Ambiguous	Bill of Rights	Total
Adopted		1	5	6
Rejected	5	1		6
TOTAL	5	2	5	12

There have been objections of various kinds made against the consti-tution. Some were levelled against its structure. . . . I know some respect-able characters who opposed this government on these grounds; but I believe that the great mass of the people who opposed it, disliked it because it did not contain effectual provision against encroachments on particular rights. . . .

It has been a fortunate thing that the objection to the government has been made on the ground I stated; because it will be practicable on that ground to obviate the objection, so far as to satisfy the public mind that their liberties will be perpetual, and this without endangering any part of the constitution which is considered as essential to the existence of the government by those who promoted its adoption.[7]

Translating this into blunt language: "It is easy to satisfy the losers because their rhetoric indicated a desire for bill of rights items, which of course we winners approve. So we can carry out our promise about amend-ments with a bill of rights alone. Having thus carried out our promise we need make no alterations in the essential consolidation of the structure of government, which is what the extreme Antifederalists really want, but which we Federalists know would be a disastrous back-pedaling from the victory we have achieved."

This assertion depends on two factual assumptions: (1) Federalists, even group 1 Federalists, do not object strongly to a bill of rights; and (2) members of groups 4 and 5 desire bill of rights amendments more than they desire alterations. Only group 6 and group 7 Antifederalists care about alterations in the structure and power of government.

Concerning the first factual assumption, the best evidence is that the House and Senate, with large Federalist majorities, submitted nine or ten bill of rights items as amendments. And the state legislatures, mostly Feder-alist, ratified all of the bill of rights items, rejecting only the alterations

7. Rutland, *Papers of Madison*, 11:119–200. Also in *Documentary History of the First Federal Congress*, 11:820–21; cited from *Congressional Register*, 1:423–37.

Table 17.3   Action on Items Proposed by Two, Three, Four, or Five States

	Alteration	Ambiguous	Bill of Rights	TOTAL
Adopted		1	11	12
Rejected	15*	1	5	21
TOTAL	15*	2	16	33

* The Congress adopted and the states rejected an amendment that pay increases apply only to members of the next Congress.

about the size of the House and the control of House elections. So Federalists seemingly had no serious objections to a bill of rights. Why, then, was the question so much discussed in the campaign?

Some writers conclude that the Federalists at Philadelphia simply made a bad mistake. Agreed. But why did this group of otherwise astute politicians do such a silly thing? After all, they had the good sense to push their agenda control much farther than they might otherwise have done, and this in itself was almost enough to win. Why then did they fail on an important rhetorical matter?

At this distance of time, it is difficult to recover the intentions and emotions of 1787, but it seems that one important disadvantage for an overwhelming parliamentary majority is that it can fail to obtain adequate evidence of the state of popular opinion. Knowing that they had a majority in the Philadelphia convention of forty-eight to seven, or about 85 percent, they simply refused to take Mason and Gerry seriously when, just at the end of the convention, they proposed a bill of rights. These two men had by then become mere nuisances for the Federalist majority, which consequently felt free — mistakenly, of course — to ignore them. So the Federalist failure to include a bill of rights probably derived from an indifference to a tiny minority, especially since the Federalists were, in mid-September, eager to start the process of ratification, especially in Pennsylvania. But of course this gave Mason and Gerry a wonderful opening to attack the Constitution. Mason's objections started out, "There is no Declaration of Rights." Like Mason, Gerry listed his objections, ending with "and . . . the system is without the security of a bill of rights" (CC 138B, 227A).

Whatever reason the framers had for omitting a bill of rights, the Federalists were, it seems to me, deeply embarrassed by the omission, especially because it turned out to be so frequent an argument against the Constitution. Although responses to Antifederalist criticism were only about a quarter of the Federalist campaign, two-thirds of that quarter dealt with the issue of liberty. The best way Federalists could finally demonstrate that the Antifederalists' charges were false was, of course, to adopt a bill of rights, which is why, I believe, Federalists at both the state and national levels welcomed the first ten amendments.

As for the second factual assumption in Madison's argument, the initiative for the discussion of bill of rights items clearly came entirely from Antifederalists. As indicated in table 4.1, they devoted 28 percent to this subject specifically and another 21 percent indirectly (by discussing the effect of political structures on liberty). The main alternative subject, the dangers of consolidation, received only 21 percent of their emphasis. So Antifederalists devoted more attention to issues of liberty and bill of rights items than to issues of structure that could be cured only by alterations.

Thus was the trap laid for the group 6 and group 7 Antifederalists. They called the bill of rights "a tub for a whale," which was a metaphor they got from the preface to Jonathan Swift, *A Tale of a Tub*: "That Sea-men have a custom when they meet a *Whale*, to fling him out an empty Tub, by way of Amusement, to divert him from laying violent Hands upon the Ship."[8] Several unreconciled Antifederalists from groups 6 and 7 repeated this metaphor. For example, George Mason, writing to his son during the time that Congress was considering the bill of rights, corrected his wrong impression:

> You were mistaken in your suggestion that the Publication you saw of Mr. Madison's, was a certain Indication of proper Amendments to the Government being obtained. It was indeed natural enough to think so. But the *Fact* was, Mr. Madison [knew that he could] not be elected, without making some such Promises. By them he carried his Election; and in order to appear as good as his Word, he has made some Motions in Congress on the Subject; and to carry on the Farce, is now the ostensible Patron of Amendments. Perhaps some Milk and Water Propositions may be made by Congress to the State Legislatures by way of their th[r]owing out a tub to the Whale; but of important and substantial Amendments, I have not the least Hope.[9]

Aedanus Burke, a group 7 Antifederalist from South Carolina, took up the same metaphor, suggesting that serious amendments to satisfy Antifederalists were a waste of time:

> I do not mean to insist particularly on this amendment, but I am very

8. (1704), ed. A. C. Guth Kelch and D. Nichol Smith (Oxford: Clarendon Press, 1958), 40.

9. Robert A. Rutland, *The Papers of George Mason*, 3 vols. (Charlottesville: University Press of Virginia, 1970), 3:1164.

well satisfied that those that are reported and likely to be adopted by this house, are very far from giving satisfaction to our constituents, they are not those solid substantial amendments which the people expect; they are little better than whip syllabub; frothy and full of wind, formed only to please the palate, or they are like a tub thrown out to a whale, to secure the freight of the ship and its peaceable voyage.[10]

Madison justified their cynicism, threatening that amendments for alterations would bring defeat to amendments of all kinds. In the debate in the House considering a proposed amendment to allow citizens to instruct their legislators, Madison remarked, "I venture to say that if we confine ourselves to an enumeration of simple acknowledged principles, the ratification will meet with little difficulty. Amendments of a doubtful nature will have a tendency to prejudice the whole system; the proposition now suggested, partakes highly of this nature."[11] In short Madison wanted no amendments about which Federalists themselves might have doubts.

So Madison and Burke were right. Hardly anyone disagreed with the Bill of Rights and hardly any of the group 6 or 7 Antifederalists were satisfied. But Antifederalists had fallen into a pit of their own digging. It was they who made a great issue of the absence of a bill of rights and they were perforce satisfied with the bill of rights kind of amendments that touched not at all on their "true" desires. What they really wanted most of all was prohibition of congressional regulation of its own elections and a return to something like the system of requisitions (see table 17.1).

But they could not get these changes. The pit they dug for themselves was the fact that in their public presentations they had devoted only 22,551 words, a mere 1 percent, to the fact that Congress controlled its own elections and only 101,293 words to taxation, a mere 5 percent, and almost none of that concerned requisitions. (Instead they referred to anticipated tax increases.) They had not told people they wanted less consolidation in these two ways, so they could not expect Federalists to take these proposed amendments seriously when it came time to prepare amendments.

This, then, is the most self-destructive interaction of rhetoric and heresthetic. The Antifederalists' rhetoric precluded for them the effective heresthetic of recommended amendments. Suppose it is true, as Jackson Turner Main and Herbert Storing claim, that Antifederalists were mostly upset by consolidation. If so, they could not get what they wanted because they attacked the Constitution mainly as illiberal rather than as consolidating. Thus was the biter bit.

10. *Documentary History of the First Federal Congress*, 11:1278.
11. Ibid., 11:1270.

V

Conclusions

18

Rhetoric and Heresthetic

M Y REASON for surveying the detail of the most important ratifying conventions (Pennsylvania, Massachusetts, New Hampshire, Virginia, and New York) is to reveal how rhetoric and heresthetic fit together in the campaign. Campaigns are more than rhetoric, and they are more than maneuver. In fact, they are some combination of the two, and the main elements of the rhetoric and heresthetic of the ratification campaigns can be summarized as follows:

Rhetoric

1. *Themes*: The main themes of the two sides were quite different. Federalists emphasized the crisis for the Union and the states, with strong secondary emphasis on the defense of the Constitution, on the dangers of populist state legislatures, and on the success of the Federalist campaign. Antifederalists emphasized the dangers to liberty inherent in the Constitution, with strong secondary emphasis on the threat to the states in consolidation.

2. *Negativity*: These main themes are surprisingly negative, which implies that each side targeted marginal voters rather than the whole body of citizens.

3. *Dispersion of Issues*: Neither of the two sides frequently discussed the main themes of the other side. They followed the Dominance Principle (emphasizing themes on which they had little opposition) and the Dispersion Principle (abandoning themes on which the other side had as good an argument as their own).

Heresthetic

1. *Proposal of a New Constitution*: The nationalists had, since at least 1779 and 1780, been agitating for reformation of the Articles of Con-

federation. Having failed on the imposts of 1781 and 1783 and in the Annapolis convention of 1786, they called a convention to revise the Articles as soon as they finally obtained solid control of Congress in 1787. Because their dominance in the convention of 1787 was unchallenged, they boldly proposed a nationally centralized new Constitution, their first heresthetical move to replace the Articles.

2. *Forward Agenda Control*: To replace the Articles, they needed control of the agenda, even after the next election. Ordinarily, of course, the right of control runs from election to election. But the nationalists of 1787 arranged a method of ratification that set the agenda for the next nine months, long after most states had held elections.

3. *Closed Rule, Initially*: One important feature of agenda control was a closed rule that required an up or down vote and precluded the kind of bargaining for amendments by which Virginia, New York, and Rhode Island had defeated the impost acts.

4. *Speed*: In most states, Federalists pushed for a quick decision before Antifederalist rhetoric could have much impact. In five states this strategy was successful, and in two more the delays were trivial. Antifederalists were never able to overcome the lead that the Federalists thus established, although the Antifederalists for the first time adopted a strategy of their own: delay and, if possible, a second convention. Unfortunately for the Antifederalists, they were not successful in coordinating their strategy and consequently could not accomplish as much by delay as Federalists accomplished by speed.

5. *A Quasi-open Rule*: When Federalists found that they could not carry Massachusetts with a closed rule, they devised a quasi-open one, namely, a promise to propose amendments once the Constitution had been ratified and the new government established. This strategy prevented time-consuming negotiation over amendments prior to ratification and delayed the negotiations, if they were ever to occur at all, until after the ratification. Thus, in another way this quasi-open rule precluded the delaying tactics that had defeated the imposts.

THE RELATIONSHIP OF RHETORIC AND HERESTHETIC

The use of Antifederal rhetoric to reject those amendments most desired by Antifederalists, as discussed in chapter 17, is a curious and probably unique outcome. However interesting as a heresthetical device, it does not tell us much about the deeper relation of rhetoric and heresthetic. What one wants much more to know is the relative effect of these two arts of language on the outcome of ratification and other, more recent campaigns: Did the Federalists win because they had the better argument or because they had the better strategy or both?

I have already indicated that the division between the two sides was about half and half. Main's (unexplained) estimate is 48 to 52 in the Antifederalists' favor, while Evelyn Fink and I estimate 50 to 46 (see chapter 2). So the two sides came out just about even in terms of popular support. The Federalist support was more widely distributed: huge majorities in one large state, in two medium-sized states, and in three small ones, along with a huge majority in the delegation if not in the election in one more medium-sized state. As against this, the Antifederalists had huge majorities in only two states, one medium-sized, the other small. The real battle took place in only four states: Virginia, where Federalists probably won the election; New Hampshire, where Federalists probably won the election in the end; and Massachusetts and New York, where Federalists probably lost the election but carried the convention.

In a sense, however, popular vote does not count: The real issue was whether or not the Federalists could win over $9/13$, or about 70 percent, of the state conventions. Because Federalists started out with much more widely distributed support (seven sure states as against only two for Antifederalists), the question actually was, Could the Federalists get half of the four closely divided states? In the end, of course, they won the two necessary elections and carried the conventions in the other two. So the question of the relative significance of rhetoric and heresthetic boils down to these two more precise questions: What gave Federalists the more widespread popularity? and How did the Federalists win the four marginal states?

The wide distribution of the Federalists' popularity derives, I think, from the fact that nationalists had for many years been hammering home the danger of a weak central government. The drumbeat of warnings had its intended effect and explains why the nationalists obtained more than $9/13$ support for the impost in 1781 and 1785, why they carried most of the elections in 1786, and, finally, why twelve states sent delegates to Philadelphia. Of course, prior to September 1787, the nationalists did not support any particular reform. But during the summer of 1787, while the convention met, newspaper comment was extremely and almost universally nationalistic and hence wildly enthusiastic about the (unknown) outcome, while provincialist comment was practically nonexistent.[1] Of course,

---

1. John K. Alexander, *The Selling of the Constitutional Convention: A History of News Coverage* (Madison: Madison House, 1990). Alexander believes the press was, during the summer of 1787, extremely biased against Antifederalists, but he admits that the bias was the socially

when the nationalists offered their specific reform, provincials had something concrete to criticize, and their rhetorical response was intense. But the plain fact is that for about a year before the unveiling of the Constitution, nationalist opinion was ascendant, and the Federalists prospered from that fact.

The Federalist argument that crisis necessitated reform can thus be said to have been powerful and persuasive. Demonstrably, it had already convinced a majority of legislators in twelve states, although not all of these were also convinced of the necessity of the extreme centralization later proposed in the Constitution. The persuasiveness of the crisis argument accounts, I believe, for the Federalists' widespread success — both for their widespread initial support and for their continuing, though attenuated, support well into 1788. It is the main reason Federalists had seven sure states and at least four more that they were ultimately able to win.[2]

And this also demonstrates, I believe, that the Federalist rhetoric was a necessary and fundamental part of their success. Had they not convinced many people throughout the Union of the existence of crisis and had they not shown that the Constitution was an appropriate response to the crisis, then they could not have had the widespread support necessary to carry 85 percent (11/13ths) of the states. So I conclude that Federalists' rhetoric as well as the rhetoric of their predecessor nationalists was a necessary condition of Federalist victory.

Can one say the same about Federalist heresthetic? Almost certainly, yes. The apparent national consensus on the need for reform was, of course, shattered by the publication of the Constitution. Almost immediately Antifederalists produced a powerful rhetoric of opposition. And as time went on, they won many supporters. And with consensus lost, Federalists needed more than rhetoric to win in the several states.

The shattering of consensus derived from two features of the situation in September 1787. One was the fact that the framers had gone much beyond what people generally had anticipated in the spring. The other was that the Constitution supplied a focus for Antifederal response.

---

prevailing one. He asks, "What prompted the publishers to champion the Constitutional Convention and then the Constitution so ardently?" And he answers, "Because they thought the Union must be reformed," and "as best it can be discovered [this] view was the popular one in America," 220.

2. Many contemporary writers in the Charles Beard tradition have tried to show that the economic and political crises were subsiding in 1787–88. See, for example, Merrill Jensen, *The New Nation: A History of the United States during the Confederation, 1781–89* (New York: Knopf, 1950). But, of course, the facts are irrelevant. Popular opinion, whether right or wrong, is what counts. And popular opinion in 1787–88, under nationalist-Federalist tutelage, generally agreed that there was a crisis.

To consider the first feature, the framers, emboldened (as I pointed out in chapter 11) by the requirement of 9/13 and the closed rule, had written a Constitution almost as centralized as Madison's initial proposal. So the framers themselves, especially the group 1 nationalists, had, in their eagerness to write the strongest possible Constitution, alienated many who were less enthusiastic than they about reform. Probably any concrete proposal for reform would have displeased some persons, but the framers deliberately invited intense dispute. Something like the simple impost could easily pass with 9/13 — that had already been demonstrated. So the framers produced a much more extensive reform that might be difficult for 9/13. Once published, the Constitution thus was, objectively, a basis for sharp division.

The second feature of the shattered consensus was that the Constitution provided a focus for criticism. Many provincials had had little to say in response to the nationalist barrage over the previous year. Nationalists of course picked out the worst excesses of provincial behavior in order to attack the status quo. So the defenders of the status quo were, perforce, required to defend these excesses. And, given the Dominance Principle, who indeed among sensible provincialist politicians would wish to defend Shays' violence or Rhode Island's insistence on issuing devolved paper money, at least as these were displayed in the stylized "facts" of journalistic presentation. To do so would simply attract to one's self, for no good reason and in support of no particular program, the obloquy of defense of what in stylized form was almost indefensible. So the proto-Antifederalists of 1786 and the first nine months of 1787 had had relatively little to say. But the publication of the Constitution reversed positions. It gave provincialists a specific target: now they could confidently attack a reform they despised rather than defend embarrassing excesses. And they attacked with intensity.

Once consensus dissolved, the Antifederalists made considerable headway. It seems likely that the immediate popular response to the Constitution was favorable or at least neutral. Federalists initially wrote about the Constitution in simple explanatory terms without defensiveness, apparently believing that defense was unnecessary. But within a couple of weeks the situation changed sharply — by 5 October Wilson aggressively defended the Constitution (see chapter 6), a sure indication that a substantial opposition had come into existence. As prophesied by Gouverneur Morris and Hamilton (see chapter 12), the opposition grew with time. And in those states in which nationalism had been fairly weak (for example, Massachusetts, New York, and Virginia) and in which the backcountry disturbances of 1786 had occurred (for example, New Hampshire, Massachusetts, Rhode Island, and North Carolina) Antifederalism progressively flourished throughout the ratification campaign. As a consequence, the previous consensus for reform evaporated in several states at least, and strong parties faced each other.

This was a triumph for Antifederalist rhetoric. Indeed, they had won over about half the voters within at most nine months, whereas it had taken the nationalists many years to reach consensus. This was a real challenge for Federalists. It meant that they could not win simply by persuasion because Antifederalists had absorbed those who might be persuaded. And here the Federalists' heresthetical skill played a role.

Federalists had to win at least two of the five possible states: New Hampshire, Massachusetts, New York, Virginia, and North Carolina. As it turned out, North Carolina was impossible, so that meant taking two of the remaining four. As recounted in chapter 13, Federalists won Massachusetts, the first up of the four, by the remarkable maneuver of abandoning the closed rule. Why Antifederalists acceded to this device is hard to ascertain, especially since they knew well that the promise of amendments lacked a guarantee. Yet enough did accede, possibly because they were crypto-Federalists who wished for a way out of their opposition. Regardless of the reason, the device worked, bringing Federalist victory in Massachusetts. Once publicized, the promise probably helped to make possible the Federalist adjustments in New Hampshire and the Federalist success in the Virginia elections. If so, the quasi-open rule in Massachusetts, purely heresthetical, turned the narrow margin in three states.

Another heresthetical maneuver turned the margin in New York: the Federalist insistence that ratification prior to amendment was necessary for participation in the new government. Antifederalists who did not want to be left out were obliged to vote for unconditional ratification. Thus ratification in four marginal states depended on the combination of a strong Federalist minority (dependent, of course, on previous rhetoric) and clever heresthetic.

I conclude, then, that the persuasiveness of the nationalist-Federalist arguments over the previous several years provided the bulk of the Federalist voters. But clever manipulation in three conventions supplied the necessary margin of victory. Such is probably the case in most campaigns. Winners must have the better arguments; but, when the race is close, they must also have the better heresthetical skill.

And this suggests the true relation between these two arts. Persuasion seems to be a long-term project that provides the basic strength of a side's campaign. But in a zero-sum game (in which category fall binary choices in elections) both sides build similarly sized coalitions over time.[3] And this is where the short-term projects of heresthetics enter the decision. This does not mean, however, that one art is primary or more necessary than the other. If several necessary conditions are themselves sufficient, there are no degrees of necessity. Each condition is absolutely necessary, though in different ways. Thus, in the absence of rhetorical preparation, no heresthetical maneuver could have won marginal states like Virginia for the Federalists; rhetoric was unconditionally necessary. Conversely, without heresthetical maneuvers, the Federalist rhetoric, which persuaded nearly but not quite half, would have failed to carry Massachusetts, New Hampshire, and New York. Heresthetical maneuver too was unconditionally necessary. In general, victory may not be possible without superior rhetoric in the long term and superior heresthetic in the short term.

RHETORIC AND HERESTHETIC IN THE ACHIEVEMENT OF AN EQUILIBRIUM OUTCOME

How is it that in a political choice situation laden with preference cycles — as the constitutional choice certainly was in 1787 and during the ratification campaign — an electorate is able to decide on anything at all? If a cycle exists, every alternative in the cycle can be beaten and displaced by some other alternative. So, for a temporarily victorious alternative a there is some socially preferred alternative b, which adroit politicians can (and do) use to supplant a. However, some alternative c is socially preferred to b and can supplant it and so forth ad infinitum until a can supplant some n and the cycle can start around again.

As I pointed out at the beginning of chapter 6, politicians who think they are likely to lose have a strong incentive to initiate this chain of successive displacements in the hope of identifying some preferable alternative with which they can win. (This is indeed what happened right after the Constitution was presented to Congress. First came the proposal of a second convention, followed soon by numerous suggestions for amendments, and so on). If, therefore, the polity lacked devices to sort through the numerous alternatives to bring about a socially acceptable decision, it would either reject all possible alternatives or adopt one that would soon be overthrown. That is, if the electorate did find a majority for some alternative in the cycle, that choice would be out of equilibrium and hence

3. William H. Riker, *The Theory of Political Coalitions* (New Haven: Yale University Press, 1963).

highly unstable. Then another alternative or the status quo ante might soon supplant the initial one.

Yet none of this happened in 1787–88. Instead, the electorate adopted a Constitution that, with a few formal modifications and quite a few more informal ones, has survived for more than two centuries. It seems the leaders of the polity must have hit upon an equilibrium outcome, in spite of the probable initial existence of a cycle in September and October 1787. How can this have come about? What devices did these leaders use to arrive at and adopt a stable and enduring winner?

This is a concrete form of a theoretical question that has deeply bothered students of politics in recent years. Although Duncan Black proved the median voter theorem, which established the conditions under which an equilibrium outcome exists in a one-dimensional policy space, he soon also demonstrated that the equilibrium vanished in two or more dimensions.[4] Then Richard McKelvey proved that in a two- or more dimensional policy (or outcome) space all the alternatives were, generically, in one huge cycle, which thus precluded any possible equilibrium outcome. (Because an equilibrium of voting is an alternative that can be defeated by no other in a binary contest, it follows there cannot be an equilibrium in a cycle, where, of course, every alternative loses to at least one other.)[5] Yet observation of the real world suggests that there are a vast number of voting equilibria: majority decisions that cannot be upset. And so follows Gordon Tullock's question: "Why so much stability?"[6]

The first answer and still the dominant one is that, somehow, people use institutions to reconstruct the issue space into one dimension in such a way as to satisfy the median voter theorem. In particular, Kenneth Shepsle identifies legislative committees as institutions that funnel the decision process onto one dimension.[7] It is certainly true that committees play an important role in the process of arriving at equilibria. Thus, treating the whole electorate as a decision body, the Constitutional Convention served as the equivalent of a legislative committee by deriving a concrete and unique proposal out of a huge and inchoate — and probably cycling — set of previously discussed possibilities.

4. Duncan Black, "On the Rationale of Group Decision Making," *Journal of Political Economy* 56 (1948): 23–34; Duncan Black and R. A. Newing, *Committee Decisions with Complementary Valuation* (Edinburgh: William Hodge, 1951); and Duncan Black, *The Theory of Committees and Elections* (Cambridge: Cambridge University Press, 1958.)

5. Richard D. McKelvey, "Intransitivities in Multi-Dimensional Voting Models and Some Implications for Agenda Control," *Journal of Economic Theory* 12 (1976): 472–82.

6. "Why So Much Stability?" *Public Choice* 37 (1981): 189–202.

7. "Institutional Arrangements and Equilibrium in Multi-dimensional Voting Models," *American Journal of Political Science* 23 (1979): 27–59.

In spite of the importance of committees and other funneling devices, there are many other institutional and noninstitutional features of the process of reducing the number of dimensions. For example, Keith Poole and Howard Rosenthal, looking at the whole history of legislative decision in the United States, from 1789 to 1985, observed several periods in which politics became two-dimensional and then reverted to a new kind of uni-dimensionality.[8]

To examine the process in the 1780s, I distinguish between the outcome space and the policy space. The outcome space includes what the participants think is ultimately important — such matters as prosperity, security, and so forth. The policy space includes the alternative methods by which leaders propose to achieve the goals in the outcome space — such alternatives as constitutions, bills, and so on. These two spaces are related in the sense that particular policies are intended to achieve particular goals. However, supporters and opponents of a policy may disagree on how or whether it achieves a goal, and one or both may be wrong. And even if the relation between policy and goals seems simple, it is well to remember that rhetoricians often have a motive to confuse the relation. For example, as I showed in chapters 3–5, rhetoricians have a motive to exaggerate the disastrous consequences that could develop from the alternatives espoused by the other side.

In spite of this befogged relation, as leaders move back and forth between these spaces, they do in fact clarify the relation, oftentimes to the point of producing stability. To interpret this process I review briefly the development of these spaces from the early 1780s to the early nineteenth century, with emphasis, of course, on the role of the campaign of 1787–88.

The nationalists of the mid-1780s wanted to strengthen the federal government. That is why they were called Federalists and their opponents were called Antifederalists even before the Constitutional Convention. Long before 1787, these nationalists had identified and agreed upon a number of areas of reform (for example, for financing the center, for governing interstate commerce, and so on). But they had not, except for the impost, agreed on specific measures. So they can be said to have imposed a dimension of consolidation on the outcome space along with the usual economic dimension(s). But the only concrete proposals in the policy space were the imposts and the Annapolis convention, and just how these would produce outcomes on the issue of economic consolidation was unclear, especially since the impost, if adopted, might have ended up being collected by state officials.

8. "Patterns of Congressional Voting," *American Journal of Political Science* 35 (1991): 228–78.

The Philadelphia convention changed all that by producing a concrete proposal on which all factions of the nationalist movement could agree. Furthermore, the nationalists, who overwhelmingly dominated the convention, established an agenda for ratification in such a way that if, roughly, a simple majority agreed that the Constitution was better than the status quo, it would win.

This heresthetical maneuver reduced the campaign to a single, clear-cut issue dimension: Consolidation versus the Status Quo. For nine months after publication of the Constitution the overwhelmingly dominant dimension of American politics concerned the degree of consolidation as defined in the range between these extreme points. In addition, the closed rule (that is, the exclusion of amendments) forced a choice between a proposal near the extreme nationalists' ideal on this dimension and the status quo, which twelve states had already rejected by sending delegates to Philadelphia. Naturally, this forced choice effectively prohibited compromises based on the introduction of new dimensions. One dimension was imposed, regardless of how much many moderates would have liked to complicate it.

Once the proposed Constitution was before the public, ideological harmonization took place. Although this harmonization structured politics in two dimensions, one provided by Federalists, the other by Antifederalists, the convention's imposed dimension of consolidation split the ideological space into two halves, as depicted in figure 9.1 (p. 135).

The main forces for harmonization in this instance as in all others are the Dominance Principle and the Dispersion Principle. As editorialists and pamphleteers unconsciously, though rationally, followed these principles, they emphasized those themes that seemed more successful relative to consolidation and rejected those that seemed less successful. Thereby rhetors winnowed out the less persuasive themes, and on each side they were left with a couple of main themes that were compatible with each other.

On the Federalists' side, the harmonization was easy. Their main claim, that the Constitution alone could alleviate the crisis, simply continued the already well-rationalized nationalist argument. Their secondary claim, that populist state legislatures threatened liberty and public order, fit easily with the theme of crisis. Both themes were attacks on provincialism and on the institutional status quo. On the Antifederalists' side, harmonization was equally easy. The main theme was that the Constitution threatened liberty, and the secondary theme was that consolidation would damage state governments. Both themes are thus justifications of the institutional status quo.

The harmonized rhetoric on each side thus supported the dimension that the framers had drawn on the feature of consolidation. That is, a heresthetical step followed by a rhetorical step generated coherence on the subject of consolidation. There was an additional heresthetical step in this case when the Federalists in several states changed the location of the proposed Constitution in the rhetorical space, moving the dividing line between supporters and opponents from line a to line b in figure 9.1. Although this kind of maneuver probably often occurs and in this case was decisive for Federalist victory, it is not a necessary part of the clarification of issues and of organization for decision. What is significant, however, is that agenda manipulation and rhetorical manipulation both contributed to the simplification that eliminated voting cycles and produced a definitive and stable decision.

APPENDIX
RHETORICAL THEMES, 1787–88

AF: Antifederalist F: Federalist Cx: Constitution

Code number and source	Themes	Summary sentences	Total printed words
Liberty Generally			
1001 AF	The Cx endangers and destroys liberty (as intended).	27	30105
1005 AF	Peroration: Americans should defend liberty against the Cx.	15	11403
1151 F	Liberty depends on the Cx, which prevents anarchy, conquest: Americans should work for it.	23	78400
1152 F	Liberty depends, not on the Cx, but on social conditions like equality, democracy, opinion, and popular control of government.	15	26493
1158 F	The AF theme of liberty is alarmist propaganda and threatens liberty.	9	16939
Civil Liberties Generally			
1501 AF	The Cx is defective without a bill of rights.	27	35407
1502 AF	The supremacy clause, federal judiciary, and consolidation together threaten civil liberties.	11	21095
1503 AF	Wilson's arguments ("all not given is reserved"; diversity precludes bill) are ingenious, but fail to protect rights.	18	13656
1551 F	Wilson's argument: a bill of rights is unnecessary in a federation.	8	24417
1552 F	The Cx declares many specific rights.	4	1629
1556 F	A bill of rights is not necessary for limited government.	8	6708
Specific Liberties			
2001 AF	Free speech, which is necessary for liberty, is unprotected and threatened by the Cx.	26	21705
2051 F	Free speech, protected by states and Congress, is not threatened. The AF issue is demagoguery.	13	9745
2301 F	The Cx endangers jury trial because appeals on fact override juries, because there is no jury trial in civil cases, and because federal courts and large territory threaten juries of the vicinage.	49	50429

Code number and source	Themes	Summary sentences	Total printed words
2351 F	Trial by jury in civil cases is not abolished.	9	21804
2354 F	Appeals on fact are desirable.	4	4125
2401 AF	The prohibition of ex post facto laws is unenforceable and screens public defaulters.	3	4627
2452 F	The prohibition of ex post facto laws is desirable.	4	5723
2502 AF	The Cx does not protect religious freedom.	15	10203
2551 F	The Cx avoids religious tests.	10	13854
2801 AF	The Cx lacks procedural guarantees (e.g., habeas corpus, "search and seizure," "bail," and "right to hunt").	10	13025
2851 F	The Cx omits property qualifications, improves naturalization, defines treason precisely, avoids impossible guarantees (e.g. "cruel and unusual," "excessive bail," and "right to hunt,"), and properly assigns habeas corpus.	10	9375
Tyranny			
4002 AF	The Cx is aristocratic, oligarchic, despotic, tyrannical, monarchical; good administration cannot save a bad constitution; the people will discover and overcome Cx-al tyranny.	47	48988
4051 F	The Cx is republican, not aristocratic, and guarantees against plutocracy; furthermore lack of energy induces despotism.	21	27660
4102 AF	The senate is aristocratic because of its long term and executive power.	6	3361
4152 F	The senate, unlike upper houses in Britain and Rome, is not aristocratic.	9	14941
Consolidation			
5004 AF	Merely electing senators won't preserve states from consolidation.	5	15397
5006 AF	The Cx consolidates states, destroying liberty, as shown by various provisions.	38	49812
5010 AF	Consolidation is impractical for the U.S.A.	6	10271
5020 AF	The Convention was to repair defects, not to consolidate (see also 14004).	5	11896

5039 AF	The Cx annihilates states, threatening liberty and civil war (also 5006).	27	40373
5051 F	Alarm about consolidation is sophistical.	13	10501
5053 F	Proof that the Cx does not consolidate: states retain functions.	37	87580
5082 F	Dangers of weakness justify consolidation.	10	13694
5552 F	The Cx is partly federal, partly national, partly concurrent.	17	27641

Direct ad hominem Remarks

8007 AF	AFs praise, defend nonsigning delegates.	33	49898
8012 AF	Afs praise, defend AF publicists and politicians (who, furthermore, are not job hunters).	19	18033
8056 F	Fs attack nonsigning delegates.	23	34404
8062 F	Fs attack AF publicists and politicians.	41	43617
8501 AF	AFs attack Washington.	21	15624
8503 AF	AFs attack Franklin.	4	2551
8505 AF	AFs attack Washington and Franklin.	5	8796
8513 AF	AFs attack F publicists and politicians.	22	11053
8514 AF	AFs attack Wilson.	22	24936
8551 F	Fs cite, praise, defend Washington.	22	37194
8553 F	Fs cite, praise, defend Franklin.	7	16256
8554 F	Fs cite, praise, defend Washington and Franklin.	12	10107
8570 F	Fs cite, praise, defend F publicists and politicians.	28	56815

Characteristics of Opponents and Allies

10108 AF	Fs support Cx to obtain federal jobs.	6	3603
10116 AF	Fs arguments are weak, sophistical, false, scurrilous.	16	8574
10136 AF	Fs are conspirators against liberty.	14	10321
10152 F	AFs oppose because have or want state jobs.	21	8988
10155 F	AFs are demagogues, Shaysites.	11	11859
10158 F	AFs are provincial, tory, sinister, hypocritical, alarmist, sophistical.	46	55227
10172 F	AFs arguments are weak.	30	38314
10304 AF	Fs are aristocrats.	14	8427
10305 AF	Great names ought not be decisive.	19	19191
10360 F	Revere the framers, do not attack them.	9	13140

Inadequacy of the Articles of Confederation

| 11052 F | The Articles were a wartime expedient inadequate for peace time. | 4 | 8057 |
| 11053 F | The Articles are commercially inadequate. | 3 | 3496 |

Code number and source	Themes	Summary sentences	Total printed words
11058 F	The Articles are constitutionally inadequate.	30	69171
11060 F	The Articles are militarily inadequate.	7	9046
Advantages of Union			
12053 F	Union is better than separate confederacies.	41	84146
12151 F	Union is necessary and must be coercive to overcome localism.	19	81861
12350 F	Union is necessary for defense.	45	59162
Crisis of 1787			
13001 AF	AFs acknowledge crisis.	20	15225
13002 AF	AFs deny crisis.	15	27821
13052 F	The Cx will save U.S.A. from crisis.	9	39547
13056 F	The crisis is severe.	17	67484
Comments on the Federal Convention			
14004 AF	The convention was called only to amend, not to rewrite, the Articles.	11	27363
14005 AF	Secrecy of the convention: it prevented popular input and concealed dissension.	8	9567
14051 F	Even if the convention exceeded authority, which many deny, it still wrote a fine Cx.	13	11195
14052 F	Great men, without faction, produced a great Cx by compromises.	15	61765
14054 F	Unqualified masses delegate framing to the elite.	3	1032
14101 AF	There were no AF delegates.	3	10748
14151 F	Pennsylvania chose delegates fairly.	6	627
Republicanism			
18151 F	The Cx is republican and democratic because power comes from the people.	39	138412
18253 F	Union and republicanism cure the disease of faction.	19	23421
18257 F	The extended republic cures faction and makes U.S.A. great.	20	55928
18302 AF	Large republics lead to consolidation and despotism, and void republicanism.	22	33222
Slavery			
19001 AF	The Cx unwisely permits importation of slaves to continue.	16	18805

| 19251 | F | The Cx limits the slave trade. | 11 | 14843 |

Constitutional Principles

20501	AF	States should be legislatively equal.	28	58625
20503	AF	States should be proportionally represented.	2	2016
20552	F	Equality of states in senate is a necessary compromise.	15	26634
20801	AF	The Cx violates the separation of powers as in the relations of senate-president, congress-president, congress-court, etc.	23	35877
20851	F	The separation of powers controls government power.	44	73338
20860	F	Conventions, censors, etc. are inadequate controls on government.	16	11008

Constitutional Structure

21011	AF	Congress controls its own elections.	18	22551
21057	F	The method of electing congress is fair and safe.	20	23674
21101	AF	Congress, too small, with long terms, will be easily corrupted.	37	47247
21104	AF	Congress lacks rotation in office and annual elections.	7	4095
21105	AF	Counting slaves for representation.	3	4118
21107	AF	The system needs fair representation.	4	3366
21152	F	While the three-fifths rule is dubious, it is a necessary compromise.	10	6861
21154	F	The House is the right size, neither too small nor too large.	28	39757
21158	F	Biennial elections are safe.	14	11511
21301	AF	Congress has excessive power (as in the supremacy clause and the necessary and proper clause).	17	17576
21350	F	Congress is structured for energy and liberty.	21	25231
21501	AF	Unicameral legislatures are best, as in Pennsylvania, to avoid aristocracy.	3	17818
21551	F	Bicameralism and long senatorial terms prevent bad legislation.	22	19533

Senate

| 22201 | AF | The Senate is too powerful. | 15 | 16313 |
| 22252 | F | The Senate is not too powerful. | 17 | 24389 |

President

| 24001 | AF | The President is an elective monarch, who with a long term, veto, practical | 35 | 41609 |

Code number and source	Themes	Summary sentences	Total printed words
	immunity from impeachment, and without a council, will dominate Congress. The president should be plural. The vice president is unimportant.		
24052 F	The electoral college method of election protects against excessive power and corruption.	11	5150
24054 F	Proposed improvements in the executive.	4	1225
24057 F	Age restrictions, term length, reeligibility guarantee experience, restrain the president, and protect against legislative dominance.	25	33926
24151 F	Energy in the (single) executive is necessary and not dangerous.	23	22187
24153 F	AFs misrepresent the reasonable powers of the President.	12	9730
24210 AF	The unrestrained power to pardon is dangerous.	4	6473
24261 F	The pardoning power is safe.	8	8307
24351 F	The veto is conditional, good for energy, and a council is thus unnecessary.	16	22754

Judiciary

26001 AF	The judiciary, with unrestricted jurisdiction, will oppress.	34	27275
26004 AF	The federal court's treaty jurisdiction is, admittedly, necessary.	3	479
26152 F	The federal courts are well constructed, offering fair trials, and could even be more national.	6	9305
26201 AF	The federal judiciary will absorb and dominate state courts, which are really the only necessary courts.	21	31028
26204 AF	Complexity, distance of federal courts makes for injustice.	10	20522
26251 F	The federal judiciary will not oppress or absorb state courts.	14	13980

Amendment

30001 AF	The Cx is nearly unamendable.	4	4658
30152 F	The amendment procedure prevents rigidity and provides for new states.	6	4824

Taxation and Finance

43001 AF	The Cx will be expensive, the U.S.A. will need excises besides the impost, and the U.S.A. will overtax — which is unfair to requisition-paying states.	26	37851
43002 AF	The federal government will preempt and monopolize state tax sources, especially for defense; but the states need taxes too.	49	64072
43051 F	The federal government needs revenue, especially for war.	13	19334
43054 F	Federal taxes won't be heavy and won't preempt states because, inter alia, of efficiency in collection.	40	72244

Treaties

45001 AF	Supremacy of treaties allows the president and Congress to dominate states.	8	6643
45051 F	The treaty power of congress and the federal courts is necessary for foreign affairs.	23	27635

Commercial Powers

46002 AF	The federal power over commerce hurts states.	6	4360
46152 F	The federal commerce power is necessary to expand trade.	12	8522

Standing Armies

48101 AF	Standing armies and federal control of militia threaten liberty.	54	64394
48103 AF	AF responses to F's assertion about standing armies and militia reveal F's sinister intentions.	9	6975
48151 F	Standing armies are necessary, exist in the states now, and will continue to exist if the Cx is not ratified.	43	68876
48252 F	Standing armies will be controlled under the Cx by public opinion and representation and won't be used to collect taxes.	29	36820

National Defense

51001 AF	Tyranny weakens defense.	11	15910
51052 F	The Cx, by providing military strength, obtains international respect, threatens Britain, and prevents war. National	54	78988

Code number and source	Themes	Summary sentences	Total printed words
	powers and national taxes are necessary for military strength.		

	Federations		
53152 F	Legislation for states (including requisitions), rather than persons, weakens confederacies.	19	55903
53157 F	Despite Montesquieu, the federal form is ideal for large territory.	10	84711
53160 F	Historically, confederations have failed.	16	53725
53251 F	It is more likely that states will encroach on the union than the union on the states.	13	25262
53257 F	Compound government with a strong center and concurrent authority makes for a workable federation and avoids civil war.	8	57689

	Paper Money		
81001 AF	Paper money is desirable.	3	4682
81051 F	The Cx prohibits paper money, thus preserving morality and prosperity.	10	15686

	Probable Effects of the Constitution		
84001 AF	Undesirable effects are anticipated.	8	7907
85051 F	Ratification will generate peace and prosperity.	23	28589
85054 F	Ratification will encourage manufacturers, foreign trade (by navigation laws), and commerce generally.	43	96087
85951 F	With the Cx, West Indians will migrate here.	5	6605

	Events of the Campaign		
88001 AF	AFs condemn F editors for limiting discussion and Wilson for subverting newspapers.	27	22584
88006 AF	AFs condemn the post office for a conspiracy to delay AF news.	37	58464
88013 AF	Ratification by conventions and by nine states violate the Articles.	10	15394
88051 F	Publius and Pennsylvania debates are published.	7	11818

88052	F	Wide discussion shows that the press is not limited, but writers should publish their names.	19	9086
88060	F	The post office is impartial.	4	8454
88301	AF	The Cx can be adopted only by force.	5	4196
88705	AF	The campaign is going against the Fs.	66	93019
88751	F	The ratification campaign is going well.	145	265340
88951	F	Ratification by nine states is justified.	4	3148
90001	AF	Eastern states are advantaged over Southern by the Cx, especially by navigation laws.	8	10781
96199	F	The minority properly acquiesces (Mass., Conn., and Pennsylvania — except the malicious).	10	20511
96201	AF	Abuse of R.I. is unjustified.	8	2959
96251	F	R.I. rejects.	16	32164
96253	F	Conn. and N.J. lose by other state tariffs.	8	7769
96257	F	N.H. is endangered by Canada.	6	15217
96902	AF	There are false reports of North Carolina's ratification.	8	2590

Campaign Strategies

97051	F	Ratify! because this is the last chance and we can do no better.	32	36074
97054	F	The choice is stable government versus anarchy.	14	21765
97105	AF	Amend prior to ratification. We cannot ratify and amend subsequently because amendment is difficult.	39	45207
97152	F	Adopt and later amend.	8	8587
97201	AF	Some desirable amendments are discussed.	23	52382
97301	AF	A second convention is desirable.	25	28602
97501	AF	Be cool, slow, cautious.	34	49980
97511	AF	Haste is suspicious.	11	26371
97551	F	Discuss, then ratify.	12	11179
97555	F	Speedy ratification is essential.	12	8469

Avoid Procedural Delay

97601	AF	Oppose Cx for it leads to despotism.	7	11332

Comments

98053	F	The Cx is almost perfect.	27	53218
98101	AF	AFs present a moderate appearance.	25	31212
98151	F	Fs present a moderate appearance.	18	34745
99060	F	God favors the Cx.	19	32854
99998	F	Formalities.	7	5488
		Total	3268	4947253

Index